CONTROVERSIAL MONUMENTS AND MEMORIALS

AMERICAN ASSOCIATION FOR STATE AND LOCAL HISTORY

BOOK SERIES

ABOUT THE SERIES

The American Association for State and Local History Book Series addresses issues critical to the field of state and local history through interpretive, intellectual, scholarly, and educational texts. To submit a proposal or manuscript to the series, please request proposal guidelines from AASLH headquarters: AASLH Editorial Board, 2021 21st Ave. South, Suite 320, Nashville, Tennessee 37212. Telephone: (615) 320-3203. Website: www.aaslh.org.

ABOUT THE ORGANIZATION

The American Association for State and Local History (AASLH) is a national history membership association headquartered in Nashville, Tennessee, that provides leadership and support for its members who preserve and interpret state and local history in order to make the past more meaningful to all people. AASLH members are leaders in preserving, researching, and interpreting traces of the American past to connect the people, thoughts, and events of yesterday with the creative memories and abiding concerns of people, communities, and our nation today. In addition to sponsorship of this book series, AASLH publishes *History News* magazine, a newsletter, technical leaflets and reports, and other materials; confers prizes and awards in recognition of outstanding achievement in the field; supports a broad education program and other activities designed to help members work more effectively; and advocates on behalf of the discipline of history. To join AASLH, go to www.aaslh.org or contact Membership Services, AASLH, 2021 21st Ave. South, Suite 320, Nashville, TN 37212.

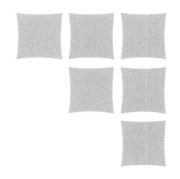

CONTROVERSIAL MONUMENTS AND MEMORIALS

A GUIDE FOR COMMUNITY LEADERS

EDITED BY DAVID B. ALLISON

ROWMAN & LITTLEFIELD
Lanham • Boulder • New York • London

Published by Rowman & Littlefield
An imprint of The Rowman & Littlefield Publishing Group, Inc.
4501 Forbes Boulevard, Suite 200, Lanham, Maryland 20706
www.rowman.com

Unit A, Whitacre Mews, 26-34 Stannary Street, London SE11 4AB

British Library Cataloguing in Publication Information Available

Library of Congress Cataloging-in-Publication Data Available
ISBN 9781538113738 (pbk. : alk. paper)
ISBN 9781538113745 (electronic)

∞™ The paper used in this publication meets the minimum requirements of
American National Standard for Information Sciences—Permanence of Paper
for Printed Library Materials, ANSI/NISO Z39.48-1992.

Printed in the United States of America

CONTENTS

PART ONE: MUSEUMS, CONTROVERSY, AND THE PAST

PART TWO: THE CIVIL WAR, RECONSTRUCTION, AND THE INSTITUTIONALIZATION OF RACISM

PART THREE: NATIVE PEOPLES AND WHITE-WASHED HISTORY

PART FOUR: IDENTITY POLITICS AND THE RATIONAL AND SYMPATHETIC MINDS

PART FIVE: COMMUNITY RESPONSIVENESS
AND HISTORICAL RECONTEXTUALIZATION

FIGURES

TERMS

Community leaders—Vocally engaged in public discourse and often activists for particular local causes and efforts. Community leaders may hold a variety of titles, but they are typically highly engaged individuals in the politics and activities of towns, cities, and rural localities.

Empathy—Characterized by active listening and an attempt to understand the experiences of other people. Empathy is crucial to reconciliation and dialogue.

The Lost Cause narrative—Historians use this term to refer to the broad-based reinterpretation of the causes of the American Civil War and the motivations of the Confederacy and its leaders that arose in the late 1800s. The Lost Cause narrative downplays the role of slavery in the Civil War by emphasizing the nobility of the agricultural South and its advocacy for states' rights.

Memorial—Traditionally freighted with the burden of helping the public to "never forget" a tragic event or to elicit a somber reflection on an individual's life. The word "memorial" is sometimes used interchangeably (even within this book) with "monument."

Monument—Monuments can be considered a subset of memorials, but often have a perception of being more celebratory or overtly "patriotic" than their umbrella group of memorials. Statues are the most common form that monuments take.

Public art—Art intended to be viewed by the public, typically in outdoor settings and can be in many different mediums. Over time (at least a generation removed from its installation), public art may be perceived to be more akin to a monument than to public art.

Public historians—Historians who do their work primarily outside of academia. Some public historians engage with the public as museum professionals. Others may be government employees or prefer to focus on the local history of their communities as informal public historians.

Restorative justice—Aimed at bringing about reconciliation rather than retribution, restorative justice was the goal of South Africa's Truth and Reconciliation Commission's work to bring justice for black South Africans in the wake of the end of apartheid.

Statue—A work of art done with three-dimensionality. A statue can be created in many mediums and can be representational or abstract.

Vergangenheitsbewältigung—A German word literally translated as "the struggle to overcome the negatives of the past." This word has been used since World War II to refer to how Germans have tried to reconcile with the crimes of Nazism.

ACKNOWLEDGMENTS

The sustaining fire for *Controversial Monuments and Memorials: A Guide for Community Leaders* was the countless number of people who responded to my entreaties and emails with interest, enthusiasm, and engagement. With a subject as fraught and complex as this one, I found myself constantly humbled. The contributors to this book span such an incredible range of expertise— professors, museum geeks, community leaders, politicians, public historians, and scholars. Each one shared generously of his or her time and intellect, and each one has enriched and enlivened my understanding of the never-ending interplay of past and present. Thank you to all of you.

When I first "jumped ship" from the world of history museums to work for the Denver Museum of Nature & Science, Bob Beatty at the American Association for State and Local History (AASLH) told me that I'd be back to history. At the time, I was dubious. But now I know that Clio's inexorable pull is just too strong, and I truly can't escape it. Bob's unflagging work to encourage, make connections, edit, send articles, swap stories, and review drafts was essential to transforming ideas into reality. Bob also connected me with Eric App, whose insightful comments and "iron sharpening" provided valuable critical feedback from a very different perspective than mine and enhanced this book's introduction.

I also want to thank Charles Harmon at Rowman & Littlefield for his keen editing eye and support throughout the process. Thank you also to Katie O'Brien at Rowman. Additionally, Vondra Shaw Abbott, a volunteer librarian at the Denver Museum of Nature & Science, helped me to find books and articles early in the process.

Many colleagues at the Denver Museum of Nature & Science provided just the right support or ideas at just the right time. Tina Martinez, Dr. Steve Nash, Justine Zollo, Liz Davis, Jared Vázquez, Julia Spalding-Beegles, Treloar Bower, George Sparks, Hugo Valdez, Tanya Breeling, Dr. Chip Colwell, Nancy Walsh, John Servold, Dr. Michele Koons, Jose Zuniga, Lindsey Housel, and Jennifer Moss Logan are among the many to whom I owe a hearty round of thanks.

My delight in reconnecting with Jill Ogline Titus—a friend from my undergraduate days at Taylor University and a stellar contributor to this book—reminded me that my history professors from Taylor helped to shape and spark my emotional and intellectual connection to the past. Thanks must go out in particular to Drs. Steve Messer, William Ringenberg, and Tom Jones. Of course, my graduate thesis advisor from Indiana University–Purdue University, Indianapolis (IUPUI), Dr. Nancy Robertson, is also owed thanks for her good work in cleaning up my writing and sharpening my thinking during the long years of getting my master's degree.

The connections I have had the joy to make through my career in museums have been so helpful in pointing me toward important thinkers and writers on this topic. I want to thank Kemi Ilesanmi, JJ Lonsinger Rutherford, and Melanie Adams for their assistance.

My friendship—given sustenance through periodic breakfasts—with Danny Gardner has been a boon for the past year or so. Thank you, Pastor!

Noel Balasingham, a dear friend, started a journey with me into the "issues and tissues" of life many years ago that continues with this book. My personal transformation with regard to privilege, social justice, and the restorative power of faith can be traced in large part to my friendship with Noel. Thank you, brother.

With a short timeline and the many twists and turns of this project, my family (Mom, Dad, Larry, Linda, Katy, Peter, Elizabeth, Lena, and Abigail) has been a steady rock of love through everything—my beloved and beautiful Molly most of all. Ultimately, this book is for the newest member of our family. This is for you, dear, sweet Michael, with hope that it will honor your ancestors.

INTRODUCTION

CHARLOTTESVILLE, MEMORY, AND HOW TO READ THIS BOOK

Tension hovered thick in the air in Charlottesville, Virginia, on August 12, 2017. The night before, young men and women with tiki torches had walked through the University of Virginia's campus yelling Nazi slogans and chanting, "Blood and soil, we'll take our streets back."[1] Antifascist (Antifa) and Black Lives Matter protesters stood in the streets ready to face that same group of neofascists as they assembled to protest the removal of a statue—a silent, carved piece of stone whose meanings had been contested nearly from the day it was constructed and whose unseeing visage would loom over three deaths that hot day in August.

In the early afternoon of August 12, after riot police had dispersed some of the crowds and the violent clashes of the morning had begun to wane, counterprotester Heather Heyer was killed after being run over by a car driven by a white supremacist from Ohio. Later that afternoon, two Virginia state troopers were killed in a helicopter crash while observing the crisis from above.[2] Some have said that the Civil War is still being fought in the South.³ On this day, the fight moved out of the ideological and rhetorical and became deadly once again.

◼ ◼ ◼

Earlier that summer, Jason Kessler, a resident of Charlottesville and an "alternative right" blogger, stood on the steps of the Lincoln Memorial and said, "Lincoln was a traitor. Our entire country would be better off if the South had won the Civil War. Now the same carpetbagging cowards that call us racist are trying to tear down our monuments."⁴ Kessler continued his tirade by invoking free speech and encouraging his fellow alt-right activists to join him in Charlottesville.

Hundreds of neofascists, southern nationalists, and white supremacists heeded Kessler's call and descended upon Charlottesville. While Kessler's reason for assembling these marchers might have been obscured by the long litany of grievances and hatreds espoused by the multifarious hate groups who answered his call to action, the touchstone issue for Kessler was a proposal initiated by Charlottesville's vice mayor, Wes Bellamy—the lone black representative on the city council—to remove a statue of Confederate general Robert E. Lee from the formerly named Lee Park.⁵

In an interview with National Public Radio (NPR) one day after the deaths in Charlottesville, Bellamy reflected on what ignited hate and inflamed the alt-right. Asked by the interviewer if he thought that the removal of the statue of Robert E. Lee from the center of town precipitated the events of August 12, Bellamy said, "I don't think it's about the statue. This is about white supremacy. And this is about the notion of different individuals of the majority race. And they believe that they are superior to anyone who is not of the, quote, unquote, 'white pure race.' They want to try and invoke fear."⁶

To Bellamy, the removal of the statue of Robert E. Lee was just an excuse for racists to make themselves visible and to spread fear. It became a rallying cry that emboldened white supremacists to display their deepset pride in their racial identity. The threat to remove Confederate statues encouraged white nationalists to stridently vocalize and violently act upon their belief that white people have an unassailable right to control the United States, including shaping the narratives of its past. Lee's Charlottesville statue was a mere vessel for the rage of racist ideologues who sought not to prevent the destruction of history but to use history to reaffirm their faith in the supremacy of the vision of a white America and to distort it in service of their intolerance and bigotry.

Charlottesville, Virginia, statue of General Robert E. Lee, ca. 1920–1950. Photo by Theodor Horydczak. Courtesy of the Library of Congress.

The motivation behind erecting and the reasons for keeping monuments and other historical markers is the impetus for *Controversial Monuments and Memorials: A Guide for Community Leaders*. Public historians, community leaders, and museum professionals cannot merely "get the history right" and then hope that we can overcome deliberate misconstructions of history and the ideological obfuscation of those who shrink from facing the realities of history and engagement with the past. Polarized rhetoric will not move us toward true understanding. Rather, we must seek common ground through dialogue. Extremist positions—"tear down all Confederate monuments today" on the far left and "preserve them at all costs" on the far right—are not productive.

We need to face head-on the tough issues that communities across America—and analogous locales overseas—deal with as reconciliation between societies today and the past collide. The events of the summer of 2017 that culminated in the tragedy in Charlottesville are outgrowths of ongoing dialogues and disputes about controversial history that encompass numerous historical situations and touch every part of the history of the United States.

Controversial Monuments and Memorials presents voices from the front lines of the ideological battles over memorializing the past. These are individuals deeply immersed in the theoretical and historical work of memorialization and who have actually worked to contextualize, remove, or reinterpret monuments. These case studies implore us not only to be more thoughtful and critical of our assumptions but also to push for change and to let our knowledge drive us to positive action.

It is my hope that as people read this book, they will also listen and reflect before taking actions (or sides) on the debates occurring in their own communities. Now is the time for community leaders, museum professionals, and historians to fully engage with the public. Introspection, awareness of our own biases, and thoughtful community responsiveness are the tools that will make this engagement meaningful and lasting. I hope that this book will provide a road map through the statues and memorials that continue to weigh down our collective American psyche.

Stone relics of bygone times stand in prominent places throughout this country. For most people, these statues are part of their everyday landscape in the same way that a Subway or Starbucks might be: instantly forgettable, silent sentinels that stare blankly into the distance. They are the forgotten remnants of the past, collecting bird excrement and slowly wearing away as the years pass them by.

When we erect a statue or a memorial, we are telling those who come after us that what we have built is worth remembering. We are giving the people of the future tangible, visible clues about what we value. We are saying that they need to pay attention to what this chunk of granite or hunk of metal *means*. We implore the denizens of the future to sit up and to listen to their past—which is our present as well as our own unique memory and interpretation of the past. Monuments and memorials say more about us as the erectors than they do about history itself.

Along with cemeteries and places of worship, memorials and monuments are firmly in the realm of the sacred in American society. Inviting reflection, admiration, reminiscence, and/or patriotism, monuments are built reminders to people and events that we deemed worthy of enshrining in durable stone or long-lasting metal. How do we endow these items with meaning and how does that meaning change as values and standards shift? Consider the following brief example as an illustration of how a statue's meaning can transform over time.

I am a Hoosier. I lived in Indianapolis for a little more than ten years (2001–2012), and during that time I was privileged to enjoy the ascendancy of Peyton Manning as a star quarterback for the Indianapolis Colts. Culminating in a Super Bowl win in 2008, the Colts went from perennial losers and also-rans to the cream at the top of the National

Football League's milk carton. On October 7, 2017, the team dedicated a statue of Peyton Manning outside of Lucas Oil Stadium, where the Colts play their games. I thought about this statue and what it represents in the context of the statues from the past.

If I were to get into the shoes of an Indianapolis resident a hundred years from now (let's say the year 2120, just to keep the number nice and round) and I came upon this statue of Peyton Manning, what might I think about it? Let's suspend disbelief for a few moments and make some conjectures about what the future might be like as we enter into this thought exercise.

We are gazing at a statue of a middle-aged white man wearing some sort of shirt with padding and a helmet with odd bars in front of his mouth. He appears to be physically fit, and he is holding an oblong ball as if he is about to throw it. Since football is no longer played in the year 2120—it was proven by scientists in the late 2010s that it damaged players' brains and led to catastrophic health conditions—the specifics of the sport he is supposed to be playing elude us. Clearly people in the past appreciated the sport that he played, but to us it seems ridiculous to memorialize a mere game—and one that celebrated bodily harm—by building a large statue in honor of a player of that game. Who decided that this statue should be built here? What did this person do that was so worthy of remembrance? Should we still countenance this statue even though it represents a barbaric sport that caused lasting harm to thousands of people? What of Peyton Manning's descendants? Will they be upset if we decide that it is time to move on from the past?

By future casting in this way, we can see the dilemma that our forebears left for us when they built memorials and monuments. Some memorials seem unlikely to ever be controversial. But when we let the unknowns of the future drive the interpretation of monuments, we find that the pedestals upon which these monuments stand quickly give way to the disintegrating power of changing values, new ways of perceiving the past, and the simple and inexorable grind of the ascendancy of the new at the expense of the old.[7]

Yet, while the example above is useful as a tool for thinking about how a Peyton Manning statue may be viewed in the future, it is not as directly applicable to the case studies and the stories that this book will tackle. Because most of these case studies are so deeply tied to power systems, white supremacy, black and native resistance to oppression, and the ongoing and systemic racism within American society, the Peyton

Manning example is only useful as a way to think about the statues we are currently erecting, not the ones that reflect many years of contested history and the tension of the social systems of racism in America. The fact that statues are freighted with ever-changing meanings is the point of the Manning illustration.

The Importance of Thoughtful Consideration of Monuments

Slavery was the cause of the Civil War. Many amateur historians, high school teachers, and laypeople will point to economic factors or states' rights as the cause of the Civil War. But, as W. Todd Groce argues in chapter 3, from the very beginning of the Civil War, southern leaders of the Confederacy were explicit about why they wanted to secede from the United States—they wanted to preserve slavery.[8] In addition, the necessary question in response to the specious alternative suggestion about the cause of the Civil War is this: What rights did the southern states want to preserve? The answer, of course, is the right to own slaves. And what agricultural economic system did the southern states want to retain? The answer, of course, is an agricultural system based on chattel slavery.

Once we have acknowledged that slavery was the cause of the Civil War, it becomes easier to see how the destruction of that profitable system wrought by the South's defeat resulted in a desire among some to change the war's narrative and to infuse the military defeat with nobility and purpose. Widespread racism—which persists to this day as the most trying and unshakable of American traditions—led to this counternarrative becoming inextricably tied to white supremacy.

Historians and thoughtful community leaders must resist offering a milquetoast response to the debates of our time. Pulling the comfortable blankets of ignorance over our heads keeps our voices silent. Hiding from the troubling dawn of newly emboldened white nationalists, jingoistic celebrants of military escalation, and self-righteous media bullies will not result in a society that anyone would care to be part of. We must rise to the challenges of our time and face them with the tools of reason, empathy, and context. Museums become effective public servants and engaged community members when we embrace this approach.

Here it is important to separate individuals from the system and time period in which they exist. Vilifying all people who fought for the South is not profitable, nor is it useful to simplify the complexities of history as simply "good" or "evil." History is at its best when it acknowledges that the rational decision makers of the past were as fully human and fallible as we are today.[9] Moreover, when we approach the past from a place of humility, we set ourselves up for insights into the shared humanity and desire for love, security, and relationships that define our species and that thread through all recorded history. These threads are why the stories of the past are compelling to us and why we can relate to people who lived thousands of miles away from us, thousands of years in the past. This is why the case studies and chapters included in this book can help us to further our understanding of the past in the context of the present controversies in tangible, actionable ways.

Statues Are Not Always
What They Seem to Be

At supper the other night, I asked my daughters (they are eleven, nine, and seven years old) about statues. The glory of having three elementary school daughters is that they are a fantastic built-in focus group and they will always say *exactly* what is on their minds. At first they talked about playing Pokémon Go! at the statue park (Benson Sculpture Garden in Loveland, Colorado) with their cousins. Their grandparents live in Loveland, and so strolling through the sculpture park hunting for Ponytas is a great way to spend an afternoon (and clearly quite memorable).

I followed up by asking about sculptures of famous women that they might have seen before. What ones did they remember of women and girls? My nine-year-old daughter cut in very quickly: "Daddy, they're all naked!" My daughter's all-too-true statement highlights the history of objectification of women in Western society and the lack of "heroic" statues built to honor female historical figures in the United States. Even statues that showcase a generic "Lady Liberty" often portray her as a buxom, yet demure, figure. As with many historical situations, when you lift up a corner of an issue, whole worlds are revealed below. In this case, the stories of women and statues could become an entire book, as could the juxtaposition of statues as works of art versus statues as items of commemoration.

Let's take a closer look at the issue of statues as public art. Where is the line between fine art and civic memory? Statues as art are saddled with multifarious meanings and can be idiosyncratic to the artist's message and the shared experiences of public art. As an example, all visitors to Denver who pass through the airport are greeted by a huge thirty-two-foot-tall statue of a blue horse rearing up, with glowing orange eyes and a wild wind-swept mane. Locally and colloquially known as "Blucifer," this controversial work of public art—actually titled *Mesteño*—was designed by artist Luis Jimenez to evoke the West and signify the hopeful strength of the ascendant American West.[10] What Jimenez hoped to achieve with the sculpture was unique to his artistic vision and seemingly propelled by the value he placed in the prevailing narratives of the region. Yet this work of art also attempted to reframe the narrative from a different perspective. *Mesteño* represents the vantage point of a Mexican American artist who saw the traditional heroic vision of white, eastern immigrants pushing and pioneering westward as incompatible with the reality of the amalgam of cultures that actually formed the backbone of Jimenez's view of the true western ethos.[11]

Whether Jimenez was successful in his effort to reframe the narrative of the West is immaterial to the fact that he earnestly strived to do so. Yet the meaning of his work of art ultimately gave way to the prevailing public opinion, which was decidedly *not* informed by Jimenez's life story and perspective. Statues, then, fall into two general ideological camps. A statue can either affirm the existing society status quo and depict scenes and people from the past as heroic or challenge the prevailing ideologies and push for new understandings of the world. Most of this book will grapple with statues that definitively fall into the former category. Primarily military focused, statues of leaders and soldiers from the major American wars are the most well-known monuments in the United States. As we will discover through contributions by F. Sheffield Hale, Thomas Seabrook, Jill Ogline Titus, Modupe Labode, and W. Todd Groce, monuments to Confederate generals and soldiers were primarily erected in the late nineteenth and early to mid-twentieth centuries and have been the nexus of much recent debate and action in communities across the nation.

While this is not necessarily a new discussion, it came to the fore in 2015 as cities throughout the South commenced removing and reinterpreting statues representing the Confederacy. In that year, the massacre of nine black parishioners of the Emmanuel AME Church in Charleston by Dylann Roof, who espoused a hatred for blacks and admired neo-Confederates, set off a spate of discussion and debate about Confederate iconography.[12] Not only was the Confederate battle flag lowered from the South Carolina statehouse, but the wisdom of allowing monuments to the Confederacy to stand also began to be questioned in earnest.[13] The violence and death of Charlottesville in 2017 and the destruction of monuments in other cities further propelled discussion about the meaning of monuments to the Confederacy and caused municipalities and museum professionals to question why and how they display Confederate-related paraphernalia and to call into question the purpose of Confederate statues.

The immediacy of the events that led to a reconsideration of Confederate monuments and the visceral reaction (from both supporters and opponents) to the hundreds of statues and memorials to the Confederacy that stand throughout the United States results in a preponderance of the chapters herein focused on statues memorializing the Civil War and the Confederacy. The sheer number of statues to the Confederacy in the United States—well over one thousand—thrust these figures into the forefront of the debates around reinterpretation and removal.[14] But it will be important for us to contextualize the issue of reinterpretation and memorialization by examining examples of contentious statues and memorials that have nothing to do with the Blue and the Gray.

How to Read This Book

Community leaders and public historians have approached reinterpreting, removing, or reimagining controversial statues in a multiplicity of ways. Think about these case studies and chapters as facets to the gemstone of historical understanding and community engagement. Each facet will illuminate different aspects of the gemstone as they catch the reflected light from the strains of American exceptionalism and white supremacy that give power to these statues.

The chapters in this book will help to frame the uniquely American story of memorialization. The first section, "Museums, Controversy, and the Past," takes on the interpretation of the past and the philosophical traps that museums—and, by extension, historians and the general public—fall into when they seek to pin the past into their own insect Schmidt's box schemas.[15] To drive home the importance of contextualization, Modupe Labode provides a comprehensive and incisive look at the recent history of memorialization in the United States in her compelling chapter, "Confronting Confederate Monuments in the Twenty-First Century." You will also find a chapter by W. Todd Groce of the Georgia Historical Society, which contains a powerful repudiation of those who would attempt to derogatorily use the term "revisionist history." In his chapter, Groce provides definitions of history and the past that are useful for us as we begin this journey: "History is the meaning that the present gives to the past; as society changes, so, too, does our interpretation of the past." Groce also weaves in a much-needed call for the integration of the humanities with STEM education.[16]

The next section, "The Civil War, Reconstruction, and the Institutionalization of Racism," is not so much the story of the Civil War as the story of how the Civil War and the end of slavery became a touchstone for the racial divides that have animated the memorialization in the United States since the end of that war. My framing chapter, "Remembering the Civil War," opens this section to provide a cohesive narrative of Civil War memorialization for easy reference. I will also share some of my personal connection to Civil War history as a way to illustrate the importance of our personal stories to our evolving conception of the past. The chapters included in this section are grouped together because they all address monuments related to the American Civil War. Despite this thematic tie, you will find that each chapter is distinct in outlook and in the solutions suggested—a product of the region and context from which each author emerges. Jill Ogline Titus begins with a powerful story from Gettysburg—the most famous of all Civil War battle sites. She draws in documentation that shows strong connections between Civil War memory, the civil rights movement, and the Cold War—a surprising and fascinating tale. Next, Thomas R. Seabrook's chapter is focused on Virginia's monuments to the Confederacy and presents compelling evidence that World War I and women's groups like the United Daughters of the Confederacy drove the conceptualization and building of statues hand-in-hand with the Lost Cause narrative. Julian C. Chambliss shares a moving example of African American agency in wresting control of the narratives of the Civil War—both through the civil rights movement and in response to the ongoing persistence of Confederate iconography in society. Stuart W. Sanders shares the unique spin on the memorialization of two very different Confederate leaders that occurred in the former "border state" of Kentucky. F. Sheffield Hale from the Atlanta History Center presents some poignant examples for how museums can provide resources for opening critical community dialogue around Confederate monuments. Closing this section is an article originally published in *Civil War Times* from *HistoryNet* that chronicles soundbite opinions on what to do with Confederate statues from a wide swath of stakeholders and scholars.

The section following, "Native Peoples and White-Washed History," draws in the other primary strand of white supremacy and violence from American history—the systematic removal and annihilation of native peoples from their lands. Gerard Baker's case study from his experience as one of the first American Indian superintendents of the Little Bighorn Battlefield National Monument in Montana provides a poignant example from a fascinating moment in history. William S. Walker's chapter delves into the complexities surrounding Theodore Roosevelt's legacy and—in particular—the equestrian statue of Roosevelt that stands outside of the American Museum of Natural History. My chapter weaves in the legacy of Columbus, Father Junipero Serra, and a story from the early 1990s that gives a fascinating glimpse of how a few key individuals drove the reinterpretation of a monument about Connecticut's Pequot War.

The next section, "Identity Politics and the Rational and Sympathetic Minds," is simultaneously the most difficult and the most pressingly urgent part of this book. Historians are often loath to wade into the politics of the present and to critically examine our own biases. I am no exception. I found the chapter "Group Behavior, Self-Examination, and Clearing the Air around Controversial Issues" the most difficult to write from an objective, disinterested standpoint—and perhaps that is the way it should be. Waiting passively on the sidelines of debates that historians need to be part of does no one any good. You'll find George W. McDaniel's chapter here. A Vietnam veteran, McDaniel has a unique perspective on war-related monuments. His call for an examination of the meanings of these statues from the perspective of veterans is illuminating. I paired McDaniel's chapter with a reprint of a speech that New Orleans mayor Mitch Landrieu gave in May 2017 after the city took down the last of its Confederate statues. Landrieu's ability to meld historical context and civic pride is stunning in its bravery and forthrightness. To close out this section, Jose Zuniga ruminates on that most insightful example of American popular culture—*The Simpsons*. Zuniga pauses with a bit of levity to remind us that statues and history are malleable and that our yellow cartoon analogs have much to teach us about ourselves.

The final section, "Community Responsiveness and Historical Recontextualization," shares how community action and civic dialogue can be the motor that drives historical recontextualization and healing. My chapter, "'The Struggle to Overcome the Negatives of the Past,'" provides a wider lens for memorialization and takes us to other countries that have attempted to make peace with their violent and racist pasts. Understanding how other countries have struggled with the weightiest issues in their past helps to illuminate how the United States might approach the similarly weighty issues of slavery and the legacy of the Civil War. In her chapter, Linda Norris draws in many disparate strands of memory and ways to remember the painful pasts from around the world in a case study drawn from her work with Sites of Conscience. Also included in this section, Vanessa Cuervo Forero reveals the power of the arts to unify communities and drive change with her case study from New York City. The Missouri History Museum (MHM) has been an active leader in working with the St. Louis community around issues of race and civil rights. Elizabeth Pickard's case study about the ACTivists program at MHM and its work to bring to light previously untold stories of civil rights and black activism in St. Louis draws into its orbit current events like the shooting of Michael Brown in Ferguson. This case study is instructive for how museums might contextualize polarizing current events in new ways. Brian Murphy brings a case study from Project Say Something in Alabama highlighting the importance of community dialogue coupled with historical context. Ben Wright shares the fascinating story of the creation and reinterpretation of Confederate statues at the University of Texas at Austin. He describes how they ended up in the Briscoe Center—the school's on-campus museum—and how their placement in a new context has been received by museumgoers. JJ Lonsinger Rutherford's chapter about *El Movimiento* in Colorado provides a clear description of the challenges and strength that come from deep engagement with community around difficult topics.

My hope is that you will plumb this book for what you need. Rare are the books that are worth reading cover to cover. I hope this one might come close to that ideal, but I won't hold it against you if you choose to seek out the parts that are applicable to your situation. Skip around if you'd like. Please use this book in the ways that are most helpful for your situation and match your interests.

■ ■ ■

As quoted above, Wes Bellamy saw the violence in Charlottesville as symptomatic of a strain of white supremacy that laces itself through all of American history. But he also saw a way out of the darkness of that hot August day. Bellamy saw a hopeful future for Charlottesville: "The city and the people that I know are loving, caring, resilient people. . . . The Charlottesville that I know is a place that will rally around each other. And we are going to love each other. And we will be stronger because of it."[17]

Similarly, in 2015, at Reverend Clementa Pinckney's funeral at the Emmanuel African Methodist Episcopal (AME) Church in Charleston, South Carolina, then President Barack Obama made a similar plea. Pinckney and eight other parishioners of the church had been murdered by Dylann Roof, a white supremacist hoping to start a race war. In his remarks, Obama reflected on the long history of violence against blacks in the United States, but then he sought to carve out a vision of hope for the future: "The good news is I am confident that the outpouring of unity and strength and fellowship and love across Charleston today, from all races, from all faiths, from all places of worship indicates the degree to which those old vestiges of hatred can be overcome."[18]

Loving each other leads to strength. Resilience emerges from a community that cares for each other. These are the touchstones that will fuel transformation and promote true reconciliation with the painful past. Stone memorials and monuments represent worlds of ideas and carry vast oceans of meaning. How will you bring love, strength, and historical truth as new light to the shadowed edifices and crumbling statues of our collective past?

No matter where you find yourself in these pages, I fervently hope that you will bring with you the love, strength, and courage that Wes Bellamy spoke of. Our interpretation of the people of the past become as hard and pitted as the statues that memorialize them if we do not carry empathy and courage with us. Historical events become a calloused drudgery of names and dates without the strength to face the challenges of a complicated past. A love for the stories of the failures and redemptions of flawed human beings can drive newfound empathy and a triumphant vision of a more just society. It is only when we fuse our historical brains with our hearts that we can emerge on the other end with collective actions that can transform our world. Taking down statues or reinterpreting them does not "erase" the history they purport to represent. Rather, it allows us a better reflection of who we are as individuals and, perhaps most important, as a nation.

1

MUSEUMS, CONTROVERSY, AND THE PAST

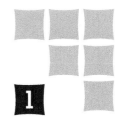

HISTORY AS LEGEND AND MYTH AS FACT

DAVID B. ALLISON

Monuments and memorials fall within a unique realm of historiography and public discourse. Meant to be permanent reminders of events and people deemed worthy of preservation, monuments and memorials are history made visible and accessible to all. This chapter will explore the intersection of public understanding of history and how historians have attempted to reconcile popular conceptions of the past with the historic record. Following a short exploration of these themes, chapters by Modupe Labode and W. Todd Groce implore museum professionals to critically examine assumptions as we wade into discussions about the disputed past.

History and Popular Memory

David Glassberg, in *Sense of History: The Place of the Past in American Life*, writes that "every person is his or her own historian, creating idiosyncratic versions of the past that make sense based on personal situation and experience."[1] Guests to museums, then, are not merely passive recipients and empty vessels into which information is poured, but are rather continually constructing their own meanings about the past and its relation to their lives. Clearly, however, the way that museums present the history and the prejudices and biases their leaders bring to the design process will affect the meaning that individuals construct for themselves. Glassberg's analysis supports this idea. He continues later, "But our individual memories are not solely the product of idiosyncratic recollection; they are also established and confirmed through dialogue with others."[2] Glassberg conceived the exchange of ideas typified by dialogue as the most important transmitter of culture and values. By promoting dialogue (through exhibits, interpretation, and programming), museums engage the public in essential historical meaning-making.

As we take this lens of understanding to memorials and monuments, it behooves us to ask ourselves why the public and historians and museum professionals seem to be at odds about what meaning "should" be drawn from events of the past.[3] Some historians view the public's meaning-making as intrinsically tied to uninformed opinions that have no relation to the well-researched "facts" that they attempt to promulgate.[4] This sort of intellectual arrogance belies a deep-set fear that their perceived authority will degrade under a crass popularization of cut-rate "Disney-fied" history.[5] The never-ending pendulum swings of popular crazes for particular time periods and people of the past are driven by the popularity of TV shows and movies set in the past. As such, historians face the unenviable task of making their voices heard amid a scrum of flashy productions featuring beautiful people and places.

The shine of 1920s England that was polished into a bright, melodramatic gem by *Downton Abbey* is only now beginning to wane.[6] The high-pressure world of advertising glamorized by *Mad Men* sparked a rabid interest in 1950s America.[7] The Netflix show *Stranger Things* has elevated 1980s Middle America to full-on nostalgic bliss for Generation Xers and older Millennials.[8] In years past—notably for Westerns during the 1960s and 1970s—television shows and movies helped to create armchair historians and amateur history enthusiasts by stimulating the imagination through thrilling stories and iconic landscapes that spoke to a deeply entrenched concept of American exceptionalism. Historians may shudder at some of the inaccuracies or exaggerations that these popularized views of the past showcase, but it is important to sleuth out the

The glamor of 1920s English high-class wealth as portrayed in *Downton Abbey* drove the public's interest in that time period.

lessons that these shows may have for us around how the public prefers to consume history and how what we do is perceived.[9]

Ultimately, the public's constantly shifting peccadillos for the various time periods as presented in popular media reveal an underlying interest and passion for the "foreign country" of the past.[10] Likewise, genetic testing kits and resources from companies like Ancestry.com provide millions of people with the means to explore more deeply their own family history.[11] Despite stagnant attendance at many history museums throughout the country, the sheer number and continued viability of history museums speaks to an ongoing interest in the past that is shared by large swaths of the American public. The Institute for Museum and Library Services (IMLS) issued a news release in 2014 that stated that there were 16,880 active history museums and historical associations in the United States![12]

Postmodernism, Truth, and the Challenge of Relativism

A large peloton of leading historians who have grappled with troubled histories of commemoration and memory have taken to task postmodern relativism in surprisingly vehement terms. Noted Civil War historian David Blight was recently quoted in the *Washington Post* saying, "This Trump-era ignorance and misuse of history is forcing historians—and I think this is a good thing—to use words like 'truth' and 'right or wrong.' In the academy we get very caught up in relativism and whether we can be objective and so on, and that's a real argument."[13] For Blight, extreme reliance on relativism can become a barrier to an informed perspective on historical events. Why is it important for historians to clarify their epistemological approach to the trajectory of history?[14] And what philosophical forebears still impact the public's perception of history?

Kevin Walsh writes that "modernism can thus be considered as a set of discourses concerned with the possibilities of representing reality and defining eternal truths."[15] Postmodernism, then, is distinct from modernism because it rebuts the assumption that there are eternal truths and that reality is unchanging once the nature of reality has been identified by scientists, historians, or other data-driven knowledge producers.[16] While most historians would not forswear the central tenets of postmodern thinking, the dangers of blatant disregard for historical fact and contemporary historiography should be disconcerting to historians and the public alike.

The distinction between what has "actually happened"—which we call the past—and how we interpret the past—which is what we call history—can be a problematic concept as we consider controversial history and disputed memory. Terms like "revisionist" are lobbed with derision at historians who have punctured previous historians' interpretations and posited a different understanding of the events and people of the past.[17] This begs the question—why would a historian consider altering well-established traditional understandings of the past?

Fundamentally, historians change the narratives of the past for two primary and intertwined reasons. The discovery of new evidence is certainly the easiest to understand and justify of these reasons. Examples of these sorts of physical discoveries abound and have rewritten history many times through the years. A theoretical example of a future discovery could be when Dallas resident Trixie LaRue cleans out her attic and finds a previously unknown document behind a box of tax returns from 1963 that reveals the real reasons why Lee Harvey Oswald shot John F. Kennedy. Or, even more likely, an intrepid archaeologist poking around in the dirt of the Piedmont discovers evidence of settlements with Viking-era artifacts that indicate that the Norse had ventured even farther down the coast of North America than previously thought. These sorts of tangible, evidentiary proofs that morph how historians view the past are typically only disputed when their authenticity is in question or when they may be thought to be overselling (or underselling) their impact on the historical record.

The second reason for changing the predominant narratives of the past—a response to shifting values, changing political and cultural ideals, and new scientific or philosophical theories—is more difficult and fraught with pitfalls, but is no less valid. The interpretation of the past is only useful for people in the present insofar as it can be understood and deciphered through our existing schemas and perceptions of our place in the world. Concerned dilettantes may bemoan the fact that the people of the past cannot defend themselves and explain "their side" of the story in rebuttal to historians' interpretation of their lives. Ultimately, however, the people of the past are dead and gone, and the present's prerogative—predicated on our own values and mores—must prevail.

It becomes easier to swallow the ascendancy of the present when we look at examples of interpretations of the past from historians of the past. Historians are no less a product of their particular place and time than the people they write about. Perhaps one of the most striking illustrations of the sweeping changes to prevailing understandings of the past centered on a young historian named Frederick Jackson Turner and his "frontier theory" of American development.

In 1893, as Chicago hosted an outsized World Columbian Exposition, Turner challenged the dominant narratives around America's unique character. Instead of viewing America as an offshoot of English and European cultural patterns, Turner proposed that America's past and its destiny were inextricably tied to the West and the pioneer ethos of the frontier.[18] Prior to Turner, historians—who mostly lived and worked east of the Appalachians—had been heavily biased toward an eastern-focused interpretation of the past that viewed America's development from the Atlantic Ocean inward toward the frontier, with impacts from native peoples and Spanish settlements in the West minimized or elided from their histories of the country. Turner's frontier theory did not rely on any new evidence; instead, it gathered its strength from a new examination of evidence in light of transformative cultural developments in the United States that originated from the West. He pointed to the rise of unions, the subjugation of native peoples, and the individualization borne of the self-sufficiency of pioneers as reasons why eastern historians had their interpretation of the development of the United States all wrong.[19] While Turner's theory is no longer preeminent among historians, his reinterpretation had opened new avenues to understand and decipher the past and continues to inform historians' perspectives about the United States' trajectory to this day.

Historians, then, have an obligation to continue to question their assumptions as new theories and cultural ideals emerge from the *zeitgeist*. Revisionism is not the nasty pejorative that some would attempt to make it into. Rather, thoughtful historians and museum professionals will acknowledge that the past, while fixed forever in time, must bend to the demands of new evidence and to the extraordinary pressures of the present as history unmakes and remakes itself in an unending cycle.

Museums and the Interpretation of the Past

As we cast our gaze past the work of historians and toward museums and public spaces and how they conceptualize and present difficult history, we must do so with an understanding of the limitations of these venues. Museums contextualize and help their visitors construct meaning about history—but they do so within the frame of the values and interpretations of their founders, their board, and the culture within which they find themselves. Living history museums provide an excellent case study for how the interpretation of the past at museums is wholly determined by the whims and vagaries of trends and by the strongly held opinions of those in power.

Most of the large living history museums in the United States had their advent with wealthy industrialists like Henry Ford (Greenfield Village in Dearborn, Michigan), John D. Rockefeller (Colonial Williamsburg in Virginia), or Eli Lilly (Conner Prairie north of Indianapolis in Indiana).[20] Their founders set out to educate the public in the values and ideals that they treasured with these museums—and to do so using a technique that attempted to convey a careful verisimilitude. Living history museums, perhaps more than other types of museums, aim to present a complete picture of the past. Fires are lit in carefully reconstructed hearths, enactors in waistcoats and breeches take on the accents and mannerisms of the time period, and historic breeds of livestock graze happily in unkempt fields.

Despite this façade of authenticity, the decisions made by leaders at these museums speak to the inability of museums to extricate themselves from the foibles of their founders and the inevitable concessions to modernity that comfort-seeking visitors expect. No matter how well researched the constructions of the past are at living history museums, creative choices have to be made in order to "fill in the blanks" left by an incomplete historical record. By the 1970s—the high-water mark for interest in colonial and pioneer-era history—most living history museums conveyed the image that life in the "Good Old Days" of the 1700s and 1800s was somehow purer and more honest than life in the present time. Learning from the mistakes of the past was less important than wallowing in the glory of the successes of the early European settlers and pioneers. These pioneers, not coincidentally, were predominantly presented as white, male, and dedicated to their country—the very same values that seemed desperately under attack by the counterculture of the late 1960s and early 1970s.

Living history museums became oases of backlash against the trends of a swiftly modernizing and demographically fragmenting America. The perceived disintegration of a monolithic, primarily white and religious culture in the 1970s—which was often spurred by an increasingly urbanized society—led to an upsurge in celebrations of rural and small-town Americana. Living history museums capitalized on this momentum by focusing on agricultural stories and on bucolic settings that bore little resemblance to the reality of life in the time periods they sought to portray.[21]

During this time, proponents of living history often couched their descriptions of the museums in the language of authenticity and presenting the past as it actually was. By doing so, they subtly made living history a sanctuary for people who wanted to celebrate America's past while at the same time lamenting its present. Historian Thomas Schlereth, in an article that appeared in *Museum News* in 1978, critiqued living history museums for their celebratory treatment of U.S. history. He argued that living history museums relied on 1950s-era consensus historiography—which sought to unify Americans under a narrative of progress and increasingly "civilized" behavior—and presented the past as blind worship of American myths and heroes.[22]

As social history and new voices from women and minorities began to chip away at national metanarratives of unity and unswerving faith in the pluck and rectitude of colonial- and pioneer-era politicians and military leaders, living history museums also began to change. Some museums worked to integrate new interpretations and perspectives into their presentations. Others maintained a celebratory, nationalistic approach to the enactments—and still do so to this day.[23]

Ultimately, the history experience at living history museums is formed not only from the messages designed into the vignettes they create but also in the interaction between the museum's staff and the public. The importance of that information as constructed rather than received points to a critical aspect of agency and to the idiosyncratic reception of messages at museums and historic sites. The public (and the staff who work at museums) are not blank slates upon which history is transmitted in a binary modality. Rather, both staff members and the public are simultaneously transformed through dialogue and shared experiences, which are informed by prior knowledge and beliefs.[24]

An additional layer to add to this dialogic connection with patrons centers on the role of material culture and artifacts in our interactions with audience. Why do we choose the things that we do to display? Sometimes our exhibits are driven by aesthetic sensibilities that seek to show off the most beautiful, representative items from a time and place. Often, however, the artifacts we display are there simply because they are the only bits of ephemera left, everything else having been lost or destroyed long ago. Perhaps what we choose to throw away says more about who we are than what we choose to fetishize in museum collections? Archaeologists' interest in middens and the garbage leavings of past civilizations imbues refuse with a significance that those items were never designed to have when they were created and used for day-to-day purposes. So, too, are museum collections but a dim reflection of the actual role that objects played in the past. Disgorged from their context and purpose and packed into boxes and cases designed to preserve and never again to serve the useful purposes for which they were designed, museum artifacts become a hollow attempt to reanimate the past with soulless, decontextualized "stuff."

Technology as a tool for museums also bears brief mention here. The past few years have brought significant growth and development to the technological capabilities of the leading virtual reality (VR) and augmented reality (AR) platforms. Many museums have experimented with creating virtual worlds for their guests to give them a better, more comprehensively immersive glimpse of the past.[25] Often, museums end up being a sort of proxy "third space" for the community—a place where people can come to interact with each other and to learn about the world in all its complexity and beauty. Does ceding the role of traditional community gathering place to a virtual environment mean that the unique relationships that form between individuals at museums would move to the digital environment? If our individual selves are subsumed into pixilated avatars strolling through fantastical VR environments with other, similar avatars, would we lose the ability to empathize with and learn about people who are different from us? Would we be susceptible to breaking up into microcommunities of like-minded individuals who have scarce incentive to interact with each other?

Despite the difficulty inherent in using artifacts and technologies to tell effective stories in museums, objects and digital environments can work in concert with live, person-to-person interaction to present effective gestalt representations of the people and events of the past. Ralph Waldo Emerson wrote, "The glance reveals what the gaze obscures." The power of museums comes from the clarity and emotional impact of story-driven, human-centric presentations of the past. Although lacking in the copious amounts of research and detail of scholarly treatises, emotionally resonant, impressionistic museum experiences provide new revelations and transformative interactions to audiences every day.

As these interactions take place, the narratives about the past that we have come to trust constantly influence our reception and incorporation of new information and ideas. The psychology of why people come to put faith in certain narratives—the complicated layering of personal tragedies, family influences, learned behaviors, and religious belief—is beyond the ken of this book. However, if we can "set the record straight" and get our history as close to accurate as possible, we may be able to gird ourselves with the necessary historical tools to address the painful past and memorialization with informed empathy. Modupe Labode and W. Todd Groce reinforce this high calling in their chapters, which commence directly after the next paragraph.

The next section, "The Civil War, Reconstruction, and the Institutionalization of Racism," will begin to construct a narrative that can provide guidance for museum professionals and community leaders as we approach our shared history with eyes fixed on truth and open to new ways of perceiving the United States' past. Many of the chapters that appear at the end of the next section are superior in form and argument to how I frame them—and the content overlaps quite a bit—but it seemed important to provide an overview from both a historical and a personal frame in order to set the stage more effectively for those chapters to shine. It is hoped that they will supplement and enhance the contributor chapters in meaningful ways. If they do not, the fault is all mine.

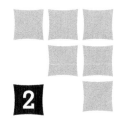

2

CONFRONTING CONFEDERATE MONUMENTS IN THE TWENTY-FIRST CENTURY

MODUPE LABODE

Editor's note: Here Modupe Labode expands on an essay she wrote for AASLH's Winter 2016 History News. *She notes some of the ways that history museums have been complicit in championing the Lost Cause and other white-culture-dominant narratives and issues a strong call to action for museum professionals. In addition, Labode provides a clear outline and discussion of the four primary strategies for dealing with objectionable memorials—alteration, reinterpretation, creating new monuments, and removal.*

From the late nineteenth century to the present, monuments valorizing those who fought for the Confederate States of America have stood in public places. Although small groups of people have consistently argued that these monuments do not belong in public spaces, until recently, most communities resisted calls to remove or interpret these memorials. However, two tragic incidents of bloodshed have opened a broader conversation about these monuments. In June 2015, a white supremacist named Dylann Roof murdered nine African Americans at a prayer meeting at Mother Emanuel AME Church in Charleston, South Carolina. Sharonda Coleman-Singleton, DePayne Doctor, Cynthia Hurd, Susie Jackson, Ethel Lance, Clementa Pinckney, Tywanza Sanders, Daniel Simmons, and Myra Thompson died that night. In August 2017, Heather Heyer, a white woman, died when she was struck by a car driven into a group of people protesting a white supremacist rally in Charlottesville, Virginia. Two state troopers, H. Jay Cullen and Berke M. M. Bates, also died that day as they were helping police to cover the riot. Roof wielded the Confederate battle flag, along with other symbols, as a marker of his white supremacist beliefs. James Alex Fields Jr., who drove the car that killed Heather Heyer, was in Charlottesville to take part in a rally of white nationalists and others who opposed the city's plan to remove a Confederate monument.

Landscapes in the United States are studded with monuments and memorials that various groups and individuals have placed to remind others about past events. These markers create a commemorative landscape.[1] No monument is neutral or objective, as such objects embody an interpretation of historical memory. The meaning of these symbols, and the commemorative landscape they create, shifts over time. As communities debate the meaning of these monuments, they often call on historical societies and museums to contribute their expertise. Yet many history organizations appear to be uncertain about what they should do or say or have opted to maintain official silences. Any statement, some organizations fear, could alienate local politicians, donors, friends, and neighbors. Silence, however, speaks volumes, and may convey the message that interpretation of the past is not relevant in these discussions. To help orient museums and historical societies as they engage in these community discussions, this chapter briefly surveys the origin of Confederate monuments and memorials, and then discusses some of the strategies that communities have used to engage with these monuments. Although the focus of this chapter is on Confederate monuments, examples of other memorials will be considered as well.

Confederate Monuments and "The Lost Cause"

Monuments to the Confederacy range from the grand statuary on Richmond, Virginia's, Monument Avenue to mass-produced statues placed in courthouse squares. These monuments are scattered throughout the country, although the majority are in the South.[2] In addition to monuments, the Confederate cause is memorialized by buildings named for officers and officials, school mascots, and the Confederate battle flag.[3] Monument building was an integral aspect of a social, political, and cultural movement that celebrated the "Lost Cause" in official and popular culture. The set of ideas takes its name from *The Lost Cause*, an 1866 tract by Edward Pollard, in which he chronicled the Civil War from the Confederate perspective. This ideology celebrated a mythical antebellum South, in which aristocratic whites presided over a bucolic South. The white men were chivalrous; the white women were gracious; and slaves, secure in a benign patriarchal institution, were loyal to their owners. Proponents of the Lost Cause argued that this romantic and wholly false vision was what the South had fought to defend, and what the United States had destroyed. White history professionals, working in museums and historical societies, lent official support to this distorted interpretation of the past. Popular culture spread Lost Cause interpretation nationwide through novels, plays, and films, including *The Birth of a Nation* and *Gone with the Wind*.

From the late nineteenth century, numerous energetic organizations—many of them run by Southern women—evangelized for the Lost Cause. Before World War II, these groups placed monuments in towns and cities throughout the region. Scholars Kirk Savage and John Winberry have documented that over time the preferred site for these monuments shifted from cemeteries to civic spaces, such as parks and courthouse squares.[4] Obelisks, plaques, and statues not only honored soldiers but also asserted that the values for which the Confederacy fought, including white supremacy, had not been defeated. In the late 1800s and early 1900s, anyone would have understood the connection between Confederate monuments and the ongoing economic, legal, social, and political subordination of African Americans. Racial violence, in the form of lynching, racial cleansing, and everyday harassment, enforced this social order through terror.

In addition to Confederate memorials, southerners created monuments that directly celebrated white supremacy, such as the commemoration of the 1874 Battle of Liberty Place, in which the White League led a coup against a New Orleans government made up of white and African American men.[5] Another subset of monuments placed before World War II focused on the "faithful slave," who presumably remained loyal to his owners. A particularly notorious monument was the "Good Darky" statue of a deferential black man, who tipped his hat to passersby. This statue stood for decades in Natchitoches, Louisiana.[6]

After World War II, segregationists wielded the Confederate battle flag to signal opposition to school desegregation and the civil rights movement. During the 1950s, Georgia, Alabama, and South Carolina incorporated the battle flag into their state banners.[7] Into the twenty-first century, branches of southern heritage organizations continue to place Confederate monuments throughout the South and in places as remote from the Confederate heartland as Iowa.[8] This most recent wave of Confederate monument building is in part a response to the changes in the memorial landscape, as civil rights activists began erecting markers and monuments and renaming streets to commemorate the civil rights movement, African American history, and sites associated with slavery and lynching.[9]

Challenging Confederate Monuments

For generations, most communities met calls to remove Confederate monuments with indifference or hostility. In discussions about Confederate monuments, it is common to hear some people speculate that "no one" complained about the monuments until recently. However, African Americans challenged these monuments when they were first established. Mamie Garvin Fields, quoted by Dell Upton, described how, in the 1890s, Charleston's African Americans confronted a monument honoring John C. Calhoun: "We used to carry something with us, if we knew we would be passing that way, in order to deface that statue—scratch up the coat, break the watch chain, try to knock off the nose." The statue was so marred that in 1896 white Charlestonians reinstalled it on a massive column.[10] African Americans also expressed displeasure with the "loyal slave" monument at Harper's Ferry and thwarted an attempt to place a Lost Cause monument to the "mammy" in Washington, DC.[11] In the early twenty-first century, African Americans in small towns in North Carolina lobbied to have Confederate monuments in their communities relocated or removed, while a community in Richmond, Virginia, protested a large image of Robert E. Lee that was part of a civic commemoration in their neighborhood.[12] These protests serve as a reminder that a significant part of the U.S. populace clearly understood the message of Confederate monuments—as edifices celebrating secession and white supremacy.

Many proposals to alter or interpret Confederate symbols in public spaces draw on strategies that have developed over decades of dealing with memorials. The most common strategies include alteration, reinterpretation, creating new monuments, and removal. These alternatives are not exhaustive strategies for engaging with Confederate monuments.[13]

Altering Monuments

Altering a Confederate monument has the potential to make profound changes to its meaning. In Maury County, Tennessee, two African American heritage organizations led the effort to alter the local war memorial by adding the names of county residents who had fought for the United States. In 2013, a ceremony was held dedicating a stone slab engraved with the names of fifty-four African American men who served in the United States Colored Troops (USCT) and four white men who fought for the United States. Many of the men who served in the USCT troops had once been enslaved and were fighting to end slavery and ensure permanent freedom for their families.[14] The simple listing of names on this slab may prompt viewers to reconsider their previous ideas about the men who fought in the Civil War and their motivations.

Many alterations to monuments—such as graffiti—are unauthorized. Confederate monuments have regularly been targets of graffiti bearing pointed political commentary, such as "Black Lives Matter" or significant dates in antiracist history.[15] In New Mexico, two monuments depicting settler conflict against native peoples in a positive light were altered by unknown people. In the 1970s, someone chipped out the word "savage" from a Union monument in Santa Fe describing warfare against "savage Indians." The absent spot remains. Someone also removed the spurred foot from the statue of conquistador Juan de Oñate. This act references Oñate's 1599 order that each adult Acoma Pueblo man who survived the suppression of a rebellion have a foot amputated and serve decades in slavery. A new foot has since been attached to the monument. (More information about the Oñate statue can be found in chapter 11 of this book.) These unauthorized acts of alteration at the very least indicate deep dissatisfaction with a monument's blunt, triumphant message.[16]

Interpreting Monuments

Reinterpreting monuments through reading rails or plaques allows the original structure to be preserved. Ideally, the viewer is able to develop a complex interpretation of the monument, but also of memorialization more generally. Qualitative evaluation would help historians understand whether reinterpretation actually achieves this goal. If the reinterpretation is conducted in collaboration with people who have divergent positions on the monument, the project itself may provide an opportunity for discussion and, potentially, understanding.

Ari Kelman and Kenneth Foote have analyzed what they consider a successful reinterpretation of a monument in Denver, Colorado. (Note: I had a small part in the process of reinterpreting this monument.) The Union soldier monument has a tablet listing the battles in which Colorado Territory troops fought. Among the military encounters was the "Sand Creek Battle." The Sand Creek Massacre, as the tragedy is more accurately known, occurred in 1864, when Colorado Territory troops attacked a peaceful, undefended village of Cheyenne and Arapaho people and killed more than 150 children, women, and men. When a state legislator learned how the monument described the massacre, he wanted the offensive name removed. However, representatives from the Northern Cheyenne, Northern Arapaho, and the Cheyenne-Arapaho tribes of Oklahoma, many of whom were related to victims of the massacre, all preferred reinterpreting the monument, not its alteration or removal. A complex array of factors made reinterpretation possible. The nations had ongoing relationships with the State of Colorado and the Colorado Historical Society, as well as long experience engaging with nonindigenous people concerning representing the Sand Creek Massacre. Among nonindigenous power brokers, there was consensus that the Sand Creek Massacre was indefensible, and during the discussions about what to do with the monument, those who sought to minimize the massacre were marginalized. If comparable factors do not exist, reinterpreting monuments may seem a half-hearted measure, undertaken as an unsatisfactory middle approach between those who advocate preserving and those who demand removing a monument.[17]

"Countering" Monuments

A common suggestion is that communities "counter" a Confederate monument with another monument that is the antithesis of the values represented by the Confederacy. This suggestion is often appealing because it avoids removing a monument and appears fair. However, Dell Upton calls attention to the insidious and dangerously inaccurate message conveyed by what he calls a "dual heritage" strategy. The Confederate monument usually is not diminished when a monument commemorating the civil rights movement, for example, is placed it its proximity. Instead, it appears that the monuments represent equally legitimate values.[18]

Several efforts successfully avoid this form of equivalency. In Lexington, Kentucky, an African American fraternity lobbied for a state historical marker in a space previously dominated by Confederate monuments. The marker called viewers' attention to the history of this public space as a site where enslaved people were sold. Unlike the Confederate memorials, the marker focused on an important aspect of the city's history that it had previously ignored and made the direct connection between the Confederacy, white supremacy, and slavery. The site's meaning has changed yet again when the city removed the Confederate monuments in 2017.[19]

Removing Monuments

Until recent years, removing a monument from public space was an option that many historians, historic preservationists, and government officials abhorred. For some, removing a monument seemed to violate principles of historic preservation or indicated an unwillingness to confront the past. Others optimistically noted that the memorials could provide opportunities for dialogue and education. After the violence in Charleston and Charlottesville, however, more cities have been willing to consider removing or relocating Confederate monuments. Often an ad hoc commission or existing committee has the task of creating recommendations for further action. Commissions in Baltimore and

Charlottesville, for example, have included historians and generated instructive reports.[20] New Orleans, Baltimore, Lexington (Kentucky), and St. Louis are among the cities that have removed monuments to the Confederacy. Out of the national spotlight, commissions throughout the country are determining the fate of Confederate monuments. As their decisions indicate, the desire to retain monuments in public places remains strong.[21]

When communities remove Confederate monuments, they are then faced with deciding what should happen to the now-vacant space: should the monument's existence be erased, or, as Kirk Savage has suggested, should a piece of the monument remain—perhaps an empty column—to remind passersby of values the public has renounced?[22] Communities also have to contend with relocating a large piece of outdoor sculpture. Some Confederate monuments have been relocated to cemeteries, while others languish in warehouses. Consistently, some suggest memorials be placed in less prominent locations or in museums. Historian Aleia Brown, writing about the Confederate battle flag, questions the ability of many museums to provide adequate interpretation of this racially charged object. Her concerns also apply to interpretation of these monuments in museum spaces.[23]

Confronting Confederate symbols and memorials is a complex, difficult task, in part, because if discussions are taken in good faith, people must grapple with important issues of race, power, and history. The stakes are high, given the polarized climate in the United States. Some people worry that discussing these issues causes racial dissent. However, it is important to recognize that these conversations are already occurring in private or semiprivate spaces, from kitchen tables to the internet, and are already affecting people's public actions and statements. Museums also need to discuss these issues among their own staff and volunteers. As Julia Rose argues, history workers must engage the process of learning about and engaging "difficult history" themselves in order to have any hope of facilitating learning among visitors.[24] The ability of museums to preserve, care for, and interpret the contentious past is dependent upon these conversations. Many museum workers have complicated relationships to the history of slavery and the Confederacy, which they are reluctant to discuss with their coworkers, or anyone outside of their families. Yet without honestly engaging the difficult past represented by Confederate symbols, the ability of history museums to engage in their core mission—interpreting the past—will be compromised.

Reading List

American Historical Association. "AHA Statement on Confederate Monuments," 2017. https://www.historians.org/publications-and-directories/perspectives-on-history/october-2017/aha-statement-on-confederate-monuments.

Bruggeman, Seth C., ed. *Commemoration: The American Association for State and Local History Guide.* Lanham, MD: Rowman & Littlefield, 2017.

Cox, Karen L. *Dixie's Daughters. The United Daughters of the Confederacy and the Preservation of Confederate Culture.* Gainesville: University Press of Florida, 2003.

Documenting the American South. *Commemorative Landscapes of North Carolina.* http://docsouth.unc.edu/commland/.

Doss, Erika. *Memorial Mania: Public Feeling in America.* Chicago: University of Chicago Press, 2012.

Savage, Kirk. *Standing Soldiers, Kneeling Slaves: Race, War, and Monument in Nineteenth-Century America.* Princeton, NJ: Princeton University Press, 1997.

Southern Poverty Law Center. *Whose Heritage: Public Symbols of the Confederacy,* April 21, 2016. https://www.splcenter.org/20160421/whose-heritage-public-symbols-confederacy.

University of North Carolina Library. "A Guide to Researching Campus Monuments and Buildings: 'Silent Sam' Confederate Monument." http://guides.lib.unc.edu/campus-monuments/silent-sam.

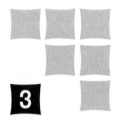

HISTORY, MEMORY, AND THE STRUGGLE FOR THE FUTURE

W. TODD GROCE

Editor's note: This chapter by W. Todd Groce has been expanded and adapted from an article that appeared in AASLH's History News *Winter 2016 issue. Groce provides an eloquent explanation and defense of historical revisionism and pleads for further integration between STEM education and the humanities.*

As **another** academic year gets under way, I am reminded of a study released in 2011 that reveals how little American students know about their nation's history. According to the National Assessment of Education Progress, only 20 percent of fourth graders, 17 percent of eighth graders, and 12 percent of high school seniors are proficient in history. Additional studies have demonstrated that this glaring lack of historical knowledge is not confined to the young but is a pervasive problem even among adults.[1]

For example, two years ago after the Charleston shooting, participants in a survey about Confederate symbols were asked two key questions: First, could they correctly identify U.S. Army general William Tecumseh Sherman? Second, could they name any Civil War battles? Those who failed to answer any question correctly (i.e., could not name a single Civil War battle or identify William Tecumseh Sherman) were more than twice as likely to favor the Confederate flag than those people who answered the questions correctly. In sum, the study revealed the opposite of what one would expect—those who most adamantly supported Confederate symbols were also the people least likely to know anything about the history of the Confederacy.[2]

What's fascinating about these studies is that they have appeared at a time of intense debate about history. Since the shooting in Charleston in 2015 and the violence in Charlottesville in summer 2017, Confederate iconography has undergone a dramatic reexamination. The passion with which we are arguing about the removal of the Rebel battle flag and statues of Confederate heroes seems to disprove the findings of the experts. How can we square our supposedly poor understanding of history with this keen interest in the future of historical symbols? If we are ignorant of the history, why do we care so much about it?

The answer: There is often a profound difference between how we remember the past and what the evidence suggests actually happened.

Everyone, even an individual without a formal education, has some notion of what he or she thinks happened in the past. This notion usually derives from family stories, school and religious instruction, political leaders, or movies we've seen. It shapes how we perceive ourselves, the way we interact with others, and the decisions we make, big and small, every day.

This personal understanding of the past can be termed "memory" and should not be confused with "history." In fact, memory is frequently at odds with history. According to Yale University professor David Blight:

History is what trained historians do, a reasoned reconstruction of the past rooted in research. . . . [However,] memory is often treated as a sacred set of absolute meanings and stories, possessed as the heritage or identity of a community. Memory is often owned, history interpreted. Memory is passed down through generations; history is revised. Memory often coalesces in objects, sites, and monuments;

history seeks to understand contexts in all their complexity. History asserts the authority of academic training and canons of evidence; memory carries the often more immediate authority of community membership and experience. Bernard Bailyn has aptly stated memory's appeal: "its [memory's] relation to the past is an embrace . . . ultimately emotional, not intellectual."[3]

Unlike history, memory is a static, fixed narrative we typically learn as children designed to be passed down, unaltered, from one generation to another. Any deviation from this story, any attempt to provide context, meaning, or a new understanding, is often condemned as "historical revisionism," a phrase that carries an ugly, threatening connotation. If we could just get back to the "facts" and rid ourselves of "political correctness" and its corrupting influences, these critics charge, we would get at the "true" story once again.

What many people don't realize is that all history is revisionism. Any time someone picks up a pen or sits at a keyboard and writes the story of the past, they are engaging in revisionism—a revising of the story to give it meaning, context, and usefulness to the present generation. Historical revisionism isn't something new. It has been going on as long as people have been writing about the past.

In fact, one of the first and best examples in this country of historical revisionism can be seen in the explanation given after the Civil War by former Confederates for why they attempted to break away from the United States. During the secession crisis of 1860–1861, Confederate leaders were very explicit in stating why they were seceding. In newspaper editorials, speeches, and the secession ordinances they pointed to one issue and one issue only—the preservation of the institution of slavery, which they considered threatened with extinction by the election of Abraham Lincoln as the first antislavery president in the nation's history.

Three days before the 1860 presidential election, the *Charleston Mercury*, one of the South's most influential newspapers, called for a secession convention if Lincoln won, stating that "the issue before the country is the extinction of slavery. No man of common sense . . . who is not prepared to surrender the institution [of slavery], [and] with [it] the safety of the South, can doubt that the time for action [secession] has come—now or never."[4]

Two months later, in January 1861, the delegates to the Mississippi Secession Convention stated unequivocally, "Our position is thoroughly identified with the institution of slavery, the greatest material interest in the world." This position—the defense of slavery—was repeated by every seceding state, including Georgia, as the reason for breaking up the Union.[5]

Future Confederate general Henry Benning, Georgia's official commissioner to the Virginia Secession Convention, explained Georgia's position in a speech in Richmond in February of 1861. "What was the reason that induced Georgia to take the step of secession?" Benning asked the Virginia delegates. "That reason," he said, "may be summed up in one single proposition. It was a conviction, a deep conviction on the part of Georgia, that separation from the North was the only thing that could prevent the abolition of her slavery. This conviction was the main cause. If it were not for the first conviction [preventing the abolition of slavery] this step [of secession] would not have been taken." Benning went on to warn that if Virginia did not join Georgia in forming a new nation, then abolition would come to the South, and white Southerners would one day face the horrifying prospect of "black governors, black legislators, black judges, black witnesses, everything black. Is it to be supposed that the white race will stand for that?"[6]

Another Georgian, Alexander Stephens, vice president of the Confederacy, proudly proclaimed that the Confederacy was the first explicitly proslavery government ever formed. In speeches given in Atlanta and Savannah in March 1861, Stephens said that slavery was the "immediate cause of the late rupture and revolution." Rejecting Thomas Jefferson's concept that all men are created equal, Stephens declared, "Our new government is founded upon exactly the opposite idea; its [the Confederacy's] foundations are laid, its cornerstone rests upon the great truth that the negro is not the equal of the white man; and slavery—subordination to the superior race—is his natural and moral condition. This, our new government, is the first in the history of the world based upon this great physical, philosophical, and moral truth."[7]

By the end of the nineteenth century, however, it was no longer morally justifiable or politically expedient to say that the war had been fought over something as ignoble as defending slavery. So when former Confederates began writing those first histories of the conflict, they changed the reason for secession—and wrote slavery entirely out of the narrative. States' rights, constitutional liberty, and defense of home against an illegal Yankee invasion—rather than slavery—became the new cornerstone of the Confederacy. Organizations founded during the 1890s, such as the United Daughters of the Confederacy and the Sons of Confederate Veterans, which were dedicated to defending the reputation of the Confederate soldier and his cause, launched a campaign to introduce this new interpretation into the curriculum and textbooks used in schools across the South, ensuring that several generations of Southerners would be indoctrinated with this "secession without slavery" version of the "War Between the States," as they renamed it.

This historical revisionism wasn't confined to just the printed word. The hundreds of monuments that were erected during the period from about 1890 to 1920 on every state capital and courthouse square from Virginia to Texas were part of the attempt to shape this new narrative about states' rights, defense of home, and secession without slavery. Inscriptions such as *"Died for states' rights guaranteed under the Constitution"* on the Confederate monument at the state capitol in Austin, Texas, and "These men died for the principles of the Declaration of Independence" on the monument in Augusta, Georgia, were typical.

It all sounded good—but it wasn't based on fact. In no way did all the backfilling about states' rights even remotely resemble the explanation given for secession by the Confederates in 1861. This rewrite of the Civil War's history—known by historians as the Lost Cause—was so successful that in 2017 we are still fighting over the cause of the war. One reason why we cannot agree on what to do with Confederate symbols is because we cannot agree on what the Confederacy was fighting for in the first place.[8]

As the historian David Blight points out, memory is deeply emotional rather than intellectual. During the 150th anniversary of the Civil War, the Georgia Historical Society installed two new historical markers about the March to the Sea that attempted to demythologize the subject. Despite decades of scholarly research demonstrating that Sherman's destruction was primarily limited to foodstuffs, livestock, factories, and railroads, the suggestion that most private homes were not burned triggered an angry reaction from those raised on stories of white Southern victimization.

At the end of the dedication ceremony for the Sherman's March marker in Savannah, I was accosted by an older woman who grew up as I did, steeped in the Lost Cause. "Some of us still remember," she angrily declared. Obviously she wasn't alive during the Civil War. But memory is not confined to eyewitnesses. It is transmitted across time. "My grand-mother told me that Sherman burned all the houses to the ground. Are you telling me she was a liar?" Fortunately, I was able to recover suffi-ciently to reply, "No, I genuinely think your grandmother believed what she had been told as a little girl during the 1880s and 1890s as the myth of the Lost Cause was being created. But that doesn't make it history."

Demythologizing the past and supplanting memory and lore with history is not easy. It's difficult to think anew about something that seems familiar, to look at the past dispassionately and with a sense of wonder rather than defensiveness. The recent backlash over the removal of the Confederate battle flags and monuments shows just how deeply attached we can be to "our heritage"—a term synonymous with memory—and how that heritage, and even our identity, can appear to be under attack when called into question by history.

I know from personal experience the power that the Lost Cause has exerted upon the collective memory of the South. I grew up during the 1960s and 1970s in Tidewater, Virginia, and West Tennessee steeped in the myth of the Lost Cause. As a child, all I learned was that the Civil War was about brave Southern soldiers fighting to repel a Yankee invasion. It never crossed my mind that the conflict was in fact a rebellion against the U.S. government or that it had anything to do with slavery. It wasn't until I entered graduate school in the mid-1980s that I was confronted with historical scholarship that challenged my beliefs and helped me to realize that my imperfect understanding of the war was based on myth rather than history.

If history and memory are not interchangeable terms, the same can be said of history and the past. Although the past never changes, history does. History is the meaning that the present gives to the past; as society changes, so, too, does our interpretation of the past.

For instance, when I was a teenager in the 1970s, Harry Truman was considered one of the worst presidents in American history. In the immediate aftermath of Vietnam, Truman's domino theory looked fool-ish and his anticommunism seemed inflexible, simplistic, and dogmatic.[9] Today, however, in the post–9/11 era, Truman is considered one of the best presidents, a man of principle who understood and exercised real leadership. Truman has become such a hero that President George W. Bush even drew comparisons between his stand in the War on Terror and Truman's stand in Korea. Because America is in a different place today than we were forty years ago, how we relate to Harry Truman and the meaning we give to his presidency has changed dramatically.

Another example: prior to the civil rights movement of the 1950s and 1960s, hardly anyone outside the academic community talked about slavery's role in triggering secession. In fact, African Americans seemed irrelevant to the conflict. Today, however, we understand just how seminal slavery was to tearing apart the nation and the vital role that African American soldiers and sailors played in defeating the Confederacy. Did the facts change? No, but society did. Black political participation and leadership encouraged historians to reexamine the history of the war and helped restore the centrality of African Americans to the story of our nation's greatest crisis.

Ironically, at a time when the clash between history and memory is more heated than ever, there are educators and politicians who consider history increasingly irrelevant as a subject of academic study. For some time now, the advocates of STEM education have warned that, in order for America to remain competitive, our schools must emulate the educational curriculum of China and other countries, or doom our nation to a long, hard fall from its position of economic supremacy. They have waged a successful campaign to funnel millions of dollars into programs designed to teach science, technology, engineering, and math, while history teachers, as well as those who teach English, music, and art, are fighting hard to justify their existence.

But we must have both STEM and the humanities if America expects to continue to be the economic and political leader of the world. The humanities inspire creativity; STEM is the tool with which we make that creativity into reality. It is at the nexus of these two disciplines where real innovation can be found.

As an academic discipline, history is particularly suited to sparking innovation. Not only does it teach us tolerance for the frailties of humankind and develops in us a national identity, but it also prompts us to ask why, and to see other ways of solving problems.

Genuine innovation—the kind that sets us on a new course—requires an understanding of how the world we live in was created. We cannot really conceive of what is possible if we do not know where we have been or how we got to this point. History gives us this broad knowledge and perspective. It can also inspire us to emulate the innovators of the past, to see in their lives and accomplishments that taking a risk and challenging convention can lead to success in the long run.

Maintaining our competitive edge requires the ability to solve problems, to communicate clearly and persuasively, and to think independently and critically about the world around us and the people who aspire to govern us. The study of history teaches these skills. Meeting the challenges of the future—whether social or economic—also requires an appreciation for our democratic ideals, our unique political and economic systems, and a knowledge of what truly makes America great, in all its complexity and diversity. Once again, history points the way.

Mastery of STEM is important. But by itself it is insufficient. Recent studies have revealed that while international students may score better in math and science than their American counterparts, they are unprepared for university and fall behind, demonstrating that it takes more than just calculus and physics to spark curiosity and creativity. Ironically, the countries that have discovered the shortcomings of a single-focused STEM education are looking to the United States, with our emphasis on the arts and humanities, as a model for how to effectively prepare young people for the challenges of the future.[10]

Indeed, many of the great American innovators were educated in the humanities. At Reed College, Apple cofounder Steve Jobs studied Eastern religions, not computer science. As a student at Brown University, CNN founder Ted Turner was a classics major who read Thucydides. The two books that most influenced the young Thomas Edison (who didn't go to college) were *School of Natural Philosophy* and *Advancement of Science and Art*, which his parents encouraged him to read along with heavy doses of English literature (Shakespeare and Dickens) and history by Gibbons (*Decline and Fall of the Roman Empire*) and Hume (*History of England*).[11]

The background of these three great innovators demonstrates that developing new ideas and technology requires a well-rounded education, one that teaches us not *what* to think, but *how* to think. Like those of yesterday, the innovators of tomorrow—those creative minds that will keep America competitive in the global economy—need science and math. They also need the inspiration, perspective, and critical eye that only history and the humanities can bring.

It is this kind of critical and creative thinking that we will need if we are to resolve the long war between memory and history. We must look beyond the myths and lore that have shrouded our past and seek an historical understanding of how we got to this point. If we are willing to take the past on its own terms and accept it as it happened—even if that contradicts what we have always believed—then maybe we will find a measure of reconciliation with our history and with one another that has escaped us for so long.

Ultimately, how we decide to see our past—through either the lens of history or that of memory—will determine the future and the kind of people and society we will become.

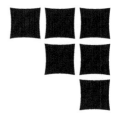

2

THE CIVIL WAR, RECONSTRUCTION, AND THE INSTITUTIONALIZATION OF RACISM

4

REMEMBERING THE CIVIL WAR

DAVID B. ALLISON

> The Civil War is, for the American imagination, the
> great single event of our history.
>
> —Robert Penn Warren[1]

I **first visited** Gettysburg when I was in middle school. We had a National Park Service (NPS) guide along in the van with our family to give us a guided tour. The peaceful Pennsylvania hills and woods were made alive by the vivid stories he told, and I imagined the cannons booming through the valleys and ranks of soldiers arrayed on the ridges, bayonets glinting in the summer sun. I was enamored by what I perceived as the valor of battle, and I thrilled with pride hearing about the gallant Hoosiers from the Iron Brigade who helped to hold the Union line north of the town on the first day of the engagement. We dutifully went to the visitor center, and in the name of education, my parents bought me a book about the arms and equipment of the Civil War.[2]

I remember poring through the stunning sketches of cannons, rifles, swords, and uniforms in that book and re-creating glorious battles in my mind. My curiosity about the Civil War did not slake as the years passed. I sought out historical fiction set during the Civil War and was pleasantly surprised on my sixteenth birthday when a friend gave me a used copy of Bruce Catton's *Civil War*—a monumental "three volumes in one" book that I demolished in no time and have continued to read at regular intervals throughout my life.[3] Catton's beautiful prose and propulsive narrative is endlessly entertaining, and the human stories he relates keeps the book as fresh as if it were written yesterday. Catton's words about remembering Gettysburg are worthy of being quoted at length:

> One day they would make a park there, with neat lawns and smooth black roadways, and there would be marble statues and bronze plaques to tell the story in bloodless prose. Silent cannon would rest behind grassy embankments, their wheels bolted down to concrete foundations, their malevolence wholly gone, and here and there birds would nest in the muzzles. . . . There would be neat brick and timber cabins on the hillsides, and people would sleep soundly in houses built where the armies had stormed and cried at each other, as if to prove that men killed in battle send forth no restless ghosts to plague the comfortable civilians at night. The town and the woods and the ridges and hills would become a national shrine, filled with romantic memories which are in themselves a kind of forgetting, and visitors would stand by the clump of trees and look off to the west and see nothing but the rolling fields and the quiet groves and the great blue bank of the mountains.[4]

As I learned more about the Civil War, I continued to treasure the "romantic memories" that Catton referred to. But I also began to realize that war is not an enjoyable lark and the complex ideas around race, equality, and constitutionality in its aftermath could be just as fascinating as the war itself.

As a student teacher in my last year of college, I was placed in Hartford City Middle School, in the county seat of Blackford County, Indiana. I taught eighth-grade U.S. history, and one beautiful fall day, I found myself on a field trip with the students to the local Civil War Days event. After some demonstrations and a few desultory lectures by costumed educators, the culminating battle reenactment commenced. Copperheads and Confederate sympathizers were common throughout Indiana during the war, and Indiana remains heavily culturally influenced by the South, but this corner of that traditionally conflicted state apparently did not harbor too many enthusiastic Confederate reenactors, because I happened to spy the leader of the Rebels trying to convince some uncomfortable-looking bystanders to join his group for the battle. His solicitations went mostly unheeded, and the "Colonel" ended up fielding a small, motley group of fifteen "men in gray" for the skirmish.

As I watched some of my students cheer on the faux Confederates as if they were attending a particularly odd football game, I thought—not for the last time—that the theater of reenactment negated the reality of the war and created a mockery of the many who fought and died. I couldn't help feeling dissatisfied with the spectacle of overweight men in crisp, unsullied uniforms running around and pretending to get shot. As the battle wound to its inevitable close with the victorious Union soldiers firing celebratory blanks into the air, I wondered why reenactments held such a strong fascination for so many people. Would those who fought at Gettysburg and the innumerable other battles during the Civil War have understood why the remembrance of the war necessitated its re-creation and revivification?

I returned to Gettysburg fifteen years ago. Arriving in town in the evening, my wife and I figured that a quick stop at the cemetery would be a good introduction to the battlefield before we headed to the hotel for the night. I'm not quite sure what I expected there, but it certainly wasn't to be instantly smote by the enormity of the place and the sheer number of graves. Tears welled up unbidden, and I could hardly even choke out any helpful anecdotes about the war to my wife.[5] The scale of the tragedy of death at that place—the lost lives of men like me, in the country of my birth—was literally staggering.

The next day, without the means or the patience for a lengthy tour, we sauntered through the battlefield, stopping occasionally to read placards, but mostly just enjoying the weather and being together. Beautiful in its solemnity, I again conjured in my mind—just like I had when I had been there as a boy—what the battle must have been like. Choking haze of smoke all around, ground trampled and muddy and groans and screams echoing through the hills. Bright, polished bayonets high in the air and flags snapping in the wind. I reenacted it all with vivid clarity in my mind. I made Gettysburg more alive than any cyclorama or movie starring Jeff Bridges and Martin Sheen could ever hope to do. In that moment, I was swept away by my imagination—a consciousness that had been seeded over the years by that "great single event" in American history, and I was ready to give myself over to fantasy even though my rational mind wanted to bring me back to the painful realities of what war really means.

In *A Righteous Mind: Why Good People Are Divided by Politics and Religion*, social psychologist Jonathan Haidt talks about the elephant and the rider of our motivations and moral sensibility.[6] He says that the elephant represents our emotional or "gut reaction" responses to situations. That elephant is huge and has a massive amount of influence over how we viscerally react to the world. The rider is our rational, deliberate responses that take the form of fact-driven arguments. The rider has a much harder time becoming the leader, since our emotive core is so powerful.[7] At Gettysburg, I am swept up in an emotional, nonrational response to the symbols and layered meanings of that particular place. It becomes more memory than history.

My reaction at Gettysburg is a microcosm that helps to explain why the American Civil War is so bitterly fought over to this day. Americans are inextricably tied to the war. Facts alone do not adequately explain the multifarious ways that it has been remembered and disputed across the country so persistently. The Civil War has become laden with a core of emotionally charged meanings that have their roots in racism, contested memory, and the overwhelming pain of a nation divided as profoundly as it could possibly be. The problematic past represented by the memorialization of the Civil War is difficult to reconcile, but its difficulty does not remove the necessity to reckon with its layered and complex meanings. This section of the book will showcase the emotional dimensions that highlight our conceptions of this defining moment in the history of the United States. Additionally, the case studies herein will show that history's handholds—the intersection of reason and emotion that illuminate how the past continues to shape our society—are a constantly

Veterans salute the flag next to a statue of Jefferson Davis in Washington, DC, ca. 1940. Harris & Ewing, photographer. Courtesy of the Library of Congress.

shifting amalgam of reinterpretation, reframing, and reification through controversial monuments and memorials to Civil War soldiers, leaders, and events.

The Civil War in Reality and the Civil War in Memory

We have already established that the Civil War was incontrovertibly about slavery.[8] Spurred by the election of the Republican Abraham Lincoln in the election of 1860, southern states moved quickly to secede from the United States and to enshrine the protection of slavery in their provisional constitutions.[9] As hostilities began, following the fall of Fort Sumter in South Carolina, southerners and northerners alike rapidly rallied behind their respective governments. Their motivations were many; yet, for northerners, a belief that the union of the United States should be preserved generally superseded other considerations.[10] Southerners likewise went to war for a variety of reasons. However, in the words of historian Richard H. Sewell, "Most fundamentally, of course, they [southerners] fought in defense of their homes and a way of life, rooted in slavery. Honor, self-determination, social and racial stability all stood in peril if the Confederacy collapsed."[11]

With the reasons for the war so clearly elucidated, how, then, did the Lost Cause narrative become such a fixture in the South during the late 1800s and early 1900s? What led to the reassertion of white power in the South during Reconstruction?[12] How did the abolition of slavery and the establishment of equal rights under the law, which had been purchased at such a high cost, become tarnished by unjust Jim Crow laws and institutional racism? How did the role of African American soldiers in the U.S. Army become so elided that by the centennial of the war in 1961 there was scarcely any mention of their sacrifices and little acknowledgment that the war had much of anything to do with the black experience in the United States?[13]

As the formerly rebellious southern states were incorporated again into the United States, three distinct memories about the Civil War emerged. Historian David Blight calls the first approach the reconciliationist vision—a perspective that sought to bring together North and South through a shared coping with the war's devastation and loss of life. Notably, Gettysburg took this path throughout most of its history as a historic site, as joint veterans gatherings sought to celebrate the valor of both North and South, while neglecting to discuss the causes of the war. The second tack was the white supremacist vision, which inflicted terror and death on African Americans through lynching, intimidation, and other violence. The third was the emancipationist vision—an approach that emphasized constitutional protections and rights for African Americans and their incorporation into the body politic.[14]

As the events of 2017 have shown, these three strands of memory are clearly still woven through the United States' national fabric. The failure of Reconstruction to guarantee rights and protections to African Americans was one of the most lasting and devastating of its legacies. Many

African American Civil War Memorial in Washington, DC. Carol M. Highsmith, photographer. Courtesy of the Library of Congress.

historians point to the economic crises of the 1870s—along with a growing indifference among northerners—as the underlying causes for the reassertion of white supremacy and oppression in the South.[15] However, it is also true that the pernicious intractability of racism and the politics of power played just as strong a role in Reconstruction's failure as these other considerations.[16]

The United States' drive to become a world power in the late 1800s and through the first part of the twentieth century saw a cultural push to justify the conquest and subjugation of native peoples through elaborate "scientific" theories about race and civilization. Black and brown people were deemed inferior, and tragic manifestations of this philosophy in the form of the eugenics movement and the reestablishment of the Ku Klux Klan are evidence that visions of equality and freedom for all were far from being realized in the United States.[17]

As the Great Depression and then World War II brought transformative change to American society, so, too, did African Americans seek a change from the daily denial of rights and oppressive social climate in the United States. While this book will not explore the many, many impactful people who gallantly fought for civil rights throughout the 1950s and 1960s, it is worth sharing one key story from this time to illustrate the ongoing emotional baggage and the deep core of white supremacy that lingered in the aftermath of the Civil War.

Fannie Lou Hamer, one of Mississippi's most outspoken and dynamic civil rights leaders, gave voice to the long years of the oppression of African Americans in the Jim Crow South. Historian Janice D. Hamlet relates Hamer's 1964 description of the toll racism had taken in her life: "When confronted by a white man who said that Whites were getting tired of the civil rights movement, Hamer responded, 'I have been tired for 46 years and my parents were tired before me and their parents were tired; and I have always wanted to do something that would help some of the things I would see going on among Negroes that I didn't like then and I don't like now. . . . All my life I've been sick and tired. Now I'm sick and tired of being sick and tired.'"[18] Hamer—and millions of other African Americans—had been swept into the struggle to regain the rights that had been lost since the reassertion of white dominance in society dating back to the end of Reconstruction. The emergence of bold, new advocacy against the violence and racism in the country during the 1960s should not, then, be a surprising development.

The Civil War Centennial

By the early 1960s, the civil rights movement and the growth of African American counternarratives had begun to challenge white national metanarratives about the history of the United States. During the leadup to the 1961–1965 Civil War Centennial, national narratives trumpeting progress and an enlightened vision of the rectitude of American democracy continued to be valued highly by most white historians and members of the public. As Robert J. Cook points out in *Troubled Commemoration: The American Civil War Centennial, 1961–1965*, in 1960, the Civil War Centennial Commission set out to convey to the public that the Civil War had been a collective, national experience—the reconciliationist perspective described by Blight and many other historians. Furthermore, the commission sought to use the centennial as a time to celebrate the unity between the North and the South that arose in the wake of the war.[19] Cook argues that as the civil rights movement challenged this white-centric understanding of the Civil War and its aftermath with regard to the African American experience, the public's perspective on the meaning of the war changed as well.[20]

Indeed, historians continue to beat the drum for an awakening to the true cause of the Civil War and a repudiation of the well-entrenched Lost Cause narrative. As you will see in the following chapters, the frontlines of these battles are often wracked with emotion and pitted with scars from the long years of white supremacy. For many southern whites, those who died fighting for the Confederacy should be viewed through sympathetic lenses. Others push back against this notion and make very different claims about how the Confederacy should be remembered. You will find all of these perspectives represented here. Statues and memorials to Confederate generals and soldiers are the final—and most visible—reminders that the Civil War is still being fought in the minds and souls of Americans.

MEMORIALIZING THE CONFEDERATE PAST AT GETTYSBURG DURING THE CIVIL RIGHTS AND COLD WAR ERA

JILL OGLINE TITUS

Editor's note: This chapter is one that Jill Ogline Titus revised and expanded from an article originally published in the Winter 2016 AASLH History News. Note the fascinating connections Titus makes between the strands of memorialization and counter-memorialization that emerged out of the crucibles of the Cold War and the civil rights movement.

A s recently as early summer 2017, Gettysburg's Confederate monuments were still rarely a cause for public debate. Although some local residents, visitors, and historians were deeply troubled by the Lost Cause messages inscribed across the battlefield landscape—particularly on the state monuments lining West Confederate Avenue—there had been no significant calls for removal or even repeated demands for broad-scale on-site contextualization or reinterpretation. But the events of the summer—both local and national—changed this situation. On July 1, the 154th anniversary of the first day of the battle, self-described armed "patriots" converged on Gettysburg National Military Park in response to rumors that Antifa protesters planned to desecrate monuments. Though no Antifa protesters appeared, the open display by "patriots" of their arsenal angered and intimidated many, and gunshots rang out when one of the protesting "patriots" accidentally shot himself in the leg.[1] A few weeks later, white nationalists descended on Charlottesville, Virginia, in "defense" of the city's Lee monument, unleashing a violent confrontation that ultimately resulted in three deaths and countless injuries and dramatically changed the national conversation regarding the appropriateness of Confederate memorials' continued presence in the public sphere.[2]

As calls for removal resounded around the country, and cities such as Baltimore; Lexington, Kentucky; and Gainesville, Florida, began to take down their monuments, serious calls for significant changes to the battlefield landscape (including removal of certain monuments, erection of new ones, and the addition of new interpretive signage) emerged.[3] Regardless of the forums in which we work, whether they be museums, historical sites, archives, classrooms, or national parks, professional historians cannot and should not try to sidestep the questions these demands raise. Should monuments located on land preserved for its historical and commemorative significance as a Civil War landscape be understood as fundamentally different in function and purpose from those standing in traditional civic spaces such as parks or courthouse lawns? Or, even if deemed to be essentially the same in function and purpose, do they, by virtue of their location warrant protection, as historical artifacts essential to understanding and interpreting the country's long struggle over the meaning and legacy of the war?

As historians have long understood, "ownership" of historical symbols such as monuments is a complicated topic. Monuments have many stakeholders—ranging from descendants of the people who erected them to the people who walk past them every day. A monument that fills some with a sense of pride and belonging can stir in others feelings of anger, hurt, and humiliation. We have long known that monuments can be powerful teaching tools and that, when read (as they must be) not as timeless symbols but as artifacts of the period in which they were dedicated, they have much to tell us about the complex and sometimes contradictory motivations of previous generations. Confederate monuments help us to understand the scope and power of the Lost Cause interpretation of the war and the myriad ways that Confederate heritage has been mobilized over generations to institutionalize and defend white supremacy. For that very reason, historians have long advocated for further contextualization of the war's memorial landscape, and many of us have contributed to these efforts though public programs, creation of interpretive waysides and digital resources, and new additions to the landscape that provide alternate narratives of the war.

But in the aftermath of Charlottesville, the question of whether educational worth trumps all of the arguments for removal has taken on new significance. Does the fact that a monument can help us understand something important about our history mean that members of a present-day local community surrounding it should be required to live with it indefinitely, even if they interpret it as a symbol of oppression or a rallying point for racism, or if it has the potential to become a flashpoint for violence? As professional historians, is it enough to just encourage dialogue, reinterpretation, and additions to the memorial landscape? Particularly when space and funds are at a premium and public safety seems potentially at risk, shouldn't removal be on the table as well?

While recognizing that not every situation is identical, many historians have embraced calls for removing Confederate monuments from civic spaces on the grounds that the unequal power dynamics they represent are inappropriate for spaces that should serve all citizens. By and large, those espousing this view have argued that these monuments' complex histories could be better interpreted in museum settings, although as Aleia Brown argued in *Slate* in the aftermath of the Charleston shooting, simply placing Confederate symbols in a museum doesn't necessarily ensure a multifaceted interpretation.[4] Calls for removing monuments at Gettysburg force us to confront the messy duality of the park as both a preserved historic/commemorative landscape *and* public land belonging equally to all Americans.

Preservation of the Gettysburg battlefield began almost immediately after Lee's retreat—within a year of the last battle, the Gettysburg Battlefield Memorial Association was already acquiring land. Monumentation followed quickly on the heels of land acquisition. By 1887, there were more than ninety monuments on the field, but only two were Confederate. Confederate monuments didn't begin to proliferate at Gettysburg until the first half of the twentieth century, and when they did, they generally took the form of state monuments commemorating all the troops from that state that fought in the battle. Of the eleven southern state monuments on the battlefield today, four of them were erected during the Civil War Centennial, and two—Florida and South Carolina—were dedicated during the one hundredth anniversary commemoration of the battle at Gettysburg.[5]

Because my research interests lie in the modern civil rights era, these Centennial monuments have always gripped my attention. The two dedicated during the battle anniversary offer a uniquely effective platform for exploring, in a site-specific way, historical events that otherwise have little concrete presence on the battlefield: the connections between Civil War memory, the Cold War, and the civil rights movement. The one hundredth anniversary of the battle of Gettysburg took place in the midst of the tumultuous summer of 1963. That May, people across the world had been stunned by the images coming out of Birmingham, Alabama: police officers turning high-pressure fire hoses on peaceful demonstrators and ordering dogs to attack children. In June, Medgar Evers had been assassinated in his driveway in full view of his children, and Alabama governor George Wallace had made his famous "Segregation Now, Segregation Forever" speech while attempting to block the admission of two black students into the University of Alabama. Three weeks before the battle anniversary, President John F. Kennedy had gone on national television to announce that he planned to send a far-reaching civil rights bill to Congress, a bill that would ultimately become known as the Civil Rights Act of 1964.

The dedication of the monument to South Carolina troops who fought at Gettysburg took a defiantly antifederal tone, which is unsurprising given its inscription: "*That Men of Honor Might Forever Know the Responsibilities of Freedom, Dedicated South Carolinians Stood and Were Counted for Their Heritage and Convictions. Abiding Faith in the Sacredness of States Rights Provided Their Creed Here. Many Earned Eternal Glory.*" This inscription was a source of friction between the National Park Service and the group that financed it, as it was very clearly a violation of Gettysburg National Military Park's "no praise, no blame" policy on monument inscriptions. But the extent to which this is highly charged, highly political language doesn't register with most visitors today because people associate "states' rights" so directly with the language of 1863. What gets missed is that "states' rights" also had a very specific meaning in 1963, and the two dedication speakers, Alabama governor George Wallace (fresh from his infamous stand in the schoolhouse door) and Congressman John May, seized every opportunity to drive that point home.[6]

With its provisions forbidding states, municipalities, and business owners to engage in racial discrimination, the civil rights bill on its way to Congress was a direct challenge to conservative concepts of states' rights. So when John May stood at this monument in the summer of 1963 and linked the South's right to resist "tyranny from Washington" to the Confederate cause and the Constitution, he was not only forcefully criticizing the bill but also directly challenging Kennedy's authority to propose it and Congress's authority to pass it.[7]

Many white South Carolinians shared May's views. In the few weeks leading up to the dedication ceremony, there had been a large anti-integration march at the South Carolina statehouse. The courts had ruled to close all state parks in response to a federal court order to integrate them, and a black student who had successfully sued for admission to University of South Carolina had his house firebombed. In inviting George Wallace—the leading symbol of southern white resistance—to dedicate this monument, the group spearheading the effort made it clear that they saw a clear connection between the Confederate cause and southern resistance to the civil rights movement.[8]

In many ways, the South Carolina monument is more of a testament to the way that a group of twentieth-century segregationists wanted the world to remember their own defense of "states' rights" than it is a tribute to the soldiers who fought at Gettysburg. But the dedication ceremony reminds us that this interpretation of states' rights wasn't limited to the South. George Wallace was a celebrity during the battle anniversary. Crowds mobbed him in the lobby of the Gettysburg Hotel and trailed him around the battlefield, begging him to sign their anniversary programs. Even as early as 1963, Wallace had political ambitions outside of Alabama, and he saw this trip to Gettysburg as an opportunity to begin cultivating a national political following. Standing next to this monument, Wallace argued that "South Carolina and Alabama stand for constitutional government. Millions throughout the nation look to the

South to lead in the fight to restore constitutional rights and the rights of states and individuals."[9]

The crowd—many of whom were not Southerners—gave him a standing ovation, foreshadowing his later success on the presidential campaign trail with similar language—race-neutral on the surface, but carefully coded. The popular response to Wallace's role in the Gettysburg commemoration challenges some of the easy North–South divisions we tend to fall into when we talk about segregation and civil rights activity. The causes Wallace fought for—limited government, states' rights, white supremacy, and a strict interpretation of the Constitution—had national appeal in the 1960s.[10]

But Wallace and May did not have a monopoly on the way that memory of the Confederate soldiers who fought at Gettysburg would be deployed during the anniversary. The group that gathered the day after the South Carolina dedication to dedicate a monument to troops from the state of Florida interpreted the legacy of the battle quite differently. The inscription on this monument echoed the themes of courage and devotion to ideals (ideals left undefined) that featured so prominently in the Palmetto State's monument, and similarly violated the "no praise, no blame" policy, but also added a Cold War twist, proclaiming, "*They Fought With Courage and Devotion for the Ideals In Which They Believed, By Their Noble Example of Bravery and Endurance They Enable Us to Meet With Confidence any Sacrifice Which Confronts Us As Americans.*"[11]

By 1963, it had become clear to millions of Americans that the United States' embarrassing record on race relations was damaging the nation's image abroad and becoming a liability in the battle between democracy and communism. At the height of Cold War competition between the United States and the Soviet Union for the loyalty of nonaligned nations in Asia, Africa, and Latin America, Soviet media channels beamed stories of voter disfranchisement and footage of beaten protesters and screaming white mobs to every corner of the world as a way of saying "don't trust the Americans—democracy is hollow when it comes to protecting the rights of racial minorities." The stakes were high. Racial discrimination was alienating potential U.S. allies in a critical region of the world, and if the trend continued, the consequences for the balance of power between the West and the Soviet bloc could be serious.[12]

The group that sponsored the placing of this monument shared these concerns about America's image abroad—and with good reason. They were Floridians—residents of a state that had just had a front-row seat to the Cuban missile crisis, and Florida was a major center of the aerospace industry (an industry deeply rooted in Cold War politics). Both ordinary Floridians and the people who represented them in Congress were in a position to be particularly sensitive to international politics and national security concerns. They did *not* want more missiles in Cuba, and they *did* want to do everything they could to help ensure that the United States would have the allies it needed to guard against Soviet expansion.

In his speech here at this monument, Florida Congressman Sam Gibbons drew upon the experiences of Florida troops at Gettysburg to argue for a vision of civil rights reform profoundly shaped by foreign policy imperatives. Gibbons called on his countrymen not to squander the sacrifice made by their ancestors at Gettysburg. "The effects of the battle that we mark now with this ceremony were largely confined to this country," he argued, "but such is not the case today; for now America's racial conflicts have immediate world-wide significance. We cannot hope to win men's minds in the battle with Communism if America becomes a land in which freedom, equality and opportunity are reserved only for the white man."[13]

Few NPS interpretive programs take place on this part of the Gettysburg battlefield (which has unsurprisingly played a major role in calls for removal of monuments[14]), so visitors to this area rarely encounter these two monuments in the company of a ranger or guide. Most visitors who interact with them do so as part of the battlefield self-guided auto tour, which includes many stops along the Confederate lines on Seminary Ridge. Very little of the broader historical context is immediately obvious to anyone disembarking from a car to examine the monuments located along the road. Despite all they have to say about midcentury politics and the malleability of historical narratives, without contextual information it's almost impossible to read beyond the surface. Thus, visitors who make the effort to engage with these monuments are generally left to do one of four things: note only "okay, these troops stood right here" and move on; unconsciously absorb the states' rights narrative presented, integrate it into their understanding of the battle and its legacy, and move on; consciously embrace this vision of "southern heritage"; or walk away angry and alienated.

What can we, as history professionals, do to rectify this? Whenever possible, we can interrogate these spaces with our visitors and students, providing them the primary sources and the interpretive framework necessary to contextualize these monuments. When in the area, many rangers and guides do their best to provide background context. We can also encourage contextual additions to the landscape. In 2016, two Gettysburg College students and I partnered with Gettysburg National Military Park (NMP) to develop content for a contextual wayside on the political uses of history during the centennial anniversary, which we anticipate will be installed at the base of the Longstreet Tower, the last major stop for most visitors before approaching the relevant stretch of West Confederate Avenue. This opportunity to interpret the civil rights/Cold War context of the 1963 battle anniversary was invigorating, and we hope the wayside will draw visitors' attention to the ways these monuments utilize the Civil War past to make statements in and about the present.

We could also flesh out the landscape in nonphysical ways—perhaps through developing a "Behind the Monuments" app for the auto tour or a series of podcasts accessible from the tour loop. Gettysburg NMP has already made good use of its blog to explore the complicated backstories and political symbolism of many of these monuments, recently running pieces on both the Florida monument and the Virginia memorial.[15] Another possibility—potentially more contentious than the others— could be developing "counter-monument" installations challenging the perceived authority of the Centennial monuments, such as an evening slideshow of images of civil rights protest in South Carolina projected across the backdrop of the monument, or an installation of the outlines of nuclear missiles in the space in front of the Florida monument.[16] I freely admit that I've yet to meet anyone who wants to partner with me on the last idea, and I don't underestimate how very difficult something like that would be to pull off. But my point is that although contextualization efforts generally begin with interpretive waysides, they don't have to stop there. Other approaches—ranging from counter-monument installations to expanded interpretation of sites on the battlefield directly linked to the theme of a struggle for liberation (such as the Brien and Warfield farms, owned by free blacks forced to flee as the Confederate Army advanced into Pennsylvania)—can also provide opportunities for visitors to exercise critical thinking skills and explore a multiplicity of narratives surrounding the history and legacy of the battle.

On a national scale, many of the conversations surrounding the future of Confederate monuments keep circling around to the question of whether removing some of these pieces from their current places on the landscape is tantamount to erasing history. Spatial context is certainly very important, and from a historical point of view, I believe something important does get lost in the transfer of a monument from its place in the public sphere to a museum setting. But are monuments and memorials "history" per se or are they specific interpretations of history that were at a certain time in the past preferenced and honored enough to be etched into the landscape? Would removing them from public display really erase history itself?

Christopher Phelps argued last year in an article in the *Chronicle of Higher Education* that changes to the memorial landscape should be seen as a natural part of the constant process of historical reinterpretation and reevaluation. Phelps wrote, "Our understanding of history changes over time, often as dramatically as that history itself. To reconsider, to recast, is the essence of historical practice. It follows that altering how we present the past through commemorative symbols is not ahistorical. It is akin to what historians do." Later in the piece, he concluded that "to remove [symbols of overt white supremacy] does not vitiate history; on the contrary, it represents a more thorough coming to terms with the past and its legacies, a refusal to forget."[17] While the analogy isn't perfect, the concept of the public sphere as a form of public historiography, a landscape that should be constantly subject to the same kind of revision and reinterpretation that characterizes historical writing (within reason, given the limitations of cost, labor, and public resources) offers a way forward out of circular conversations about erasing history. Yet accepting that point doesn't assume that all spaces are exactly the same. If we want to make the argument that museums and preserved landscapes are places for not just commemorating but also actively wrestling with our history in all its complexity and darkness, what are our strategies for inviting visitors to step into the ring themselves? How will we use these towering artifacts to illuminate the ways that narratives of the past are constructed to exercise specific meanings in the present? More important, how will we encourage visitors to question whose interests and voices are sacrificed when certain perspectives are enshrined—and, finally, why that matters not just "then" but also "now."

6

TRIBUTES TO THE PAST, PRESENT, AND FUTURE

WORLD WAR I-ERA CONFEDERATE MEMORIALIZATION IN VIRGINIA

THOMAS R. SEABROOK

I
n his 1914 speech at the dedication of the Confederate Memorial in Arlington National Cemetery, President Woodrow Wilson declared the Civil War over.[1] Any
observer looking back on this claim from 2017 might come to a different conclusion. More than 150 years after the capitulation of the Confederacy, battle lines have been drawn again, and protestors clash over
the memory of America's deadliest conflict. Many people have asked
why controversial monuments dedicated to Confederate soldiers and
leaders were built in the first place in the wake of violent ideological

clashes such as the August 12, 2017, riot in Charlottesville, Virginia. Depending on whom you ask, Confederate monuments are either poignant tributes to the sacrifices of a desolated generation or shocking symbols of white supremacy—past and present. This chapter addresses the question of monument builders' intentions through several case studies, looking at a handful of Confederate monuments built in Virginia in the 1910s. Despite the claims of many twenty-first-century commentators, white supremacy alone was not the reason they were built. Nor were monuments merely innocent memorials of collective mourning. Confederate monuments reflect the multiple hopes, fears, and biases upon which memorialists drew as they came together to express their feelings through the ancient practice of monument building.[2]

Common Soldier Monuments as Role Models

On August 27, 1914, not quite three months after President Wilson's dedication speech at Arlington, a crowd of about twenty-five hundred Hanover County residents, grizzled veterans, and out-of-towners gathered across from the old Hanover Tavern on the lawn of the 1730s courthouse where Patrick Henry once spoke out against British tyranny. That year, the reunion of the 15th Virginia Infantry was a special one, as the grand new monument to Hanover's Confederate soldiers was also dedicated. With songs, stories, and speeches, the white citizens of Hanover County spent the day celebrating the common men and women who had played their parts in the drama of the 1860s, not only to honor the heroes of fifty years past but also to impose their worldview on the physical and mental landscapes of their community.[3] Though their primary purpose may have been to remember the sacrifices of communities during the Civil War, Confederate common soldier monuments like Hanover's are hardly just stone sentinels looking backward to the past. Confederate memorialists in the 1910s erected monuments on courthouse lawns and in cemeteries, parks, and other public areas as role models to teach reluctant citizens the proper patriotic duties of Virginians in an effort to support ongoing vindication of the Confederacy.[4]

The 1914 Hanover County monument was meant to serve as an instructional reminder to future generations of the sacrifices of Hanover's Confederate soldiers. The *Hanover Progress* opined that "we have done well to record the deeds of these heroes in granite and bronze. It was our

Confederate Monument, Hanover, Virginia, 1914. Photo by author.

duty to the future generation and to the memory of the 'Boys in Gray' to do this. And that monument will stand on the Court Green in it's [*sic*] simple grandeur to remind our children and our children's children of the deeds of their forefathers and to teach it's [sic] lesson of patriotism and valor."[5] What the *Progress* failed to mention was the monument's function in the present.

Just as the Spanish-American War had done, America's entry into World War I prompted Southern memorialists to advocate U.S. military service as one way of proving the worth of the South and, by the same token, the Lost Cause. To be Southern, they argued, was to be American, implying that the defense of Southern culture was a legitimate form of Americanism. The loyal support of the South for the war was essential to the goals of Confederate memorialists, especially when faced with antiwar sentiment in rural areas. Many people of lower socioeconomic status saw the war as another way for rich men to profit from the sacrifice of the poor. Elite white men and women, invested in preserving the military value of the South, used common soldier monuments as one tool to garner support for the Great War, raising statues to anonymous and relatable heroes to appeal to the common man.[6] The dedication of Spotsylvania County's Confederate monument on Memorial Day 1918, for example, featured songs popular on both sides of the Civil War, performances by the U.S. Marine Band, and an oration by war hawk senator Claude A. Swanson.[7] The mingling of Confederate and American patriotic symbolism underscored the main theme of the day: reunion and a renewed vow to serve the United States in the Great War.

The 1919 Confederate monument in Monterey, Highland County, is an even clearer example of the conflation between the Civil War and World War I. Monterey's soldier wears a Confederate private's uniform but holds a bolt action rifle that would look less out of place in the trenches of the Western Front than on the battlefields of 1860s Virginia. Everything about the Monterey monument, whether intentionally or not, combined elements of the Civil War and World War I. The program advertising the unveiling ceremony stated, "The occasion will also be a day of welcome to the returned soldiers"—that is, the troops recently returned from Europe.[8] The inscription on the monument base reads, "*To the Confederate soldiers of Highland County a loving tribute to the past, the present, and the future.*"[9]

This language gets to the heart of memorialization. As a tribute to the present as well as the past, Monterey's memorialists intended their monument to honor the efforts of Virginia's World War I soldiers as well as its Confederate soldiers. The mixing of Confederate and World War I–era gear on the statue, whether intentional or a sculptor's error, causes the soldiers of both conflicts to blend in the imagination—a visual counterpart to the monument's inscription. This commingling suggests the righteous nature of the Confederate cause by imbuing the soldiers of 1861–1865 with the spirit of the victorious American forces of 1918. By comparing World War I soldiers with Confederate soldiers, Highland County's memorialists continued the vindication of the Confederate cause, playing on the patriotism of the period to support the continuing vindication of the Lost Cause.

Confederate Soldiers Monument, Monterey, Virginia, 1919.
Photo by author.

Memorialization and Female Suffrage

Confederate monuments were also one part of elite white Virginians'
response to the threat of female empowerment and suffrage. Invested in
maintaining the status quo of Southern life as handed down by the antebellum planter class, the United Daughters of the Confederacy (UDC)
and other often female-dominated groups used memorialization as a
form of nonthreatening political activism. These Southern women perceived changes in society during the 1910s, including the renewed growth
of the women's suffrage movement, as antithetical to their way of life.

Since one of the tenets of that lifestyle was female exclusion from politics, female memorialists found a way to express their political agency within their "proper" sphere through an avenue open to them since the Civil War—monument building. Pointing to Confederate women as models of behavior during a time of social unrest, memorialists attempted to bolster the traditional role of women as caring for and supporting men.

The threat of war and American involvement overseas exacerbated the existing struggle for female equality. Just as common soldier monuments dictated the proper role of men during wartime, stone and bronze memorials represented to women on the World War I home front the desirability of self-sacrifice. At the same time, the monuments reminded women that the advantages of females left behind to take control while men fought were, by nature, temporary. The UDC and other groups included noncombatant women in their memorialization to identify the Confederacy with their personal antisuffrage views—ultimately another lost cause. In doing so, they glossed over the unpleasant legacies of the war such as the 1863 food shortages that brought Southern women out of their homes and into the streets in protest.[10]

While the official political stance of the UDC was to have no political stance, this often translated into the idea that women should have no place in politics. This concept coincided with the position of elite white women as a class. Class was one of the most important factors in whether one supported female suffrage or opposed it. Those who opposed female suffrage tended to belong to the upper class of Virginian society. As an heir to the social world of the antebellum plantation elite, the UDC strived to uphold the virtues of women prized by Old South society. The proper sphere of women in the view of many elite white Southerners was not in public life, but in the home, supporting men in their labors and raising children to embrace correct values.[11] Elite status and a longing for the comfortable gender roles of the Old South pushed many Daughters into the antisuffrage camp. "In Virginia," historian Elna Green writes, "an anonymous Daughter announced firmly in the *Times-Dispatch* that 'no daughter of the Confederacy will be a suffragette.'"[12]

Between 1910 and 1920, more than half of the Confederate monuments and markers built in Virginia were erected by the UDC or similar local women's memorial groups. Many Confederate monuments built in Virginia during the 1910s included inscriptions honoring the women of the Confederacy. Hanover's 1914 monument, erected with the help of

Detail of inscription on the Hanover County Monument, 1914.
Photo by author.

both the local UDC chapter and the local Ladies' Memorial Association, was dedicated both to the county's soldiers *"And to her noble women who loved them."*[13] Even this simple inscription placed the women of 1860s Hanover County in a specific context. The women's function during the war was to love their husbands, brothers, and sons who were defending the Southland. Women's love was key to the morale of soldiers, giving women on the home front a key role in winning the war while retaining the antebellum gulf between women and politics or physical labor. Other monuments, such as the one at Spotsylvania Courthouse, bear the simple inscription *"Love makes memory eternal."*[14] This phrase again reinforced the work of female memorialists as essentially one of love, especially considering that "love makes memory eternal" was the official motto of the United Daughters of the Confederacy.[15]

As Confederate monuments modeled the masculine role during wartime, female involvement in monument building instilled in these same monuments meaning for women. An oration at Lunenburg County's 1916 monument ceremony in Victoria, given by Virginia state senator Patrick H. Drewry, contained praise that was also an exhortation: "The women of the Confederacy! For four years they gave of 'their all' to their country . . . full of 'the tender grace of a day that is dead' they bravely and fearlessly faced dangers that required the hardihood of men."[16] In this quote, Drewry acknowledged first that the women of the Confederacy belonged to a world that had passed away. He contrasted their "tender grace" with the "hardihood" and bravery of men, making a distinction between the proper characteristics of each separate gender. The nostalgic tone with which he described "a day that is dead" brought attention to the fact that in 1916 these comfortable and prescribed roles were shifting. One way to bring back the good old days, then, was for women of the modern age to emulate the tenderness and poise of Confederate women. This emulation of Confederate women came with a caveat, however. For a limited span of four years, Confederate women had stepped outside their sphere to take on the burdens of men before they stepped back into their proper roles as beings more suited to grace than to physical strength. Victoria's monument is an indelible symbol of the acceptable public agency of women, erected by women as a way to make their social standing as imperishable as the stone.[17]

The preserved memory depicted by monuments such as those at Victoria and Hanover was one of unity and support. By looking backward to the contributions of Confederate women, female memorialists drew a comparison with themselves as important members of a still maledominated society. In true Lost Cause fashion, Confederate memorialists brushed over the currents of dissent that scholars have traced throughout the Confederacy, creating a powerful image of faithful Confederate women intended to influence the women of 1910s Virginia.[18]

For female Confederate memorialists, monument building took on added importance as a way to create physical moorings for a way of life in flux during the 1910s. With the beginning of World War I, women increasingly took the place of men leaving for the front, echoing the social shifts of the 1860s.[19] Female Confederate memorialists were at a crossroads. Changes in society did not bode well for the leaders of the UDC and other groups. Memorialization, therefore, became one way that elite white women could reaffirm their place in society. To these women, monument building proved that women in general had ample agency within patriarchal confines. Monuments also served as physical reminders of the characteristics Confederate memorialists wanted their female contemporaries to emulate. Faced by unnerving changes in society, female Confederate memorialists looked to monuments as a way of reinforcing ideals of antebellum culture in the public eye. Their efforts stand as a reminder of not only the sacrifices of Confederate men and women but also the worries of a generation striving to hold fast to old ways in the changing world of the 1910s.

Keeping Public Space White

In addition to honoring the dead, promoting patriotism, and dampening suffragette dreams, Confederate memorialists used monuments to uphold the status quo of white privilege. Though most sources from Confederate memorialists do not explicitly mention the role of African Americans in society, memorialists' use of Lost Cause language to deny the importance of slavery or, in some cases, actively defend the institution, lays bare the debate over the causes of the Civil War that underscored the treatment of black men and women in the early twentieth century. By the 1910s, Jim Crow laws had denied black Southerners the rights and freedoms guaranteed by the Civil War and subsequent Constitutional amendments. Elite white men and women turned to the Lost Cause in their quest to combat a new wave of racial unrest and assert their social dominance.[20]

Violence, though pervasive, was frowned upon by the elite society to which most Virginia memorialists belonged. Many white Virginians instead took on African American agency via memorialization and public art. Monuments to the Confederacy were one of the ways in which white Southerners attempted to maintain their control of society through the delineation of physical space—that is, segregation. Confederate monuments constructed on public land took on added meaning as another symbol of the separation between white and black: whites could erect a stone memorial to soldiers who fought on behalf of a government

Details on the Arlington Monument. Photo by author.

committed to keeping slavery intact, while blacks were limited in their opportunities for memorialization.[21]

The Confederate Monument in Arlington National Cemetery portrays a typical Lost Cause view of African Americans' place in society. One frieze shows a white soldier handing his young child to a female slave. Another shows a male slave in uniform marching into battle alongside his master. The imagery here vindicated the Lost Cause version of slavery as a benevolent system, characterized by faithful mammies and servants willing to die for their white families. The images of slaves portrayed on the monument were meant to show, according to an official publication, "the kindly relations that existed all over the South between the master and the slave. . . . The astonishing fidelity of the slaves everywhere during the war to the wives and children of those who were absent in the army was convincing proof of the kindly relations between master and slave in the old South."[22]

The uniformed slave on the Arlington Monument served another purpose as well: showing the proper place, according to the monument's creators, of African Americans in the military. The "faithful negro body-servant" went to war at his master's bidding, not with any eye to his own fortunes. Though the citizenship status of Southern black soldiers in World War I was different from that of their enslaved ancestors, little else had changed in fifty years. The army was still segregated, with white officers commanding black units. Out of the two hundred thousand black soldiers who served in France, eight out of ten were used as laborers. The Marine Corps, for one, did not accept black recruits.[23] As the United States entered the European conflict, some white men and women feared the possible consequences of arming a large number of blacks. Added to that fear was the concern that enemy spies would attempt to use racial discord to their advantage, dividing Americans to cripple the war effort. Though pragmatists such as W. E. B. Du Bois urged blacks to "close ranks" with whites against a common foe, expecting gratitude from the white nation, race riots tore across the nation in 1917 and 1918 and lynch mobs across the South killed eighty blacks, including soldiers in uniform, in 1919.[24]

The Arlington Monument is unique among Virginia's Confederate monuments for its explicit racial content. Most monuments either ignored the cause of the Civil War or glorified the cause of states' rights. Monuments erected at Hanover Courthouse, Goochland Courthouse, Winchester, Luray, and Monterey make no mention in their inscriptions of the Civil War's purpose for white Southerners. Victoria's monument is perhaps the most direct, since it proclaims, "*We fought for the sovereignty of the States.*"[25] Prince George's monument praises the "*Undying devotion to duty and country*" of the county's soldiers but makes no claim as to what that duty was.[26] The monument at Spotsylvania Courthouse also mentions the cause but makes no clear mention of what that cause may have been.[27]

More details on the Arlington Monument. Photo by author.

By not stating the cause of the Confederacy on the monuments, memorialists implied that such was already common knowledge in the community. Monuments are repositories of established collective memory—in this case, the memory of the elite white memorialists. Inscriptions that expressly vindicated the Southern cause sent a powerful message to those who might dissent, especially African Americans who were not apt to view the Confederacy or slavery in a favorable light. Confederate memorialists cast the Union and Confederacy as two sides that were both essentially correct, the North fighting for one vision of government and the South for another under the same Constitution. This idea continued the tradition of sectional reunion based on shared whiteness to the detriment of African American advancement in the decades after Reconstruction.[28]

Amid lingering fears of the eclipse of the white race following imperial expansion, growing social unrest and the outbreak of the Great War catalyzed a backlash by elite white Southerners. Virginia's Confederate memorialists looked to the familiar white face of the rebel soldier, immortalized in stone and placed in the public square, for grounding in the midst of social insecurity. To counteract African American upward mobility, white Virginians took steps not only to segregate blacks within the public sphere but also to ensure that that public sphere remained staunchly white through the erection of Confederate monuments.

Conclusion

As they saw their world changing, Virginia's Confederate memorialists renewed their dedication to the ideals of the Lost Cause by building monuments to Confederate soldiers. These monuments served many purposes, imbued with meaning for contemporaries and future generations alike. By 1900, Southern whites had reversed the tide of Reconstruction and had placed themselves once again in positions of privilege. This privilege was never on solid footing, however, as growing challenges over the next several decades revealed. Facing perceived threats to their status, elite white men and women of the 1910s sought a return to the well-defined social order of the Old South. The Lost Cause took on new importance for memorialists as they worked to uphold the legacy of their Confederate forebears.

Studying monument building provides a deeper understanding of the creation of public memory. Memorialization is an act of the present as much as it is an honoring of the past. In the 1910s, during a time of social unrest on several fronts, elite white Virginians turned to the Confederacy as an example of the perfect society—a society where white men ruled by virtue of their military prowess, supported by the mothering love of women at home and the labor of a race unfit to wield power over themselves or anyone else. Pervasive racism was never the sole motivation for monument builders, who approached memorialization from a number of different, mainly conservative, points of view. As we look back at Confederate monuments in the public sphere today, the conversation must take into account not only the plurality of memorialists' intentions but also the evolution of our collective social mind-set over the past century. A nuanced view of Confederate monuments, an understanding of their purpose in society at the time of their placement, and an open-minded conversation about their meaning within the modern landscape, taking into account the diversity of thought and experience of people on all sides of the issue, must take precedence over sound-bite politics and sensational journalism if Americans are to move forward toward a more harmonious public interpretation of the Civil War.

DON'T CALL THEM MEMORIALS

JULIAN C. CHAMBLISS

Editor's note: This chapter by Julian C. Chambliss was originally published by Frieze.com *on August 23, 2017. Reprint and expansion is used by permission.*

What we see happening in places like Charlottesville today—after the tragic, bloody events of last weekend [August 12, 2017], and the roiling debates around Confederate memorials—has less to do with historical facts and more to do with collective memory. In Dell Upton's 2015 book *What Can and Can't Be Said*—his insightful examination of African American memorials in the United States—we are presented with two pivotal questions regarding our understanding of monuments in the contemporary South. What is possible, and what is *permitted*, to be said in public memorial discourse?

Upton's analysis of civil rights memorials acknowledges a key point too often omitted from contemporary debates.[1] New South "boosterism" invented the memorial landscape in the 1880s and 1890s. A class of merchants, manufacturers, and financiers sought to transform the South. Partnering with figures such as Henry W. Grady (1850–1889), the managing editor of the *Atlanta Constitution*, they promoted industrial growth, agrarian reform, and northern investment to reintegrate the region into the "political and economic life" of the United States.[2] This process required stripping away facts around the political, economic, and social motivation involved in fighting the Civil War and, in their place, constructing a new context that embraced a collective understanding of southern sentiment about the war that would be acceptable to northern whites. This process had nothing to do with the history of the war. Americans, North and South, knew full well that the Confederacy was created to preserve slavery, and the resolution of the Civil War meant the end of a slave democracy on which southerners relied. Indeed, as New South boosters shaped this narrative, Frederick Douglass tirelessly warned of the "failure of historical memory" at the center of the struggle to maintain black rights.[3] Douglass saw the war as an ideological struggle linked to public memory and spent the 1870s and 1880s (he died in 1895) fighting to stop this history from being lost. As historian David Blight explains, he "abhorred" the decontextualized interpretation that gained popularity in the 1880s and pushed back against the sentimentalism that would allow Americans North and South to avoid "whether benignly or aggressively— the deep significance of race in the verdict of Appomattox."[4]

Today we continue this struggle. We are not debating what happened; instead, we are quarreling about how southerners chose to *remember* it and northerners *chose* to accept it. As countless historians have tirelessly explained, the Confederate memorials that dot the landscape were erected long after the war was fought as southerners promoted the idea of a "New South"—new in the sense that a new generation of southern leaders embraced a narrative of modernization *and* preservation. A narrative that argued that southern soldiers fought nobly not to preserve slavery but for self-determination against northern aggression. Fueled by a regional identity that believed in honor, family, and religion, southerners may have lost on the battlefield, but they retained the values that defined their culture. They continued to preserve those noble values even as they grew cities and nurtured industries such as textiles and railroads.

They succeeded in reshaping and rebranding the region, but it came at a high cost for black Americans. As southern whites murdered and disenfranchised black people, they celebrated why they committed those acts by creating markers to an *idealized* version of *white* southern history. The memorials we debate today are public markers created by private groups that endorsed this white vision and supported these white actions. In truth, we should not call them memorials. A proper label would be "political markers funded by the United Daughters of the Confederacy (UDC) and gifted to municipalities across the South to celebrate the reestablishment of white rule after Reconstruction." The pattern of greatest activism linked to these *markers* between 1896 and 1919, and again between 1954 and 1965, correlates to the public proclamations of anti-black sentiments at those moments.[5] Indeed, the first period coincides with the rise of white supremacy marked by the 1896 *Plessy v. Ferguson* decision that legalized segregation and opened the door to subsequent black voter suppression, a lynching campaign in the 1890s,[6] and a series of anti-black riots in communities such as Atlanta (1906), Springfield (1908), and East St. Louis (1917). This aggression culminated in 1919 with what author James Weldon Johnson described as the "the Red Summer"[7]—a period of twenty-six race-inspired riots that erupted across the United States. The second period marked white southerners reacting *against* the landmark *Brown v. Board of Education* Supreme Court decision in 1954 that ended school segregation. In the years that followed that victory—as Martin Luther King Jr. and countless others marched in nonviolent protest culminating in the Civil Rights Act (1964), which outlawed discrimination based on race, color, religion, sex, or national origin, and the Voting Rights Act (1965), which prevented denial or restriction of the right to vote—white southerners embraced symbols of the Confederacy.[8]

Navigating the space created between history and feeling prompted me to participate in the Confederate Flag—13 Flag Funerals project organized by artist John Sims on May 25, 2015.[9] In organizing the burning and burials of the Confederate flag in the former states of the Confederacy on the 150th anniversary of the end of the Civil War, Sims commemorated—from an African American perspective—the struggle for freedom. A form of creative resistance, the project highlighted what countless black *and* white people were prevented from saying for decades. A black person burning a symbol of the Confederacy in public rejects the romanticized South and challenges the white-centric public memory that defines the region. Online threats, calls to my college for me to be fired, and calls for me to be arrested for burning the Confederate flag bombarded me as I pursued this project.[10] Yet, in confronting Confederate symbolism with a public art project, we foreshadowed a wider debate around truth in the public sphere. It reminded Americans that black people who challenged white supremacy were terrorized, beaten, or killed for doing so. It acknowledged, as should be obvious, that African Americans rejoiced in the South's defeat, suffered brutally through Jim Crow segregation, and continue today to seek freedom equal to all in the public square.

While previous ethnic white immigrants who came to United States were placed in a "melting pot" that washed away their difference and made them "white," our contemporary social space cannot be defined by the white racial status quo. The lived experience that defines the modern United States requires the legacies and memories of all our people to inform the public square we inhabit. While it may seem like an empowered white majority clinging to the past is defining our reality, in truth, today many more Americans are claiming a place for their experience to define our democracy. Together we care about the truth and reject symbols that threaten and demean. We seek a community that celebrates the richness of our diversity. This is the path we are on, but we must work hard to confront the truth of historical violence and its effect. The work of the Equal Justice Initiative[11] to document racial violence marks an important effort to create common understanding about what happens to people of color. With the truth made clear, we can move forward toward creating a public sphere that celebrates those people and institutions that helped the United States live up to its ideals.

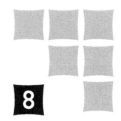

A LOST CAUSE IN THE BLUEGRASS

TWO CONFEDERATE MONUMENTS IN LEXINGTON, KENTUCKY

STUART W. SANDERS

Early in the Civil War, President Abraham Lincoln reportedly said, "I hope to have God on my side, but I must have Kentucky." As a dividing line between the North and South, the federal commander-in-chief understood the strategic and political importance of the Bluegrass State. During the conflict, nearly seventy thousand residents fought for the North while thirty-five thousand served the Confederacy. Although Kentucky was predominantly Unionist, the commonwealth eventually made a postbellum pivot to the Lost Cause. This was apparent when, after the war, Kentuckians erected more than fifty monuments to honor the Confederacy and only seven to commemorate the Union.[1]

As formerly enslaved African Americans sought economic freedom and political power, white Kentuckians forged a narrative of the war that favored the Lost Cause. Two Confederate monuments in Lexington, Kentucky, are emblematic of this shift. Moreover, the dedications of these memorials, one in 1887 and the other in 1911, show how subsequent generations of Kentuckians became more and more devoted to the memory of the Confederacy.[2]

As the Civil War progressed, loyal Kentuckians' Unionism ultimately diverged from federal policy. These Kentuckians believed that slavery would be better protected under the U.S. Constitution than out of it. Therefore, they supported the Union cause.[3] When Lincoln issued the Emancipation Proclamation, however, Kentuckians were furious at this shift in Northern war aims. Union soldier John T. Harrington of the 22nd Kentucky Infantry Regiment, for example, wrote his sister, "I enlisted to fight for the Union and the Constitution but Lincoln puts a different construction on things and now has us Union men fighting for his Abolition Platform, and this making us a hord [sic] of Subjugators, house burners, negro thieves, and devastators of private property."[4]

The enlistment of enslaved African Americans into the Union army also angered Kentuckians. When Bluegrass State slaves ran away to join the federal service, Kentuckians feared that their agrarian slave economy would collapse. Furthermore, the sight of armed African American soldiers marching through Kentucky towns reinforced longstanding fears of slave insurrection.[5]

Because of these policies, after the war Kentuckians embraced the ideals of the defeated Confederacy. As historian Anne E. Marshall contends, "The conservative racial, social, political, and gender values inherent in Confederate symbols and the Lost Cause greatly appealed to many white Kentuckians, who despite their devotion to the Union had never entered the war in order to free slaves." Kentuckians quickly supported former Confederates for political office, and multiple postbellum governors, members of congress, and state legislators were ex-rebel soldiers.[6]

In order to commemorate this shift to the Lost Cause, Kentuckians erected Confederate memorials across the state. Marshall writes that most of these monuments "appeared between 1890 and 1915, the heyday of lynching and the dawn of Jim Crow." Therefore, this timing suggests that Kentuckians erected these statues not only to honor the Confederacy but also to reinforce a racial hierarchy and to stifle black political power.[7]

This photo from circa 1920 shows the Cheapside Public Square in Lexington, Kentucky. Note the statue near the back right of the crowd. Cheapside Public Square, Lexington, Kentucky, ca. April 7, 1920. Keystone View Company. Courtesy of the Library of Congress.

The first monument to appear on the lawn of the Lexington courthouse, installed in 1887, honored John C. Breckinridge. Born in Lexington in 1821, Breckinridge served in the Kentucky legislature, the U.S. Congress, and was the youngest vice president in the nation's history. He ran for president in 1860, lost to Abraham Lincoln, and eventually became a Confederate general and the Southern secretary of war. After the conflict, he spent three years in foreign exile until it became clear that authorities would not prosecute him for treason against the United States. He returned to Lexington in 1869 and died there six years later. Less than a decade after Breckinridge's death, calls to memorialize him began. Soon the state legislature allocated funds for a statue.[8]

Placed on the courthouse grounds, the location of the statue held layers of complex historical significance. Known as "Cheapside," it was once a major slave auction site where thousands of enslaved African Americans were sold. In January 1855, for example, John Carter of Lewis County, Kentucky, sold all of his slaves at Cheapside. An advertisement listed twenty-one men and two women for sale. Their fates are unknown, but it is likely that many of them were sent to the Deep South to work on cotton or sugar plantations.[9]

Despite the site's dark history, on November 16, 1887, thousands of spectators gathered there to dedicate the Breckinridge statue. A band played "Hail Columbia" and "America." A local minister, related to Breckinridge by marriage, gave a prayer. U.S. Senator James B. Beck, who had been Breckinridge's law partner, struck a tone of reconciliation. Beck painted Breckinridge as a reluctant secessionist and a patriot and hoped that the statue would inspire future generations. Kentucky's governor, former Confederate general Simon Bolivar Buckner, referred to Breckinridge as "the greatest of [Kentucky's] citizens." The statue was unveiled as the band played "The Star-Spangled Banner."[10]

"Not a rebel flag was displayed," the *Lexington Daily Press* reported, and the "blue and gray mingled freely together." The newspaper also added its voice to calls to change the name of Cheapside to "Breckinridge Square."[11]

At first glance, the dedication of the Breckinridge statue was a paean to reconciliation. All of the music played were national songs. There was no "Dixie" to be heard. Despite this, the *Lexington Daily Press* provided clarity about the intent of the monument. With the Breckinridge statue installed at Cheapside—where thousands of enslaved men, women, and children had been sold—the *Daily Press* now saw the site as hallowed ground. "We don't want any more negro drays and spring wagons gathered on Cheapside," the *Daily Press* wrote. "It's too sacred now for them."[12]

Although spectators heard patriotic songs and speeches about reconciliation, the speakers were not calling for a reunion among all Kentuckians. Instead, they were calling for peace among *white* Kentuckians. Although they lost the Civil War, these men—former rebels who had become prominent national politicians—were stamping the ideals of the Confederacy upon this public, civic space. In 1887, white Lexington residents decided that Cheapside would become a place where the ideals of the defeated Confederacy would be honored. The Lost Cause would loom large over the site's ties to slavery.

Twenty-four years later, a new generation of Lexington residents, spearheaded by the United Daughters of the Confederacy, installed another Confederate monument there. While this memorial revered another city resident, the dedication ceremony no longer touted reconciliation. It also fully embraced Confederate iconography.

John Hunt Morgan was perhaps Kentucky's most dashing Confederate soldier. Born in Alabama in June 1825, Morgan moved to Lexington where he attended Transylvania University. He served in the Mexican War and became a successful hemp merchant. During the Civil War, Morgan commanded a Confederate cavalry brigade that made slashing raids into the Bluegrass State. Killed in Tennessee in September 1864, his remains were eventually reinterred in the Lexington Cemetery.[13]

By 1911, the ghost of John Hunt Morgan still loomed large over Kentucky politics and culture. That year, for example, U.S. Senator James B. McCreary, who had served as a rebel officer under Morgan, was elected governor of Kentucky. The United Daughters of the Confederacy, thanks to a sizable contribution from the state, raised $15,000 to build a Morgan monument at the courthouse. Dedicated that October, nearly twenty thousand spectators watched the ceremony, which included a parade of Union and Confederate veterans, school bands, politicians, and civic organizations.[14]

Unlike the Breckinridge statue dedication, the program for the Morgan monument highlighted Confederate symbols and songs. Although rebel veterans were in the audience, including McCreary and former governor Simon B. Buckner, fewer Confederate veterans spoke. Instead, a new generation of Lexingtonians, many of whom had been children during the Civil War, were publicly affirming the ideals of the Confederacy. Having grown up with tales of Morgan's exploits, it was now their turn to cherish the "Thunderbolt of the Confederacy."

Shortly after the program commenced, a group of schoolchildren formed a human "Stars and Bars" and sang "Dixie." After a number of speakers, including Lexington's mayor and the governor, the students again formed the human banner and sang the Confederate songs "Bonnie Blue Flag," and "Maryland, My Maryland." After the unveiling, the students sang "The Star-Spangled Banner," but they did so while remaining in the "Stars and Bars" formation. Such was the dichotomy of the Lost Cause in the border state of Kentucky.[15]

The 1911 ceremony was also visibly different from the one in 1887. While there were no Confederate flags on display at the Breckinridge monument dedication, rebel banners were plentiful when the Morgan statue was unveiled. In addition to the schoolchildren forming a "Stars and Bars" pattern, Confederate flags hung in windows around the courthouse. Furthermore, a massive rebel banner covered the statue before it was unveiled. According to the *Mt. Sterling Advocate*, "The principal streets of the city were gayly [sic] decorated with National and Confederate flags, while the statue was draped in huge battle flags of the Confederacy."[16]

An earlier generation—those who actually fought in the Civil War and sought postwar reconciliation with their white counterparts—kept Confederate symbols and songs muted during the Breckinridge statue dedication. Their children, however, who grew up steeped in Lost Cause mythology, literally covered the city with Confederate symbols for the Morgan statue unveiling. The Lost Cause had taken hold over another generation. Those who came of age immediately after the Civil War chose to revere Confederate iconography even though their wartime relatives most likely supported the North. The Union had won the war, but Bluegrass Confederates claimed the peace.

Today, this intergenerational devotion to the Lost Cause continues in Kentucky, leaving some modern residents to believe that slavery was not central to secession and civil war. Despite this, and knowing that it would elicit great controversy, in October 2017 the city of Lexington removed the two Confederate monuments from the grounds of the old courthouse. The statues are to be reinstalled at the Lexington Cemetery, where Morgan and Breckinridge are both buried. "It's been a very difficult issue for this community and it's now completed," Lexington's vice mayor Steve Kay said.[17]

Regardless of Kay's assessment, public historians know that the real work is just beginning. Removing these statues from a civic space has taken away their original, historic context. Therefore, the city will have to interpret them in their new setting and will have to explain why these monuments are now in the cemetery. The city should also reinterpret Cheapside and the area around the old courthouse, including information pertaining to the debate around the statues. Moving these monuments has simply opened up a different set of challenges.

In a state that remains divided, both racially and politically, arguments over the best ways to interpret public spaces can be difficult conversations, especially when they are laced with modern political agendas.

The historical memory of many Kentuckians is still tinged with Lost Cause nostalgia (thanks, in part, to the prevalence of Confederate monuments on courthouse lawns). Therefore, some residents will find interpretation referencing slavery as a cause of the war to be unacceptable. Others will roundly reject any interpretation at the monuments' new location in the cemetery that notes that Breckinridge and Morgan were waging a war on behalf of a republic built on chattel slavery. As more work remains, it is apparent that the ultimate legacy of the two Lexington statues is far from decided.

In this instance—and in others involving Confederate monuments across the country—public historians should take the lead by constructing a meaningful dialogue with key stakeholders. Public historians are uniquely situated to use museum collections, primary source materials, experience with interpretation, and the historical process to engage with communities and assist decision makers. In places like Kentucky, where the Lost Cause still weaves a thread of rebel gray through public discussions, those in the field have a responsibility to provide a long view of the Civil War and to show how echoes of the conflict still reverberate today.

Abraham Lincoln once said, "I think to lose Kentucky is nearly the same as to lose the whole game." Although Kentucky never left the Union, residents' hatred of emancipation aligned the state with the Lost Cause. Today, as Bluegrass State communities decide the fate of Confederate monuments, an opportunity arises to engage the public and to use the historical process to interpret our nation's greatest conflict in our public spaces.

9

CHALLENGING HISTORICAL REMEMBRANCE, MYTH, AND IDENTITY

THE CONFEDERATE MONUMENTS DEBATE

F. SHEFFIELD HALE

Editor's note: This chapter has been revised and expanded from an article that originally appeared in the Autumn 2016 issue of AASLH's History News *magazine. Hale shares how and why the Atlanta History Center developed the Confederate Monument Interpretation Initiative, an effort to provide resources and to open dialogue about controversial monuments and memorials.*

The current debate surrounding Confederate monuments is a symptom of a larger problem, and one that is not unique to the United States. Throughout the world, many nations have struggled with the disposition of monuments that remain in place following governmental change from autocratic rule, colonization, and other regime changes. At its core, a debate about a monument is a debate about the meaning of historical memory. In this case, how that memory is portrayed—or honored—on the public landscape. These debates essentially originate from the fundamental misunderstandings or disagreements about our collective history. This prevents our ability to build an interpretive consensus of our past. We find ourselves incapable of agreeing as a society on a true historical narrative. As a result, we cannot decide—in fact, we often cannot discuss—who tells that history, what (or whose) history is to be told, and how it is going to be expressed.

The tragedies in Charleston and Charlottesville were caused by white supremacists wielding Confederate symbolism. Afterward, communities across the country renewed consideration of the role of Confederate symbols. In 2015, the Atlanta History Center began developing tools to assist communities in conducting discussions that are based in research and historical evidence. Those dialogues must also be comprehensive in including broad inclusivity in determining the function and purpose of Confederate monuments within each community. The article, "Finding Meaning in Monuments: Atlanta History Center Enters Dialogue on Confederate Symbols," published in *History News* (Autumn 2016) outlined the History Center's approach. The History Center also gave presentations to local community groups and spoke to national and local media to promote awareness of these tools.[1]

As the debate over Confederate monuments and symbols evolves, the Atlanta History Center continues to promote historical research and dialogue. In a debate where passions often rule and logic hides, the historical perspective is central to the discussion and of the utmost importance. To be clear, though, the status quo is not an option: Confederate monuments cannot remain as they are without contextualization that delves into the true history of the monument—the motivation and symbolism of its construction. It is with this perspective that the History Center weighs in on this contentious debate.

The Charleston Shooting:
The Atlanta History Center Reacts

I became the CEO and president of the Atlanta History Center (AHC) in 2012, following a lifetime of involvement with the institution. Well aware of the reputation of the ninety-year-old organization's traditional strengths and weaknesses, my top priority has been to shake off the public's dusty impression of AHC (and history in general) and to transform it into a welcoming place for *all* visitors. I believe the key to expanding our mission is to get outside our campus boundaries as an active and informed participant in the community—sometimes when and where we are least expected.

Like many across the country, I was sickened by the tragic shooting in Charleston in 2015. Feeling called to action by this tragedy, I began to contemplate a way in which the Atlanta History Center, with its knowledgeable staff and extensive collections, including my own historic preservation experience, could best have a place in the debate over Confederate emblems. In short, all of the ingredients were present to make a meaningful contribution to the broader discussion of Confederate monuments, the Lost Cause, and how history is never as simple or removed from the present as many think.

When the Confederate Monument Interpretation Initiative began, it did so with an eye toward turning objects of veneration (Confederate monuments) into historical artifacts that could be reinterpreted to tell the story of the purpose of their creation. I also realized that the status quo of monuments remaining unchallenged and noncontextualized was simply not an option. If not clearly interpreted with proper context, the monuments must be removed. The initiative was specifically designed so that research and dialogue for decisions on removal or contextualization are conducted at the community level.

We began giving public presentations on the monuments issue in January 2016. We used international examples, such as the whole-sale eradication of Joseph Stalin statues in the Soviet Union (in 1985, I traveled to Stalin's hometown of Gori, Georgia, to see the last one), the destruction of the sixth-century Buddhas of Bamiyan in Afghanistan, and the relocation of monuments honoring colonial rulers in India and communist leaders in Eastern Europe to "commemorative parks." We discussed contemporary, non-Confederate issues, such as Cecil Rhodes in England and South Africa, and Woodrow Wilson at Princeton. We also explored the definition of heritage and asked audiences to consider the ways that those who seek to preserve "Confederate heritage" or "our heritage" invariably leave out the unpleasant parts of the Confederacy, especially institutionalized human bondage enshrined in the Confederate constitution.[2]

The cornerstone of the Confederate Monument Interpretation Initiative is a portion of the Atlanta History Center website designed as a tool to facilitate local research and dialogue. These pages offer tools for researching Confederate monuments. The Confederate Monument Interpretation Template helps guide users through important research questions and includes suggested language about the Lost Cause and its connections to Jim Crow segregation. All of this can be used or adapted to create interpretive text panels for contextualizing a monument. These text panels must be placed next to a monument to turn it from an object of veneration into an educational lesson. Similar content can also be provided on local history webpages. The History Center's website also includes a guide on how to get started on researching Confederate monuments and a page with updated listings of books and news articles concerning the debate.

A Brief Overview of the Erection of Confederate Monuments

Before discussion can begin about actions and reactions to Confederate monuments, it is important to understand the historical context of these monuments. Immediately after the Civil War, the sense of shock and grief among many white Southerners was profound. At least one-fifth of all white men of military age in the Confederacy died during the war. From the 1860s through the 1880s, most monuments were erected to commemorate Confederate dead. Often placed in cemeteries, these memorials usually took the form of obelisks, arches, or fountains, often adorned with funereal drapes.[3]

The majority of the Confederate statues in the South today are of a different character. Erected between 1890 and the 1930s, these monuments were placed on public sites, such as town squares, courthouse lawns, and college campuses. They tend to be more elaborate and celebratory, depicting soldiers at attention or generals atop horses, and their inscriptions generally focus on justifying the Confederate cause rather than mourning its dead. While feelings of mourning and loss undeniably factor into these monuments, a monument such as an equestrian statue of a Confederate general represents something other than loss. These glorify the professed moral victory of the Confederacy and affirm the white supremacy that remained in place after the end of Reconstruction. This gloss makes these statues offensive.

These monuments are the products of an era defined by Jim Crow, confirming white supremacy through veneration of the mythology of the Lost Cause. This belief system, widely held by whites in the South, denies the role of slavery as the cause of the Civil War and seeks to redefine the Confederate war effort as a moral defense of homeland and states' rights. As physical manifestations of that mythology, monuments of the 1890s–1930s period created a stronger white Southern identity (some might say nationalism) than had ever existed during the war.[4]

Conceptions and Misconceptions about the Civil War

When approaching an issue as controversial and emotional as the Confederate monument debate, a solid historical understanding is essential. At the heart of the debate are misconceptions about our collective history that have been reinforced for decades. In the context of the Civil War, this means fundamental misunderstandings about life in the antebellum South, the cause of the Civil War, consequences of the conflict, and the value and "failure" of Reconstruction. These false assumptions result from inadequate (and inaccurate) information in textbooks and classrooms, narratives passed down by family members (romanticized and illusory), and images in popular culture.

The facts of history do not change. What changes is the interpretation and presentation of history, often highly dependent on political climates. When the facts of history become misconstrued in the name of heritage (which I define as history without the unpleasant parts), we arrive at difficult situations, as we have with the Confederate monument debate today. The underlying cause of the debate is the inability of a large segment of the population to acknowledge that the primary cause of the Civil War was the desire of the Southern states to preserve the institution of slavery, which they perceived as untenable while remaining in the Union. While other factors played a part in causing the war, none played as large of a role as slavery. Notably, after the war, 3.9 million Southerners, or 40 percent of the Southern population, gained freedom from bondage, and the country was reunited. These were the important outcomes of the war. But these outcomes are the ones precisely ignored or minimized by continued adherence to the Lost Cause. This Lost Cause belief, which remains so pervasive throughout the country, makes the monuments issue extremely difficult to resolve.[5]

Another misconception regarding the Confederate monument debate is that removing them would somehow erase the history of the Civil War. To this, we say that history comprises more than our physical landscape, and, more to the point, the history presented by Confederate monuments is faulty and incomplete. Confederate monuments after 1890 represent Jim Crow America more than the Civil War. If any history is in danger of being erased, it is the history of people who would erect such statues to reinforce the white supremacist values of the Jim Crow era, not the Confederate figures the statues purport to represent. The ability to tell that dark story in the public space is what is at stake, not an attempt to "hide difficult history" (as is often the claim).

Charlottesville: A Turning Point in the Confederate Monument Debate

In August 2017, our nation was starkly reminded of the resilience of white supremacy when the "Unite the Right" neo-Nazi rally in Charlottesville, Virginia, turned violent, resulting in the death of a counterprotester at the hands of a terrorist from Ohio. The white supremacist organizations were using the removal of the Robert E. Lee statue in Charlottesville as the pretext to promote white nationalist ideology and dominate the news cycle. Confederate monuments were again thrust into the national spotlight.

Charlottesville changed the political landscape for many communities considering Confederate monuments. In this case, the removal of a Confederate monument became a rallying point for white supremacists from all over the country and a spark for violence. Such violence means that for some communities, keeping Confederate monuments is no longer an option. In Baltimore, for example, an extensive research process the previous year resulted in the recommendation of removing two

Confederate monuments and keeping two others with contextualization panels. Just days after Charlottesville, all four statues were removed.

Crafting a Community Dialogue

What we arrive at is a dilemma: how do we address this issue while taking into account public opinion, the specific history behind each monument, and the very real practical concerns of keeping or removing them? To achieve real and lasting change, and a chance of ultimate consensus, the decision-making process is more important than the ultimate solution itself. Community involvement in that process is of the utmost importance to ensure that all voices and viewpoints are heard and taken into account.

The next dilemma, however, is how to go about achieving such community engagement in a way that allows all voices to be heard and respected. In many ways, those who take a hard-line position on either side of the issue close off the opportunity for dialogue by eliminating the potential of any middle ground for cooperation.

There are some who favor keeping Confederate monuments in place. In their minds, the monuments are not offensive because the Confederacy was not offensive (or was just in its cause). On the other side, there are those who see the monuments as a visceral reminder of a painful past and a failed attempt at treasonous rebellion for the purpose of preserving slavery. Furthermore, in this view, Confederate monuments are deeply offensive and racist, despite contextualization. Therefore, monuments must be removed to ensure that they are no longer objects of veneration and no longer offend or promote violence.

Since the positions taken on each end of the spectrum of this argument often find justification in absolute moral terms, middle ground cannot exist in that framework. Rather, any position other than that held by the individual is, by definition, immoral. This is not to say that there is any historical or moral equivalency between the two positions, only that there is a political problem these opposing positions engender. The divergence in viewpoints creates a zero-sum conversation and prevents any functional community dialogue.

A possible first step in alleviating this tension is beginning a bottom-up community dialogue approach that begins with extensive research on the history and function of individual monuments (though similar, no two are exactly alike). This research is beneficial regardless of the final outcome because the process is infused and surrounded by well-researched historical facts. Taking the time to extensively research monuments also allows people all along the spectrum to evaluate their opinions in light of historical facts, promoting a healthy debate and possibly building consensus.

Some states currently have laws that prevent the removal of Confederate monuments but do not forbid the addition of interpretive text panels. Even if a state legislature considers changing these laws, the potential for contextualization remains important, both because of the benefits of accurate historical research and because of the fact that it can provide at least a temporary solution, if removal is still desired but not legally possible.

Atlanta Advisory Committee— Principles in Action

Soon after the Charlottesville attack, Atlanta mayor Kasim Reed and the Atlanta City Council created an eleven-person advisory committee to recommend action steps for Atlanta street names and monuments associated with the Confederacy. Given the Atlanta History Center's importance as a source of historical information about the city, I was appointed by the mayor and subsequently elected cochair of the committee along with Derreck Kayongo, CEO of the Center for Civil and Human Rights.

While working with this committee, I experienced firsthand the difficulties I have described. While listening to public comment in the City Council chambers at committee meetings (also broadcast on city television), some people expressed Lost Cause sentiments that would make it difficult to find an acceptable solution that included anything other than leaving each monument intact and untouched. We also heard people advocating for keeping the monuments to use them as educational tools to explain the Lost Cause and how it affected the social, political, and physical landscape. Yet others advocated for removing the monuments without further discussion, with some saying that suggesting otherwise was not a legitimate opinion. Members of the committee likewise held a variety of views, with one member stating that the Lost Cause language found on some Atlanta reconciliation monuments was "grotesque" and another ready to have all monuments removed.[6]

The advisory committee established a procedure: all monuments would be carefully researched before considering any action. This research unearthed insightful facts about the circumstances surrounding the erection of the monuments as well as their stated (and unstated) purpose and uses since. When the final recommendations of the committee were made, some decisions differed from what they most likely would have been without background research and analysis. For example, the committee's consensus decision recommended retaining the early monuments in Oakland Cemetery due to their funereal nature, educational potential, appropriate placement in a cemetery, and potential for effective contextualization by the Historic Oakland Foundation, which already conducts regular tours of the cemetery.

Like many other states in the South, Georgia outlawed the removal or obscuring of Confederate monuments in the early 2000s. Given that no monuments could actually be removed until the law is changed, the committee used an evidence-based research approach as a means of arriving at the best solution. The two reconciliation monuments, the Peace Monument in Piedmont Park and the Peachtree Battle Monument located on Peachtree Battle Avenue, were slated for eventual removal, pending a change in the law.[7] Others, such as a battlefield marker for the death of Confederate General W. H. T. Walker and the Oakland Cemetery monuments, were recommended for additional contextualization with interpretive panels. Another, a bust of Sidney Lanier, was recommended to remain unchanged because the commemoration of the poet was for his writing, not his Confederate Army service. These nuanced, balanced, and thoughtful solutions could only have been achieved as a result of the research process combined with an inclusive dialogue.[8]

History Meets Public Service: The Future of Public History

At the heart of the Confederate monuments debate is the eventual self-destruction of the Lost Cause myth. As more individuals research and challenge this false historical narrative, the once-common misconceptions about slavery, the Civil War, Reconstruction, and the Jim Crow era collapse under the weight of their own misrepresentation and distortion of the historical record. As we have seen over the past decades, the debate over Confederate symbols will not go away any time soon, nor will any of the debates that arise from the same basic root cause. The Confederate monument debate has spurred ongoing consideration of other historical figures and their legacy, such as Christopher Columbus and his role in the destruction of the Native American populations and the conquest of the Americas. Similar dissecting and challenging of dominant narratives have resulted in discrediting of long communally accepted historical "truths" in the past and will continue to do so in the future.

As these previously widely accepted historical narratives quake and eventually crack, many Americans find themselves confused and in search of a new story that brings together different segments of the population and fully explains our history. Public history can play a vital role in filling in these newly created gaps. By helping communities uncover their own history, public history institutions can help Americans make informed choices about their own present and future through an evidence-based understanding of the past. In a world of identity politics and divisions, it becomes more important than ever to empower communities to learn, grow, and understand our collective history.

As public historians, this is what public service calls us to do.

10

EMPTY PEDESTALS

WHAT SHOULD BE DONE WITH CIVIC MONUMENTS TO THE CONFEDERACY AND ITS LEADERS?

CIVIL WAR TIMES

Editor's note: The following chapter is from an article reprinted by permission from Civil War Times Magazine *and was published in October 2017. Note the wide range of approaches and perspectives from scholars, community members, and activists. Clearly, there are no easy answers. Thank you to His*toryNet *and* Civil War Times Magazine *for granting permission to reprint.*

From **Charlottesville,** Va., to New Orleans, La., the removal of Confederate statues from public spaces and the debates over their removal are making national news. Numerous other Southern communities, large and small, are reconsidering the future of the Southern soldiers in marble and bronze that stand watch over their town squares and courthouses. What will be their fates? As a bi-monthly magazine, *Civil War Times* (CWT) has a hard time being newsworthy and current. Often news stories that occur when we are putting an issue together will be "cold" by the time that issue is completed and sent off to the printer. The monument controversy, however, appears to be one that will remain topical for some time, and I feel that CWT needs to address the debate in some manner as it grows in intensity. I think it would be interesting, timely, and important for readers to hear views on monument removal. So, to that end, I asked members of the magazine's advisory board, all highly respected scholars and authors, as well as some other selected authorities, to send us their opinions on Confederate monument removal. Their interesting and thoughtful answers are diverse, and some are likely to be controversial. The removal of Confederate monuments is a complex issue. —The HistoryNet Editor

James J. Broomall

Director, George Tyler Moore Center for the Study of the Civil War Shepherd University

I am an academic historian who practices public history and advocates for preservation. The removal of Confederate monuments troubles me as much as the destruction of a historic building or the total "rehabilitation" of a battlefield. The built environment contains countless lessons if allowed to speak. Make no mistake, the bronze sentinels and stone plinths found primarily in Southern cities and towns offer an incomplete, even dangerous message if they remain silent. I can therefore appreciate why so many people wish for their removal. Confederate monuments are at once symbols of white supremacy, works of art, affirmations of the Lost Cause, and tributes to white Southerners. Yet, public history and preservation suggest that Confederate monuments can be used as tools for education, deliberation, and even protest. Interpretive signage and additional memorials or statuary offer one way to convey the thick historical and aesthetic layers associated with these relics. We can further democratize these spaces by capturing oral histories of the current monument debates, advocating teach-ins and dramatic performances, or encouraging viewers to create temporary discursive signage. Confederate monuments remind audiences of a painful past but can also give voice to contemporary social concerns and needs if they are allowed to speak.

Catherine Clinton

Denman Chair of American History
University of Texas at San Antonio

Headlines frequently call for the removal of Confederate monuments. Scholars try to learn from case-to-case how we can help communities find a place to debate how the culture of Confederate veneration affects the lives of those who live in the shadow of proslavery symbols.

Many suggest that eradication of these public symbols will create safe spaces and reduce the hostility felt by those resentful of Confederate remnants. What if monuments today might become more creative? In Germany, artists install "sto[l]perstein," stumbling blocks on the pavement adorned with names and dates of Holocaust victims. These arresting public installations remind passersby of those led to their deaths by a monstrous and unjust government.

Americans witnessed a controversy over a 2016 "Fearless Girl" statue installation in lower Manhattan. Public art can raise hackles, as well as awareness of critical issues. Perhaps we would be better served by funding counter-monuments to feed the hunger for new and different stories told with imagination. Perhaps shared spaces can become places where conflicting interpretations of circumstances might be highlighted.

Static 19th and 20th century visions set in stone might seem objectionable, but it's probably equally offensive to try to sanitize the past without a plan to feed the human desire for knowing what's come before in order to understand what might lie ahead.

Christy S. Coleman

CEO, American Civil War Museum
Richmond, Va.

In the past two years, the American Civil War Museum has fielded numerous calls regarding controversies about Confederate imagery. Many want the museum to take a firm stand to support or oppose the removal of these items from the public landscape. As an organization, we rely on our mission to guide our actions.

In short, ACWM is a resource for communities to explore the war and its legacies. We recently hosted a symposium called Lightning Rods for Controversy (aired by C-Span) to frame the conversation and give interested parties the opportunity to hear from content experts. In addition, our unmatched archival and artifact collections contain important documents and information to help address the "who, what, where, when, and—most important—why" these monuments and symbols were placed. When communities are armed with this information, we are hopeful they will make well-informed decisions with reasoned discourse with all stakeholders.

At the heart of these discussions and debates is the core question of how we choose to remember. When it comes to the American Civil War, the answer is not always "blue and gray." Americans of every background grapple with the war's legacies in contemporary times. This history is not dead or past. This history is present.

William C. Davis

Professor of History, retired
Virginia Tech University

In the passionate debate over where—and whether—the Confederacy merits remembrance today, we forget that changing values and demographics have always imperiled past generations' heroes. Nowhere is it written that heroes remain in place for all posterity. Where are the statues of George III today? New times make new heroes. Before 1968 there were no Martin Luther King Boulevards; today there are hundreds.

Removing statues in New Orleans and elsewhere is unfortunate, however understandable. Occasionally circumstances demand change. Nathan Bedford Forrest High School in Jacksonville, Fla., was all-white in 1959. By 2014 it had a substantial black student population. African Americans attending a school honoring a slave dealer (and possible abettor of the "Fort Pillow Massacre") was too surreal to be ignored.

Confederates represent a part of our history. Judge past figures by today's values, and our Capitol's "Statuary Hall" would become "Empty Pedestal Hall." Instead, consider Budapest's Memento Park. Rather than destroy statuary from the Communist era, the city moved it into one park as a "monument" to democracy's triumph.

"Lost Cause" mythology claims that Confederates seceded over self-determination. Ironically, as local populations today reevaluate who to memorialize, that argument is ascendant. Urban demographics will continue to shift, along with popular will, meaning that in the future if the people so desire, Davis and Lee may march back into town.

Gary W. Gallagher

John L. Nau III Professor of History
Director, John L. Nau III Center for Civil War History
University of Virginia

Debates about the Civil War's memorial landscape erupt periodically and usually feature the same arguments from those who want to leave statues and other monuments in place and those who want to remove them. How to deal with Confederate monuments inspires honest disagreement among well-intentioned, well-informed people, as well as some vitriolic cant from both ends of the political spectrum. In my view, eliminating parts of the memorial landscape is tantamount to destroying documents or images—all compose parts of the historical record and should be interpreted as such. I favor adding text that places monuments within the full sweep of how Americans have remembered the Civil War. I also support erecting new monuments devoted to previously slighted groups or events. The controversy over the equestrian statue of Robert E. Lee in Charlottesville is a good example of current debates. I would preserve the statue, add panels discussing its history, rename the park, and commission a memorial to the more than 250 men born in Albemarle County who served in United States Colored Troops units. Visitors to the revamped park could ponder generational changes in memorialization that underscore the contested nature of historical memory. Taking down statues, in contrast, potentially inhibits a real understanding of our past, warts and all, and can obscure important themes, movements, and eras.

Lesley J. Gordon

Charles G. Summersell Chair
Southern History at University of Alabama

In 1908, the town of Raymond, in Hinds County, Miss., held a ceremony to dedicate a monument to Confederate soldiers. Ex-Confederate Captain

William T. Ratliff assured listeners that their monument was not about defeat, but instead courage and "principles that would endure forever to show what men and women would do for a cause they believed just and right." The Nathan Bedford Forrest Chapter of the United Daughters of the Confederacy officially unveiled the statue, with an estimated 1,500 in attendance.

This statue, like the thousands found throughout the South and beyond, had a clear message: to celebrate and promote the ideals of the Lost Cause. The triumphant narrative of Confederate valor and sacrifice was meant to bolster white supremacy and silence African-American voices as much as their agency, particularly in the context of the Jim Crow South.

This campaign of obfuscation has been remarkably successful, leaving many white Americans unwilling or disinterested in grappling with the war's painful legacy. The removal of Confederate monuments—and the vigorous debate it has inspired—helps, I believe, to finally reach some sort of reckoning with that past in order to embrace a more pluralistic American society.

D. Scott Hartwig

Supervisory Historian, retired
Gettysburg National Military Park

We are all aware that the legacy of our Civil War and Reconstruction is complex, controversial, and for some, painful. I can understand the anger residents of New Orleans might feel about a monument in the heart of their city commemorating and celebrating an 1866 massacre of black citizens who were simply demonstrating for the right to vote. It was a constant reminder of a white supremacist society and I sympathize with the city's decision to remove it.

Monument removal, however, becomes more problematic when we apply it to any monument or memorial associated with the Confederacy, as if by removing these symbols we can somehow repair the past and heal wounds. But does it? It seems more likely to heal one wound and open another. A better solution to tearing down Confederate monuments is the example of the Arthur Ashe monument on Monument Avenue in Richmond. Ashe's monument reminds visitors and residents that Richmond's history is complicated and more than just the memory of the

Confederacy and its leaders. Rather than tear down monuments, build new ones, where appropriate, that tell the story of those who struggled bravely for freedom and equality.

Harold Holzer

The Jonathan F. Fanton Director
Hunter College's Roosevelt House Public Policy Institute
Vice Chairman, The Lincoln Forum

A few years ago, my fellow historians Gary Gallagher and Joan Waugh took me to view the Indian War Monument in downtown Santa Fe. There, the problem of how to contextualize a tribute to the white man's battles against "savage Indians" was addressed by the almost comical obliteration of the adjective "savage."

The effort may have been clumsy, but it may point the way to contextualizing Confederate tributes, however ill-conceived, without destroying artworks that may have both historical and aesthetic value. Some of the equestrian "icons" long on view in Richmond, for example, surely deserve to survive as stellar examples of American sculpture. Not all art is easy to digest.

But even Stalin did not order the destruction of the great statues of the tsars in St. Petersburg, though his own images suffered a far worse fate (and deserved no rescue, if only because they were so mediocre). In effect, I remain torn. I abhor the iconoclastic destruction of art—whether by the Taliban at Bamiyan, Afghanistan [where two monumental sculptures of Buddha were blown up in 2001], or by our own justifiably offended citizens in New Orleans. Using the preservation of a mediocre Jefferson Davis statue to rally neo-Nazis waving the Stars and Bars is a repugnant exercise that deserves condemnation. Do no local museums exist in these cities willing to reinstall, or properly label, the worthiest examples of the post–Civil War memorial movement?

Robert K. Krick

Noted Speaker on Civil War topics
Author of *Stonewall Jackson at Cedar Mountain*

We live in an age riven by shrill and intemperate voices, from all perspectives and on most topics. No sane person today would embrace, endorse, or tolerate slavery.

A casual observer, readily able to convince himself that he would have behaved similarly in the 1860s, can vault to high moral ground with the greatest of ease. Doing that gratifies the powerful self-righteous strain that runs through all of us, for better or worse. In fact, it leaps far ahead of the Federal politicians (Lincoln among them) who said emphatically that slavery was not the issue, and millions of Northern soldiers who fought, bled, and died in windrows to save the Union—but were noisily offended by mid-war emancipation.

It is impossible to imagine a United States in the current atmosphere that does not include zealots eager to obliterate any culture not precisely their own, destroying monuments in the fashion of Soviets after a purge, and antiquities in the manner of ISIS. The trend is redolent of the misery that inundated the planet during the aptly named Dark Ages, arising from savages who believed, as a matter of religion in that instance, that anyone with opinions different than their own was not just wrong, but craven and evil, and must be brutalized into conformity.

On the other hand, a generous proportion of the country now, and always, eschews extremism, and embraces tolerance of others' cultures and inheritances and beliefs. Such folk will be society's salvation.

Michael J. McAfee

Curator of History, West Point Museum

In Saratoga National Military Park there is a monument bearing the sculpted image of a boot and an epaulette of a brigadier general. That general's name is not mentioned on the monument, nor is it on the series of plaques honoring generals of the American Revolution in the Old Cadet Chapel at West Point, N.Y. Despite his gallant service, that man turned his back on his cause and became a traitor. For that reason there are no monuments that mention the name Benedict Arnold.

What does this have to do with the Southern monuments honoring the political and military leaders of the Confederacy? They, like Arnold, were traitors. They turned their backs on their nation, their oaths, and the sacrifices of their ancestors in the War for Independence. They did so not out of a sense of mistreatment or for money as did Arnold. They attempted to destroy their nation to defend chattel slavery and from a sense that as white men they were innately superior to all other races. They fought for white racial supremacy.

That is why monuments glorifying them and their cause should be removed. Leave monuments marking their participation on the battlefields of the war, but tear down those that only commemorate the intolerance, violence, and hate that inspired their attempt to destroy the American nation.

Joseph McGill

Founder, The Slave Dwelling Project

This nation was founded on an underpinning of slavery and white supremacy. While President Thomas Jefferson penned in the Declaration of Independence that "All men are created equal," he owned 600 people and fathered children with his enslaved Sally Hemings.

President James Madison is considered the father of our Constitution—"We the people." But Madison also owned slaves. The fact is, 12 of our former presidents owned slaves, and eight of them owned slaves while they were in office.

In our efforts to sanitize history by removing Confederate monuments that are reminders of slavery and white supremacy, we must ask ourselves: Where do we stop? As an African-American male, I do not buy into the "Heritage not Hate" defense of Confederate flags and monuments.

That said, I am in support of Confederate monuments remaining on the landscape. My reason being, Confederate soldiers were defending a way of life that was passed down to them. If we remove Confederate monuments, then we should also remove the monuments of their fathers and the fathers before them. In this sanitizing of history, we will eventually get to our Founding Fathers, some of whom were slave owners. How would Washington, D.C., look without the Washington Monument or the Jefferson Memorial?

Megan Kate Nelson

Independent Scholar
Author of *Ruin Nation: Destruction and the American Civil War*

What unites all of the participants in the debate about Confederate memorials? The belief that "retain" or "remove" are only two options.

But what about a third option? I would like to propose that Confederate memorials should neither be retained nor removed: They should be destroyed, and their broken pieces left in situ.

On a scheduled day, a city government or university administration would invite citizens to approach a Confederate memorial, take up a cudgel, and swing away. The ruination of the memorial would be a group effort, a way for an entire community to convert a symbol of racism and white supremacy into a symbol of resistance against oppression.

Historians could put up a plaque next to the fragments, explaining the memorial's history, from its dedication day to the moment of its obliteration. A series of photographs or a YouTube video could record the process of destruction. These textual explanations may be unnecessary, however. Ruins tend to convey their messages eloquently in and of themselves. In this case, the ruins of Confederate memorials in cities across the nation would suggest that while white supremacists have often made claims to power in American history, those who oppose them can, and will, fight back.

Ethan S. Rafuse

Professor of History, U.S. Army Command and General Staff College, Fort Leavenworth, Kan.

Like Ulysses S. Grant, I respect the sacrifices and hardships the common soldier of the Confederacy endured, and the character and military skill of some of their leaders, while also disagreeing with those who wish to pay homage to the cause they fought for. Say what you will about the Civil War North (and much can be said that is critical), it did fight to preserve the ability of the United States to be a force for good in the world—and did so successfully. You also have to be pretty obtuse not to appreciate there is good reason to be offended by anything that honors people who fought to defend slavery and the Southern racial order.

That being said, I cannot help but think the time and energy being devoted to the removal of monuments could be spent in more constructive ways. Moreover, like it or not, these monuments are part of our heritage and cultural landscape (warts and all) and have value as educational tools. I would not want to see the Confederate White House bulldozed or lose the fodder for discussion the Heyward Shepherd memorial at Harpers Ferry provides. Shepherd, the first man killed by John Brown's raiders, was African American. Thus, there is the very real, practical question in regards to the removal of monuments of where one stops—and who decides where that point is?

Thos. V. Strain Jr.

Commander-in-Chief
Sons of Confederate Veterans

I was contacted by the editor of *Civil War Times* about my thoughts on the removal of monuments that have been erected to honor the men that fought for the Confederacy during the War Between the States. It is my opinion, and that of many others, that these removals are an attempt to erase history. If you take the time to read the comments on social media and on the websites of the news organizations reporting these removals it is obvious that only a few people actually support the removals. What it boils down to is that the politicians are telling those that elected them that their wishes mean absolutely nothing to them.

Just this week one of these politicians that voted to remove a statue in Virginia lost in the primary for reelection and he noted that his stance on the removal more than likely cost him the election. In the end what we really have, in my humble opinion, is a group of people who are following their own personal agendas and saying, "to hell with the people" and moving forward with these removals. It isn't what we want, it is all about them.

Susannah J. Ural

Professor of History

Co-Director of the Dale Center for the Study of
War & Society University of Southern Mississippi

There's an obelisk at Karnak built to honor Hatshepsut, one of the few women pharaohs of Ancient Egypt. Its inscription captures her curiosity at how she, who ushered in a period of prosperity and peace, would be remembered: "Now my heart turns this way and that, as I think what the people will say. Those who see my monuments in years to come, and who shall speak of what I have done." Hatshepsut's successor, for reasons still debated, nearly destroyed every memory of her. But history has a way of haunting us.

In an era of great division, most factions in the Confederate monuments debate actually agree that history should not be erased. The question is in how it should be remembered. In my opinion, if citizens come together and agree to remove the monuments, they should do so. But don't hide them away in warehouses. Place them at museums or battlefield parks where historians and interpreters can help visitors learn about the motives behind the Lost Cause. That movement erected these statues to, yes, honor concepts of sacrifice for liberty and family, but these monuments were also designed to entrench a ruthless tradition of white supremacy.

Like Hatshepsut's obelisk, Confederate memorials "speak of what [we] have done." Let us do just that at historic sites designed for that purpose, where Confederate symbols, including the flag, are and should be part of the landscape from which visitors learn.

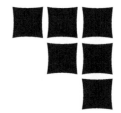

3

NATIVE PEOPLES
AND WHITE-WASHED
HISTORY

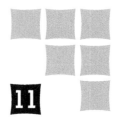

FROM COLUMBUS TO SERRA AND BEYOND

DAVID B. ALLISON

Columbian Legacies

The persistence of Columbus Day as a national holiday in the United States has consistently been a repugnant reminder to native peoples of the subjugation and annihilation of their ancestors wrought by contact with Europeans. Moreover, statues of Christopher Columbus (Cristobal Colon) in New York City, Arecibo, Puerto Rico—which is the record holder for largest statue in the Western Hemisphere—and Washington, DC, have been viewed by many as perpetuating a blindly worshipful embrace of the so-called discoverer of America. Of course, the first peoples to come to America were, in fact, the native peoples.[1] In addition, Columbus's subsequent actions in the Caribbean led to disease, torture, and enslavement for the people with whom he came into contact.[2]

But, as we have seen time and again throughout our peregrinations through controversies about monuments and memorials, a simple, dichotomous categorization of historical events and people into good and evil is rarely helpful for promoting empathy and understanding. The stunning complexity wrought by the reconnection of continents long since set geologically adrift from one another begs us to stop and listen to all the voices impacted by that event. On the quincentenary of Columbus's fateful voyage, historian James Axtell wrote, "In moral terms, the Columbian legacy was to bring into contact and often conflict not only the human populations of Asia, Africa, Europe and the Americas, but their plants, animals and organisms, their institutions, values and ideas."[3]

As contact spooled itself out across the land, the persistence of imperialism in the name of the advance of civilization resulted in a decidedly less than equal encounter. Native peoples were forced to accommodate, fight, or flee European newcomers who clung to an ideology that often negated or devalued the essential humanity of the denizens of the New World. Justification followed hot behind the debasement of native groups, as settlers, politicians, and soldiers claimed superiority over supposedly "savage" native peoples.

Due to the legacy of white domination ushered in by first contact, many native groups have pushed for renaming Columbus Day as Indigenous Peoples Day, and calls for removing statues to Columbus have increased greatly in the past decade. Some Italian American groups have strongly combated the move to remove Columbus statues—particularly in New York. Many Italian Americans claim Columbus for their own and have used pride in his accomplishments as their own shield against the mid-twentieth-century ethnocentrism that excluded and belittled people of Italian descent. The strong sentiments either praising Columbus's heroism and bravery or bemoaning the colonizing conquest of North America that his actions touched off speak to the continued complexity of history and memorialization in the United States.

These debates came to a head in November 2017 in New York City at a town hall–style event run by the city's Mayoral Advisory Commission on City Art, Monuments and Markers. This gathering aimed to open public discourse and to help government officials learn more from the community about controversial plaques and statues in New York City. The conversation focused on a large Columbus statue erected at Columbus Circle in 1892, a statue of controversial gynecologist J. Marion Sims in Central Park (see Vanessa Cuervo Forero's chapter for a thorough explanation of Sims's grotesque experimentation on African American women and the controversy around him), the Theodore Roosevelt equestrian statue in front of the American Museum of Natural History (see William Walker's chapter about this statue at the end of this section for more context),

A Christopher Columbus statue stands with a heroic pose in Connecticut in October 2011. From the George F. Landegger Collection of Connecticut Photographs in the Carol M. Highsmith's America, Library of Congress, Prints and Photographs Division. Courtesy of the Library of Congress.

and two plaques along Broadway to French World War I heroes (and later Vichy France leaders) Phillipe Pétain and Pierre LaValle.[4] After a vehement discussion about the perceived merits and drawbacks of the statues and plaques, Elena Goukassian from Hyperallergic reported, "It was clear the Sims statue seemed to be the most hated at the hearing; not one single person testified in favor of keeping it. . . . Toward the end of the four-hour-long hearing, one woman who had defended other contested statues concluded: 'Let the statues stand . . . except for Sims.' This was greeted by a roar of laughter."[5]

While some statues—such as the one to J. Marion Sims—seem to have broad consensus about what to do with them, others—such as statues to Columbus—continue to be hotly contested. In October 2017, right around Columbus Day, the statue to Columbus in Central Park was spray-painted with the words "Hate will not be tolerated," and the mariner's hands were colored red.[6] The Columbian legacy is still far from being settled. It seems likely that the annual Columbus and Indigenous Peoples Day remembrances each October will bring with them the chilly winds of disputed memory and the still-fresh wounds of the past.

Other parts of the country—notably the American Southwest and California—have also had to grapple with legacies of the subjugation and annihilation of native peoples. The visible presence of monuments and memorials to colonizers, conquistadors, and men of the cloth who attempted to convert American Indians to Catholicism are reminders to many natives of the sometimes forceful violence of Spanish rule in that part of the country. The next section will examine two such examples of controversial statues in the western United States.

Serra in California and Oñate in New Mexico

When interested tourists come to experience the past at historic sites and memorials like picturesque Spanish missions, they do so in a specific spot of land that has been populated with a network of meanings and perspectives meant for public consumption. Some scholars, such as Elizabeth Kryder-Reid, a professor of anthropology and museum studies at Indiana University-Purdue University, Indianapolis, have explored these sites. In "Sites of Power and the Power of Sight: Vision in the California Mission Landscape," she examines how the design of missions in California serve very specific interests. Kryder-Reid argues that though these missions are portrayed for tourists as beautiful expressions of Catholicism, they were historically oppressive vehicles of colonization.[7] As is often the case, those in power greatly influence how the public perceives the meaning of a physical space—even if the meaning of the space is contested.

Counternarratives from previously underrepresented and unheard voices tend to spring up when the powerful "history makers" decide to memorialize people perceived to be oppressors or agents of colonization. Geographer Katharyne Mitchell provides a further exploration of how this alternative perspective on memory production can develop in "Monuments, Memorials, and the Politics of Memory":

> Collective projects of resistance to normative memory production include those which refuse to accede to the scripting of history in the format of the dominant power. These are memories that evade the regulatory practices of the state and/or the market, with individuals and groups either forming "counter" practices associated with

dominant monuments, or creating their own places of mourning or celebration. In these landscapes of "minority" memory, those groups that have been rendered invisible in the landscape, or who have been discredited or marginalized in mainstream memorialization, oppose normative readings and/or create sites which speak to a different interpretation of historical events.[8]

With this lens of alternative interpretation of historical events, turning our attention to the many statues to Father Junipero Serra that populate California's central coast region will be illuminative.

A Spanish Franciscan friar who founded nine missions and converted thousands of Native Americans to Catholicism through baptism in the eighteenth century, Serra represents for many native peoples the brutal assimilationist practices that occurred at missions throughout the Spanish colonies.[9] After Pope Francis canonized Serra in 2015, attacks on Serra statues began in earnest. Statues in Santa Barbara, Carmel, and Monterey were all vandalized—through decapitation, graffiti, or splashes of red paint.[10] The debates about Serra's legacy continue, as Catholic leaders claim that he was a defender of indigenous peoples, while others point to his forced conversions of natives as evidence of his complicity with colonial oppression.

The small town of Alcalde, New Mexico, has also been the site of similar protestations toward statues honoring Spain's colonial heroes. In 1997, members of a group known as the Friends of Acoma sawed Oñate's right foot off his equestrian statue in Alcalde.[11] A conquistador during the 1600s, scholars have noted that Oñate helped to oversee the slaughter of eight hundred people at Acoma Pueblo and legend reports that he cut off the feet of twenty-four survivors of the massacre.[12] The symbolic removal of his foot from the statue echoes the atrocity he committed at Acoma, and the "surgeons" who did the amputating have been widely celebrated in native communities as a result. Others, however, have argued that the mixed Hispanic heritage of New Mexico deserves celebration by honoring men like Oñate. As with Serra, contested historical memories around the Oñate statue continue to open new questions about who should be memorialized and how their deeds (and misdeeds) should be remembered.

Next, we will examine a case study from Connecticut to see how one museum took positive steps to reopen the difficult history of the Pequot

War and to remove and reinterpret a statue to a colonial leader. Much of this section has been culled from notes shared with me by Laurie Pasteryak Lamarre, the executive director of the Connecticut League of History Organizations, and I am thankful to her for sharing this tale with me.

The Pequot War in Connecticut and Decolonization

Sonorous names like Monongahela and Manhatten are some of the few remnants of language extant from the original inhabitants of North America on the east coast. Having been usurped by white settlers over many years, in many places, only mellifluous place names survive. In Connecticut, the Pequot peoples have been largely forgotten, but one of their conquerors—John Mason—was memorialized in durable bronze.

Writing about Mason's deeds during the Pequot War (fought between the Pequot and English colonists and their native allies between 1636 and 1638), Lamarre remarks that the English military leader's actions resulted in "the massacre and genocide of a group of people. It enforced slavery, displacement and dispossession, repression, and attempted to erase [the Pequots]."[13] Notably, Mason had been the commander during an incident (which is often labeled a massacre) at Mistick Fort in 1637 in which more than four hundred Pequot men, women, and children were killed.[14] The immediate aftermath of the Pequot War resulted in the English colonists commandeering large swaths of the traditional Pequot lands and Mason himself receiving almost a thousand acres of dispossessed Pequot land in the town that is now known as Mystic.[15]

As part of a push to celebrate their Puritan forbears, in 1889 a statue to John Mason was unveiled in Groton, Connecticut. Lamarre notes the context of the creation of the statue: "The statue was erected at the time of 'Manifest Destiny.' It was erected, purposefully, near the site of the battle."[16] With a strong tie to the expansionist rhetoric of the late 1880s, the Mason statue was representative of a particularly celebratory colonial, white supremacist mind-set in white America during this period.

By the early 1990s, as the anniversary of Christopher Columbus's stumble into America neared, many Connecticut residents and native activists began to question the John Mason statue's value to the community and to blanch at what he represented in terms of conquest, colonization, and the annihilation of native peoples. Lamarre relates that "[on]

July 21, 1992, Lonewolf Jackson [a member of the Eastern Pequot tribe] addressed Groton Town Council as part of the citizen's petition portion of the meeting. Mr. Jackson requested that the Town remove the Captain John Mason Statue located on Pequot Avenue, in Mystic, Connecticut." Lamarre continues, "The request was supported by a petition of 900 signatures gathered in one weekend by members of the Pequot Nation and members of a community-based organization, the Southeastern Connecticut Coalition for Peace and Justice."[17]

A Groton town council resolution from 1992 notes that the combined efforts of an advisory council comprising the Groton Town Historian, representatives from the Pequot Nation, representatives of the Southeastern Connecticut Coalition for Peace and Justice, representatives from Pequot Avenue, a representative from the Mystic-Noank Historical Society, and Joseph Hickey, a representative of the State Parks Division of the Department of Environmental Protection, would decide the fate of the statue.[18] By 1995, the statue had been removed from Mystic, and by 1996 it was installed in Mason's hometown of Windsor with new plaques that contextualized Mason's life and legacy more effectively than the celebratory hagiography that had been there before. Writing about the mood after dedicating the new location and interpretation of the statue, Lamarre explains that "people left the ceremony with a new appreciation for the fact that all these officials, from their various points of view, worked very hard to find an accurate and sensitive solution to the new location and interpretation of the statue, that it had been a personal, as well as a professional, journey for all of them."[19]

Notably, the process had not been easy for the people involved in the reinterpretation and removal. Lamarre quotes from the "John Mason Statue Advisory Committee Final Report, October 20, 1993" to show the journey to reach compromise: "The path to consensus was difficult, grueling, and time consuming. Compromise was necessary from both extreme viewpoints. Those requesting the statue be removed from public view and those refusing to accept removal for any reason shifted to agree to relocation and replacement of the statue. This decision was motivated by educational and historic perspectives which can benefit the community-at-large."[20] The lessons for us when opening conversations about the controversial monuments of our time is clear—there will be no quick and easy solutions, and we must always strive for "amity for all Americans" in our reinterpretations.[21]

Joseph A. Amato, in *Rethinking Home: A Case for Writing Local History*, discusses the intimacy that residents can have with even the most ramshackle structure in a particular location.[22] Personal and shared memories are powerful influences in peoples' lives, and the loss of a historic building might have a profound effect on a community's sense of place and its members' view of themselves. Indeed, anthropologist Chip Colwell shares how the landscape of the Southwest became written with new meanings by the dominant culture in the early part of the 1900s: "The naissance of archaeology here was launched in parallel with the transformation of the Southwest into a romantic landscape—of towering mountains, dramatic canyons, and lush valleys, certainly, but also a place of history, a landscape marked everywhere by the past."[23]

Museums that blithely hold onto indigenous remains, artifacts, and other material culture are among the most pernicious and intractable remnants of a romanticizing colonial mind-set. Decolonization—the repatriation of native objects and native land—has become a new way for natural history museums to work closely with tribal groups to ensure that the tribes themselves are able to interpret their own culture in the ways that they so choose.[24] Museums like the Denver Museum of Nature & Science and the San Diego Museum of Man have been leaders in not merely following the letter of the law as outlined by NAGPRA (Native American Graves Protection and Repatriation Act) but also reaching out in meaningful ways to native groups to ensure that their voices are strongest and most prominent as they determine what is most important to reinterpret, remove, or repatriate.[25] Increasingly, museums are learning that they must thoroughly decolonize their collections to make amends for their history of rapacious looting and unethical desecrations of sacred native objects and, most tragically, the very bones of the dead.

In 1990, Rosemary Cambra, a Californian Costanoan Indian, wrote upon the reburial of five hundred thousand bones of native peoples that had been collected at Stanford University, "[After a ceremony] we wheelbarrowed three feet of dirt over the remains and then put another five feet of dirt over them with a back hoe. . . . It took two women to put the reburial idea into the minds of the Stanford [University] people." She continued, "No threats, no arguments. It didn't take a whole band or a whole tribe of 200,000 Indians to rebury these people. It was just laying down a truthful foundation."[26]

Truthful foundations must be the starting point for any discussion about controversial monuments and memorials. The next section— "Identity Politics and the Rational and Sympathetic Minds"—will explore how our identity influences our unique, yet constantly influenced and changeable, perspectives on the moral imperatives of keeping, reinterpreting, or removing public statues. I will argue that a foundation of truth—given strength through both rationality and empathy—is the most effective way to begin dialogue about historically fraught statues.

NATIVE VOICES AT LITTLE BIGHORN NATIONAL MONUMENT

GERARD BAKER

Editor's note: Baker's powerful personal story from his years in the National Parks Service—specifically from his time as superintendent for Little Bighorn Battlefield National Monument in the mid-1990s—has been supplemented with information the editor gleaned from a 1997 New York Times *article titled "Controversy over Memorial to Winners at Little Bighorn" and Baker's plenary address at the 2010 American Association for State and Local History (AASLH) Annual Meeting.*

> For a long, long time in my generation they would always say, "Keep your history to yourself. Don't ever tell the white people what's going on because they're going to make fun of you. Don't ever tell people what you've been through because they're not going to believe you." That is how I started out with history.

We knew it. We kept it to ourselves. We were never allowed to talk about our ceremonies. We were never allowed to share sacred songs.

—Gerard Baker, 2010 Plenary Address,
AASLH Annual Conference

I have had the honor to serve as the general manager (superintendent) for two of America's iconic landmarks—namely, Little Bighorn Battlefield National Monument and Mount Rushmore National Memorial. Although small in acreage, these two units of the National Park Service (NPS) are rich in history and complex interpretations. The focus of this chapter will be on my time at Little Bighorn, although the story of my years at Mount Rushmore is equally compelling and also deserves a telling one day.

I took a somewhat circuitous path to the NPS. I was raised on a small cattle ranch in western North Dakota on the Fort Berthold Indian Reservation. I am an enrolled member of the Mandan-Hidatsa Tribe. The only national park unit around us was Theodore Roosevelt National Park–North Unit, but we never heard or knew about it. What we did know was the history of our people as told by the elders. They taught us about who we are—our clans and our societies in village time and of today. My folks relocated to the western part of the reservation when the U.S. government flooded the Missouri River as part of the Pick-Slone Plan creating the Garrison Dam. We lost everything as a tribe.

My next direct contact with the federal government happened when I applied for my first NPS appointment in the summer of my college years. I thought I was applying to work on a road crew, but I ended up in the old Park Ranger Technician series and worked in a campground—as I now tell people, "I started my career cleaning toilets and worked my way down to management from there!" Once I received my degree in criminology from Southern Oregon State University, I started my NPS career in the ranger field, including a stint as a park ranger/historian and deputy sheriff, among other things.

Throughout my career, I have always found NPS to be an excellent agency. I believe Americans are truly lucky that so much park land was set aside for future generations. I also noticed that one piece was always reduced (or sometimes not mentioned at all) throughout the parks: the story of American Indians and their lands that are now NPS property. This simple fact guided me in later life as an NPS manager at various locations, including Little Bighorn. This site is known among the NPS as a starter park, a great place to get your feet wet in all areas of park management. That it was. It was also known as a controversial park because of its story, a brutal loss by the U.S. Army at the hands of American Indians, and was getting more so when I showed up as the superintendent in the fall of 1993. It was the first superintendency of my NPS career.

Prior to taking the job, I had been to Little Bighorn a few times in my life. Of course, I knew the history just like everybody else . . . we (American Indians) won! I had also had a memorable experience at the park as part of my previous NPS duties. I was invited to the site by a previous superintendent—Dennis Ditrmanson—to attend an anniversary of the Battle of the Little Bighorn. I participated not only in law enforcement duties but also as a liaison of sorts to the Indian community. It was rumored that the American Indian Movement (AIM), under the direction of the late Russell Means, would be coming to the park to erect its own commemorative plaque.[1]

I rode up with other rangers there to assist with law enforcement. I was in the backseat as we arrived at the entrance station. I rolled down my window and said, "I'm Russell Means. Where can I put this plaque?" I remember the entrance station getting a bit wild for a while until I revealed myself as not actually Means, but it showed they were ready for almost anything.

Later that week, Ditrmanson informed me he had been invited to a Sun Rise ceremony at the camp of a Northern Cheyenne elder and asked me whether he should go. My answer was yes, by all means he should go, and not only go but also wear the NPS uniform to the ceremony as an invited guest. I told him that every time he was invited to a ceremony, especially in this case (a prayer ceremony), he should go. I said that I would attend as well, but not in uniform so as not to be too noticed. I had a lot of relatives and friends at this event; plus I was trying to find out whether AIM had any weapons or explosives, as rumored. The ceremony proceeded without incident, and the only non-Indian person there—Ditrmanson—did great. I believed this opened more doors for communication that would be essential in the future.

When I arrived at Little Bighorn in 1993, the park had just experienced some very troubling times. Nine years earlier, I had taken a break from the NPS. I joined the U.S. Forest Service as an assistant district ranger and American Indian program manager. I was assigned to the position of acting district ranger for the Ashland Montana District, and I would many times stop and visit the superintendent at Little Bighorn, Barbara Booher, who happened to be the first American Indian and also the first female to be the park's superintendent.

Two major changes occurred during her service at the park. Both were issues I had to deal with when I took the job. The first was a name change from Custer Battlefield National Monument to Little Bighorn Battlefield National Monument. The second was the disbanding of the park's friends group, which was very opposed to the name change and fought nearly every action the superintendent undertook to broaden the park's interpretation to include the American Indian story—particularly selling books with American Indian perspectives, most notably Dee Brown's *Bury My Heart at Wounded Knee* (1971).

Both changes created the opportunity to tell more of the other half of the story: the American Indian story. As she and I spoke, we discussed the need for more American Indian representation in all aspects of the park's personnel. She also shared with me the pushback she was receiving. She told me of individuals going so far as to warn in phone calls, "You are going to get the s—t beaten out of you when we catch you alone."

Her tales took me back to a time when an Indian presence was an unwanted part of the yearly Battle of the Little Bighorn anniversary commemorations. I was on patrol wearing my NPS uniform and law enforcement gear when this small, non-Indian male came up to me, stood right in my face, and said, "If this was a hundred years ago, I would be the first to take your babies and throw them in the air and catch them with my bayonet!" I would find out later that he was a board member of the friends group (Little Bighorn Associates) that was none too pleased with the changes at the park. At the time, all I could do was just walk away. But it helped me think about my own time as superintendent: What should I do and how should I react so as not to escalate this situation? Stay calm and have great backup is the best answer. That backup was my staff (all of them) and, most important, my family.

All of my professional work was with the NPS. The park service was all I knew. I had some great (and some not-so-great) mentors—even before the word became popular! I learned at an early point in my career that no matter how big a park is, it was vitally important to know not

This dramatized print depicting the Battle of the Little Bighorn from a decidedly white perspective attempts to convey the bravery of the U.S. soldiers. H. Steinegger, artist. *General Custer's Death Struggle. The Battle of the Little Big Horn* (San Francisco: Published by The Pacific Art Co. of San Francisco, 1878?, March S.F.: Lith. Britton, Rey & Co). Courtesy of the Library of Congress.

only who works in all the park's divisions but also their names and a bit about them. I have always felt that all staff are equally important, and their jobs are important. This is especially crucial in more controversial sites that require a more inclusive interpretation. It is imperative that staff get on board with what you are trying to do and eventually bring the rest of the staff on as needed. I soon became familiar with the General Management Plan, which called for inclusion of more of the story from the Indian side, and including that story in other resource areas.

I toured various divisions for an update. In addition to the park, we were caretakers for the Custer National Cemetery—in particular, the areas where it was still an active grave site. Our staff had to have special skills to accomplish this task, and they did—including working with native people and organizations. Because this park is surrounded by the Crow Indian Reservation, we had a great staff that represented the tribe.

The overall message that I received from the staff at the park was how difficult it was (and would be) to change interpretation to include the

Indian story due to intense opposition of one group—the Little Bighorn Association—that pretty much worshipped George Armstrong Custer above all else. I carefully reviewed our resources and quickly grasped what we were doing currently and the direction we were headed in the future. (We were also always getting input from the regional office, which I am sure was getting it from the Washington office.) I soon realized that my role was divided into two primary responsibilities: one that led the park as its manager, and the other, even more important role of taking care of the politics of the park, its visitors, and, as it turned out, the nation as a whole. It was important to have the full support of my supervisor, John Cook, the regional director for the Rocky Mountain area. This was fortuitous, as I was hired by a different regional director, due to the fact, I am sure, that I was American Indian and had an NPS background, including speaking up in the past regarding the need to promote the American Indian story in national parks.

As we forged ahead, I ensured that the Custer story was in no way diminished. Our big challenge was giving the American Indian interpretation its due. It was a balancing act. Staff and I understood the magnitude of the battle's anniversary program. It had long been run nearly exclusively by the same aforementioned pro-Custer group with whom I had had a past negative experience. As for the Indian side of the story, I found out that even though a previous superintendent had invited one of the scouting tribes (who scouted for Custer during the battle), they were not invited to participate in anything or sponsor an event. This was a crucial flaw in the park's operation—one I was set on fixing.

I heard from the local tribes that although the previous superintendent had attempted to open doors with the various bands of Lakota Sioux, Northern Cheyenne, and the local Crow tribe, the park had not worked with them much at all. I proposed a plan to enhance our anniversary programs. My staff shared that we held many programs throughout the anniversary days. I asked what the tribes did. My team answered that they had a march up the main road to Last Stand Hill, where they held other events and activities, but staff was unsure exactly what happened then, however, as they had never attended. The Indians would walk right by the area where NPS held its interpretative programs. When I asked how staff handled this, they answered, "We just tried to speak louder so the people in their audience could hear us." Understanding how insulting this was to the tribes, I put a stop to that immediately and directed

Photograph of Curly, the supposed sole survivor on the U.S. side of the Battle of Little Bighorn. Richard Throssel, photographer. (Curly, sole survivor of Custer massacre—scout for Custer, head-and-shoulders portrait, facing left.) Courtesy of the Library of Congress.

the staff to suspend all programs until we produced a new program that included the tribes.

In order to get the tribes to participate, I decided to meet with the tribal political leaders and elders. Unlike in the past, where the U.S. government officials had tribal leaders visit our offices, I traveled to the office of the tribal chairman or president and introduced myself to them and the rest of the folks: elders and youth included. As anticipated, no matter which tribe I met with, I was lectured, as a representative of the federal government, about their tribes before and after the battle and what happened to the tribes of today as a result of this historical event. This was all shared with heartfelt emotion, and I knew how very important it was (and is) to not only listen but also seek to understand. All tribes soon agreed to participate in our anniversary program.

We did something that was controversial and made a lot of people angry. We put together a five-day program, with each day dedicated to one tribe. We invited veterans from each tribe to post the colors and raise the flag in a formal ceremony. We invited a group of singers to sing the Native Flag Song and other non-Indian groups to play the national anthem.

Pushback was immediate and somewhat unfair. One group that opposed all tribal involvement at Little Bighorn reported that one of the Indian veterans had touched the American flag to the ground four times. They neglected to acknowledge, however, that this American Indian elder was a proud veteran in his upper eighties, and the flag touching the ground was unintentional (a flag of that size gets heavy after standing at attention for a while!).

We highlighted the U.S. Army on the fifth day, inviting speakers from both the native and the nonnative side. I met many times with the elders of each tribe (as well as other organizations within the tribe) to ensure that their needs were met. I learned some American Indian groups planned to meet outside the southern boundary to reenact the battle. I also heard some younger Indians had plans to cut our fence and "count coup"—ride up on horseback and strike the Custer Monument with a coup stick.

I assembled support from other NPS superintendents to come to the anniversary programs. Many were native themselves; those who weren't had worked closely and built rapport with many tribes in their career. With them, and with the assistance of some Lakota and Northern Cheyenne, we organized a nighttime meeting outside of the park. This meeting consisted of the pipe-holders from each tribe represented in the battle, a couple young people for security, four of us NPS managers, and some of my staff, all in uniform. We sat in a tipi that was set up near one of the tribal rodeo grounds and discussed the topics that would make the anniversary a meaningful and historic event. Because we had all used the pipe, the agreements we made could not be broken. It seemed, at least for a time, to bring together some traditional enemies.[2] The Crow tribe butchered a buffalo for this event and did all they could to be great partners and hosts. When it came time for the tribes to march to Last Stand Hill, we marched with Lakota, Cheyenne, and other tribes in our NPS uniforms, including NPS director Roger G. Kennedy.[3]

We tried and succeeded somewhat in hiring for representation of the tribes that fought against Custer: Lakota, Northern Cheyenne, Crow, and other seasoned interpreters. People discovered that Little Bighorn Battlefield National Monument was a place to visit if you enjoyed history.

From the start, we had trouble with some of our visitors who came back time after time and heard the U.S. military- or Custer-centered story imparted by excellent military historians and seasonal rangers. When we hired tribal personnel, I encouraged them to tell the stories they heard about the battle from their elders, which they did.

One group remained vehement in its disapproval. This led to threatening calls to the park and also to my residence. Many times I had to stop what I was doing to visit with a very upset visitor, who had heard about our changes, complaining about "the Indian programs and the Indians kids you hired!" After an often very long explanation that described how adding the native part of the Little Bighorn story did not mean the Custer part of the story went away, visitors often left satisfied and generally appreciative of our approach.

Issues continued, however, and some complained to contacts in the regional and Washington, DC, office. Soon NPS sent us a team to teach our interpretative staff the "fundamentals" of interpretation—or, as one of my staff said, "They are teaching us how to speak 'white.'" Staff would request meetings, sometimes at my residence, to discuss what they were being taught. My recommendation was always to make the best of it, but to tell your stories your way! I have often thought that in some way we had to teach the non-Indian audience how to really listen to an Indian speaker. I don't think this has been done yet.

Unfortunately, I continued to get angry letters, calls, and sometimes in-person visits. On the positive side, I would also get visits from the FBI and other federal law enforcement personnel. The journey was fraught with difficulty, but ultimately a reinterpretation of the site benefited visitors and citizens immensely. I am very proud that we worked through it to tell a more inclusive story about the Battle of the Little Bighorn.

Here are some key lessons I've learned in reflecting on my time as an American Indian in charge of the Little Bighorn Battlefield National Monument. I learned that you need a great and supportive staff to handle the day-to-day operations at a site like the monument. The job of the manager is also to make sure your staff—those bearing the brunt of changes—is cared for. This includes getting out among the staff to see and know the site you are responsible for.

Second is the importance of getting involved in the community. Many local people had a love for history and were appreciative of getting the opportunity to explore the native story—a side that was really never presented to them. I learned that it was essential to know as many folks as I could in the regional and national offices and create a dialogue that would last all my career. The most important realization I had was knowing when it was time to leave. I felt that I had accomplished a lot at the park, particularly the incorporation of the story of the tribes in all aspects of the site and the creation of a new friends group that included tribal and nontribal members. This new group is still represented at the Little Bighorn monument today. Finally, I learned the power of listening—to your staff, your superiors, and your stakeholders. Sadly, I also learned that the NPS is still years behind in the American Indian story. But I am proud of the role I played in reversing that trend.

13

SHOULD THE STATUE OF THEODORE ROOSEVELT OUTSIDE THE AMERICAN MUSEUM OF NATURAL HISTORY BE REMOVED?

A POSSIBLE COMPROMISE

WILLIAM S. WALKER

Editor's note: In this chapter William S. Walker presents an overview of the life and legacy of Teddy Roosevelt, particularly with regard to his views on race. Read my essay "From Columbus to Serra and Beyond" (chapter 11) for more information about the town hall meeting in New York City in the fall of 2017 that addressed the TR statue in front of the American Museum of Natural History, the J. Marion Sims statue in Central Park, and a statue to Christopher Columbus.

Whehen **Theodore Roosevelt** passed away at his home, Sagamore Hill, on January 6, 1919, at the age of sixty, he was one of the most popular and, at the same time, most controversial ex-presidents in American history. After leaving the presidency in 1909, he went on two major expeditions—to Africa and South America—ran for president again as a third-party candidate, and become an outspoken proponent of the United States' involvement in World War I. Although few Americans agreed with everything that he said and did, many respected his commitment to public service as well as his leadership qualities and conservationist spirit. The tributes after he died were widespread and sincere, and suggestions for how to memorialize him were as varied—and, in some cases, as unusual—as Roosevelt himself had been.

Across the United States, many Americans wanted to immediately celebrate and memorialize the twenty-sixth president. In compiling suggestions for memorials four months after his death, the Roosevelt Permanent Memorial National Committee arranged them into fifteen different categories: Americanization; Conservation of Wild Life; A Seaside Park at Oyster Bay; A Cemetery in France; General Educational Projects; An Agricultural Endowment Fund; Monuments; Newspapers; Homes for Children; Hospitals; Museums; Clubs; Highways, Parks & Cities; Trees; and A National Holiday.[1] Overall, the suggestions fell into two broad groups. According to the *Literary Digest*, there were those who favored "some beautiful monumental memorial" and those who preferred a "'dynamic commemoration' which should perpetuate the Roosevelt ideals."[2] Into the latter category fell some of the most intriguing suggestions, such as "a Roosevelt Training School of Patriotism," which was the idea of Harvard professor Albert Bushnell Hart, or "free municipal dental clinics," which was the recommendation of M. M. Bluhm, DDS.[3] Over the coming years, individuals and groups from New York City and Washington, DC, to the Black Hills of South Dakota and Portland, Oregon, dedicated monuments and memorials of every type honoring his legacy. Although his face on Mount Rushmore may be the most recognizable of the tributes, in the decades following Roosevelt's death, schools, parks (including Theodore Roosevelt National Park in North Dakota), statues, a mountain in South Dakota, an island in the Potomac, the first Audubon songbird sanctuary, a forest experiment station in the Adirondacks, and numerous historic sites became features of the landscape that marked the enormous influence he had on American life.

Recent events, however, have demonstrated that contemporary activists view Theodore Roosevelt through a decidedly more critical lens.[4] Protesters involved with the Monument Removal Brigade and Decolonize This Place have decried James Earle Fraser's equestrian statue of Roosevelt flanked by native and African figures outside the American Museum of Natural History in New York City for the racist worldview it conveys and scholars and artists have signed a letter calling for its removal. Explaining their decision to splatter the statue with red paint, the Monument Removal Brigade has written that it embodies "patriarchy, white supremacy, and settler-colonialism." They add that "the monument not only embodies the violent historical foundation of the United States, but also the underlying dynamics of oppression in our contemporary world."[5] Their work of "applied art criticism" echoes a 1971 action by indigenous activists who similarly used red paint to mark structures on Alcatraz Island as an act of protest against the federal government's seizure of the island in San Francisco Bay. The New York–based activists had chosen the Roosevelt statue as the target for their local protest because, in their view, it was clearly "racist."[6]

James Earle Fraser was a well-regarded sculptor of the early to mid-twentieth century who undertook a number of high-profile public commissions primarily during the decades of the 1920s and 1930s. Prior to unveiling the Roosevelt statue at the American Museum of Natural History (AMNH) in 1940, he had sculpted several well-received busts of the twenty-sixth president, as well as images of other presidents and political figures, including a seated statue of Abraham Lincoln for the Lincoln Highway in Jersey City, New Jersey, and a ten-foot statue of Alexander Hamilton for the Treasury Building in Washington, DC. Historians may recognize his works from the Supreme Court Building ("Authority of Law" and "Contemplation of Justice") and the National Archives ("Recorder of the Archives").[7] He is best known, however, for his sculpture "The End of the Trail," which depicts an exhausted and demoralized native person hanging his head while sitting atop an equally hang-dog horse. Originally sculpted when he was a teenager, the sculpture was Fraser's effort to criticize white sentiments in favor of the genocide of native peoples.[8] Scholars and cultural critics have interpreted it, however, as the embodiment of the "Vanishing Indian" stereotype, an ideological and cultural construct that supported and justified the project of white settler colonialism. Growing up in the Dakota Territory in the late nineteenth century, Fraser had interacted with Sioux people near his hometown of Mitchell and, as a boy, he had developed a respect for native people and their cultures. In addition to "The End of the Trail," he crafted busts and full-size sculptures depicting native men, which reveal evidence of this respect. Nevertheless, Fraser was a white artist who had been immersed from a young age in the settler society of the western United States. His understanding of native people and culture was undoubtedly limited and filtered through the racialized worldview of the late nineteenth and early twentieth centuries, and his statue of Roosevelt must be viewed through this lens.

Fraser's Roosevelt statue at AMNH resonates visually with the racial thinking of the early twentieth century, projecting a troubling hierarchy of human groups that places whites above indigenous people and other people of color on a universal scale of human civilization. Fraser depicts Roosevelt in hunting garb riding on a horse with native and African figures walking on either side of him as his gun bearers. The statue's symbolism corresponds with overtly racist statements Roosevelt made in his writings, including his four-volume history *The Winning of the West*, and actions he took, such as his wrongful condemnation and punishment of black soldiers after the Brownsville affair in 1906. Moreover, the racial imagery of Fraser's statue matches the dominant paternalistic attitudes that many whites, including Roosevelt, displayed toward people of color in the early twentieth century.

While acknowledging these resonances between Fraser's imagery and Roosevelt's ideas, it is also important to recognize that at several points in his career, Theodore Roosevelt spoke and acted in racially egalitarian ways, and he garnered political support from both whites and people of color. Shortly after Roosevelt's death, the NAACP's *Crisis* memorialized him in an editorial as a "friend" who was the "world's greatest protagonist of lofty ideals and principles." The editorial mentioned the "hot bitterness over the Brownsville affair," but it also praised Roosevelt for his strong condemnation of white violence against African Americans during the 1917 riots in East St. Louis, Illinois. For *The Crisis*, Roosevelt was "splendidly human"—one who loved "the public eye" but was also "intent on achieving the public good." He was a

From *Puck* magazine, this illustration aims to align Theodore Roosevelt's defense of Fifteenth Amendment rights for African Americans as being in the tradition of "The Great Emancipator" Abraham Lincoln. Udo Keppler, artist. Justice versus prejudice / Keppler. United States, 1903. New York: J. Ottmann Lith. Co., Puck Bldg. Courtesy of the Library of Congress.

political figure who had made his fair share of questionable statements and decisions, but he was not a proponent of depriving African Americans of social and political rights like his successor, Woodrow Wilson, and he occasionally spoke and acted in ways that suggested a real commitment to racial equality.

In other areas of concern to contemporary activists, such as U.S. imperial actions in Latin America and Asia, Roosevelt's record is similarly mixed. His support for U.S. expansionism, especially early in his career, marked him as a full-throated champion of U.S. imperialism abroad and settler-colonialism in North America. He famously played an enthusiastic role in the Spanish-American War. More important, as president, he oversaw the latter phase of the Philippine-American War and subsequent U.S. occupation of the Philippines, and he cleared the way for the construction of the Panama Canal by encouraging Panamanian independence from Colombia. He also negotiated the Gentlemen's Agreement, which prohibited large numbers of Japanese people from immigrating to the United States. At the same time, he brokered peace between Russia and Japan and opposed the segregation of San Francisco's public schools. He was also a fervent advocate of international cooperation; indeed, despite his reputation as an aggressive warrior, he was a skilled practitioner of diplomacy.

Recently, the scholars and activists who signed the public letter calling for the removal of the Fraser statue criticized Roosevelt for being, in their words, a "frank advocate of eugenics."[9] Eugenics is defined as "the science of better breeding to improve the human race." The American Museum of Natural History—along with Cold Spring Harbor Laboratory on Long Island—was a major center of eugenic thought in the first three decades of the twentieth century.[10] The main advocates of eugenics decried the negative effects that they imagined poor people, the disabled, and "degenerate races," especially the large number of southern and eastern European immigrants who were entering the country at the time, were having on U.S. society. In this period, AMNH curator and administrator Henry Fairfield Osborn, who chaired the board overseeing the creation of the Roosevelt memorial, and museum board member Madison Grant were vocal proponents of eugenic ideas that supported and advanced nativist and white supremacist ideologies. In a 1913 letter, Roosevelt wrote approvingly of the writings of Charles Davenport, director of the Eugenics Record Office at Cold Spring Harbor Laboratory, stating that "society has no business to permit degenerates to reproduce their kind."[11] He also praised Madison Grant's racist tome *The Passing of the Great Race* in a statement endorsing the book. Moreover, at various points in his career, he professed a concern about "race suicide," the notion that people of northern and western European ancestry were in danger of dying out because of low birth rates in comparison to the birth rates of Asians, Africans, and other people of color. These positions are indefensible and provide evidence of Roosevelt's sympathy with racist and eugenicist ideas.

As with other aspects of Roosevelt's career, however, there is also evidence indicating that he was neither a nativist nor a eugenicist. As a police commissioner in New York City and governor of New York in the 1880s and 1890s, he embraced the city's polyglot ethnic mixture, and throughout his career he occasionally spoke and acted against discriminatory attitudes toward racial and ethnic minorities.[12] His actions also suggest that he favored protecting the most vulnerable members of society rather than breeding them out of existence. His father, Theodore Roosevelt Sr., whom he idolized, was a founder of the Children's Aid Society (as well as AMNH), and Roosevelt carried that patrician desire to work for the interests of poor and working-class people into his own career. During and after his presidency, he advocated for and successfully advanced governmental efforts to ameliorate the worst abuses of Gilded Age capitalism, frequently incurring the wrath of J. P. Morgan and other "robber barons." In his famous 1910 "New Nationalism" speech, which offered the clearest and most potent statement of his political philosophy, Roosevelt argued for greatly expanded government regulation of corporations and increased protections for workers, including workers' compensation, reasonable hours, and safety protections. "The absence of effective state and, especially, national restraint upon unfair money-getting," he intoned, sounding like a modern-day Occupy activist, "has tended to create a small class of enormously wealthy and economically powerful men, whose chief object is to hold and increase their power." "The prime need," Roosevelt continued, "is to change the conditions which enable these men to accumulate power which it is not for the general welfare that they should hold or exercise." Reducing the disproportionate influence of the wealthy on U.S. politics and the federal government was a central goal of his political career. For Roosevelt, monopolistic corporations and greedy men were the main danger to democracy in the United States. Branding Roosevelt, therefore, as simply a racist champion of eugenics ignores ample evidence demonstrating his commitment to improving the plight of vulnerable members of society.

The overall symbolism of memorials to Theodore Roosevelt is challenging to assess. Certainly very few people would contend that all monuments to Roosevelt be removed from the landscape. Many of them honor his career as a naturalist and conservationist. During his presidency, Roosevelt created six national parks and created or enlarged 150 national forests. He also designated eighteen national monuments and fifty-one federal bird reservations. Moreover, he was a vocal advocate of natural science, and his legacy continues to play a critical role in national conversations about the environment. In this age of climate change deniers and the dismantling of environmental regulations, lauding a Republican president who led the charge to protect our natural environment is a powerful statement. Other memorials to Roosevelt celebrate his public service and the model of engaged citizenship he embodied. Marking these two central features of his life and career—conservationism and public service—was, in fact, the original purpose of the memorial at the American Museum of Natural History.

Fraser's statue is only one part of a larger complex honoring Roosevelt, which encompasses spaces both inside and outside the museum and contains murals, texts, dioramas, and other sculptural elements. As a whole, the complex, which was designed by John Russell Pope, represents the official New York State Memorial to Roosevelt. Dedicated in 1936 by then-president Franklin D. Roosevelt, the memorial is a multilayered work that highlights many aspects of Theodore Roosevelt's life and career. (Although part of the original plan for the memorial, Fraser's statue was not unveiled until 1940.) According to the board that oversaw its creation, the first goal of the memorial was "to interpret the character of Roosevelt as naturalist and as citizen," while the second was to support the educational mission of the American Museum of Natural History for "those who wish to study nature in all its phases." The final goal was to select a design that symbolized the "spirit of Roosevelt" and "those ideals for which [he] strove." Overall, the New York State Memorial to Theodore Roosevelt is a fitting tribute to one of the state's most accomplished figures, and, given its location in and around the American Museum of Natural History, it rightly highlights the critical role Roosevelt played in promoting natural science and conservationism. Moreover, through quotations such as "A great democracy must be progressive or it will soon cease to be great or a democracy" and "If I must choose between righteousness and peace I choose righteousness," it encourages public service and active citizen engagement in social and political issues.

Fraser's statue, however, is a jarring and offensive symbol for many, and it fails to support the memorial's primary aim of honoring Roosevelt as "naturalist" and "citizen." My recommendation is to replace the statue with another that is more consistent with this goal—perhaps one

Approach to the State Theodore Roosevelt Memorial drawn for the American Museum of Natural History, ca. 1924. April 9. Photograph. Courtesy of the Library of Congress.

that mirrors the famous photograph of Roosevelt with John Muir atop Half Dome at Yosemite, or, if audiences prefer an equestrian statue, TR could be depicted riding alone in civilian clothing. In this way, New York State and the American Museum of Natural History could acknowledge the legitimacy of activists' criticisms while continuing to highlight those aspects of Roosevelt's career worth remembering and celebrating.

4

IDENTITY POLITICS AND THE RATIONAL AND SYMPATHETIC MINDS

GROUP BEHAVIOR, SELF-EXAMINATION, AND CLEARING THE AIR AROUND CONTROVERSIAL ISSUES

DAVID B. ALLISON

A s we have seen in the preceding chapters, statues have been touchstones for crucial debates throughout the history of the United States. Changing values, historical reconsideration, and morphing political expediencies result in reinterpretation and removal of monuments and memorials. The following section continues exploring these themes by focusing on the intersection of cultural and personal identities, political will, and activism. Might we be able to forge new, bold approaches to our collective understanding of how controversial statues continue to influence our political and social discourse?

In this grouping, you will find a chapter by George W. McDaniel from the perspective of a Vietnam veteran. His unique voice and call for an exploration of the real human cost of the wars that many memorials represent are a useful filter for this section of the book. Additionally, Mitch Landrieu's speech given at the removal of the last Confederate statues from public places in New Orleans is reprinted here. This speech demonstrates how historically informed civic pride can be the spur for political action. Lastly, Jose Zuniga shares how pop culture—and specifically *The Simpsons*—can provide a cheekily helpful comeuppance to historians' often over-serious approach to the study of the past as we see human nature reflected in the satire of a brilliant cartoon. Please recognize that this chapter stands slightly apart from the hugely complex and often charged contributions that fill this book—mostly because it takes a humorous tack. Despite this difference, I hope you will find that it illuminates of some of the ways in which we might approach controversial monuments and memorials.

A Statue of George III, Mob Democracy, and Violence in the United States

The birth of American democracy was rarely smooth and clean. Gangs of ruffians in Boston stoked passions and hurled insults and snowballs, giving British soldiers reason to fire on them in the later-named Boston Massacre. There is more than just deep irony that the most enduring phrase from the Declaration of Independence—"All men are created equal and that they are endowed by their Creator with certain unalienable rights"—was written by a man (Thomas Jefferson) who enslaved black Americans who toiled and suffered as decidedly unequal and without rights. The effects of pervasive unrest, unruliness, and desertions within the Continental Army—especially during the early years of the war—became part of the foment of intellectual and physical discombobulation that accompanied the advent of the United States.[1]

To further reinforce how haphazard and disorganized the revolution against the British in the American colonies was, it is instructive to recount the tale of how a mob of zealous soldiers and citizens toppled a statue of King George III in 1776. Some of the earliest statues in colonial America were of the regents of England, France, Spain, and other colonial powers. Erected in concert with a statue to the English statesman William Pitt, the statue of King George III stood on the Bowling Green in Manhattan and represented the power and absolute control that

After hearing the Declaration of Independence read to them, soldiers and citizens topple a statue of King George III on July 9, 1776, in New York City. André Basset, publisher (Paris: Chez Basset, Rue St. Jacques, 1776). Photograph. Courtesy of the Library of Congress.

the royal crown wielded over the American colonies. Shortly after Jefferson's Declaration of Independence was signed, New Yorkers reacted strongly to the statue. "On July 9, 1776," journalist David Dunlap writes, "after hearing the newly adopted Declaration of Independence publicly proclaimed, forty American soldiers and sailors under the command of Captain Oliver Brown stole down to the Bowling Green in Lower Manhattan under cover of night." He continues, "They lashed ropes around the statue, pulled until their ropes broke and then pulled again. At last, the symbol of a detested monarchy lay in pieces on the ground. Pieces of precious lead."[2]

After melting down the lead from much of the statue, the intrepid crowd reused the lead to make bullets to use in the fight against the British—perhaps meant to be the ultimate indignity for King George III—while also providing much-needed ammunition for the beleaguered Continental Army.[3] The mob removed the king's head from the statue—a symbolic act of justice meted out to a supposed tyrant—but a group of Loyalists apparently recovered it and sent it back to England.[4] In writing about the incident, Krystal D'Acosta concludes, "This was their means of protest and gaining a voice. This was their means of writing the social history they wanted to represent their values and vision."[5]

Ardent democracy taken to the extreme of a mob mentality has been common throughout the history of the United States as "We the People" seek to have our values and vision represented. Stretching from its earliest days—July 9, the day when the King George III statue crashed to the ground was a mere seven days after the final vote to adopt the Declaration of Independence—the American republic has been regularly poised on the razor's edge between uproarious violence and disorderly vigilantism on one side and peaceful negotiation and calm deliberation on the other. One has only to skim through notable trends in the country's past to bump into numerous examples of this dichotomy.

The rough, empire-forming frontier of the early 1800s led to the rapid deforestation of much of the middle part of the country and a rapacious push to move native peoples out of their homelands. This period also witnessed an increasingly sophisticated diplomatic acumen within the United States, as evidenced by peaceful resolutions to numerous border disputes.[6] The huge wave of lynching after the Civil War—4,697 total between 1880 and 1930, with 3,344 of those lynched being African Americans—reveals a racially motivated propensity for violence.[7] These same years also included elements of unbridled corporate greed that resulted in deplorable working conditions and harsh—and often violent—repression of labor union activities. During the same period, the entrepreneurial spirit of countless Americans resulted in significant scientific breakthroughs and inventions that improved people's lives.[8]

The twentieth century provides examples as well. During World War II, the U.S. government interred more than 120,000 Japanese Americans in prison camps, denying their civil rights and enforcing a racial stratification that did not extend to those of German descent, who more closely resembled dominant-culture white Americans. During these same years, the United States became a land of hope for thousands of refugees from the horrific Holocaust in Europe, though many others were denied entry. By the 1960s, vast economic disparity between black and white America and the backlash against African Americans' push for civil rights in the face of institutional racism begat a violent response in the South and in the North that impacts us today. These years also gave rise to some of the most eloquent voices calling for a renewal of the American dream of a pluralistic, just society—Fannie Lou Hamer, Martin Luther King Jr., and Bob Moses, among so many others.

What, then, do we make of the cycle of oppression / resistance to oppression and violent actions / peaceable solutions that typify the American experience? Moreover, what can we learn from the past to inform our present predicament around controversial monuments and memorials? How might we cultivate resistance to oppression and encourage peaceable solutions to the challenges of our times in the midst of the polarized quagmire of political rhetoric and mistrust that characterizes our postmodern, globalized society? The next section will briefly explore how our individual agency and identification with political, religious, and social groups influence our political activism (or political torpor) and our ability to use the past as a tool toward building a better future.

Identity Politics in a Postmodern Context

It is time to get confessional: I am in my upper thirties, my affiliation clinging to the last years of Generation X. I believe in the saving, transformational power of Jesus Christ. I am a shameless punster. I am married with four children—one of whom we adopted. I am a Midwesterner. I have a lot of student debt. I usually vote for progressive candidates. I am a museum professional. I live in a suburb of Denver. I am a lifelong *Star Wars* enthusiast. I am a white, cisgender male. I love to experiment and explore new ways to cook and bake food when I'm in the kitchen. I advocate for social justice.

Like all humans, I hold within me bundles of identities all at once. This list of identities is always expanding and includes serious, lifelong pursuits like my faith and my marriage, and trivial, banal personal interests like the half-completed *Star Wars* fan fiction that I started when I was in high school and my passion for getting just the right Maillard reaction to perfectly brown a piece of meat.[9] Sometimes my identities shift as I have new experiences—epiphanies born of reflection, from conversation with trusted friends and family, or from reading a particularly inspired novel that provides me with fresh insight into the human condition. Sometimes these identities come into conflict. Sometimes I intertwine these identities with human orders and associations and find my identity subsumed into political, religious, or advocacy groups.

When our identities migrate to the realm of groups—Methodist Church, Sierra Club, Republican, Chicago Bears fan club, Toast Masters, Democrat, Sertoma International, and on and on—we start to tap into a deep human need for belonging. Social psychologist Jonathan Haidt refers to this behavior as "groupish" and defines how this manifests itself in his book *The Righteous Mind*: "When I say that human nature is also *groupish*, I mean that our minds contain a variety of mental mechanisms that make us more adept at promoting our *group's* [emphasis his] interests, in competition with other groups."[10] Because our identities are inextricable from our conception of ourselves and because we are wired (from both a biological and a relational standpoint) to seek out other people who share our values, beliefs, and identifications, we find ourselves gathered together with other people who agree with us and who compete and argue against groups that do not agree with us.

Our propensity to join groups and to position ourselves in opposition to others becomes problematic when we begin to oversimplify or to deny the complex web of identities and human strivings of those who belong to other groups. From the lofty heights of self-righteousness and in-group reinforcement, we tar other people who disagree with us as hopelessly wrong-minded, blinded by false teaching, or (most pernicious of all) not as enlightened or as fully human as we are. We stop listening to understand and start yelling louder to prove our devotion to a righteous cause.

In *Citizenship Papers*, poet and essayist Wendell Berry warns of the dangers of the groupish desire to be right: "All of our human orders, however inclusive we may try to make them," he professes, "turn out to be to some degree exclusive. And so we are always being surprised by something we find, too late, that we have excluded." He continues, "But these surprises and changes obviously have their effect also on individual lives and on whole cultures. All of our fictions labor under an ever-failing need to be true."[11] Berry has identified the deep conundrum of our identities and our alignments with groups. In banding together and hewing exclusively to one particular conception of the world, we selectively shield ourselves from new information and create barriers to empathy. Historian James Axtell provides additional support for this notion: "In the absence of knowledge, it is easier to judge than to understand, for understanding in some depth usually undermines the rocky grounds of rectitude, often obviates the need for judgment, and sometimes leads to forgiveness, that most unfashionable virtue."[12]

If we cannot trust our identities and the opinions our groups share about what is right and wrong, what, then, creates pathways and hand-holds for us when we enter into discussions about controversial monuments and memorials and how can this endeavor lead to forgiveness? If our perspectives are irredeemably tainted by our groupish tendencies, should we throw our hands up and surrender to a nihilistic and lazy do-nothingness? I would argue that we *do*, in fact, have responsibilities to truth that exist outside of strictly group-developed beliefs and prejudices.

Here we must return for answers to the historian's passion for understanding the past through a combination of carefully reasoned scientific methods that value objective facts (the Rational Mind) and thoughtful empathy informed by a love for transcendent human desires for love, faith, beauty, belonging, and justice (the Sympathetic Mind). Balancing the Rational Mind with the Sympathetic Mind can help historians and community leaders separate honestly held, group-based opinions from misinformation and lies.[13] The distinction between these two extremes makes all the difference and takes us beyond the politician Daniel Patrick Moynihan's helpful koan, "Everyone is entitled to his own opinion, but not his own facts."[14]

When we dunk our heads into a stream of lies and deliberate falsehoods, our hair comes out dripping and matted with the mucky water of politically motivated or personally expedient denials of objectively determined fact. Washing out falsehood and rationalization takes stronger detergent than mere facts and a belief in the triumph of just "getting it right," however. Facts must be packaged as unassailable and, perhaps more important, attractive. Facts must be coddled and presented as truth worthy of embrace and susceptible to belief—a key part of cultivating the Sympathetic Mind in concert with the Rational Mind.

Facts alone are dry, callous things that stack up on each other like so much firewood, ready to be consumed by the fiery glances of angry zealots. Without the subtlety of empathy and the gentle caress of relatable stories, facts are ignored or denied as the pitiable outrage of a misguided "opposition." Where, then, is the place for righteous anger and indignant shouts? When do silent protests and whispered discomfort become action? What we do in these moments is what defines our character and cannot help but place us within certain groups that strive for justice and that champion truth. From these bastions, we must fight back against lies and mistruth of the sort promulgated by white nationalists and neo-Nazis. If we take up the sword of reasonableness while garbed in the armor of compassion, we stand a much better chance of opening critical dialogue informed by historical fact about the role of controversial statues in our society and can show that not all opinions have the same solid basis both in fact and in sympathy. Historians and community leaders do have truths to share—flabby and vacillating equivocation has no place in the land of alternative facts and beliefs unmoored from reality—and we must make our stands accordingly.

As you read the following chapters, consider your own personal story and identities. Where can you align yourself and open critical dialogue in your community? How might you infuse an understanding of the United States' historical complexity into building a "more perfect Union" through peaceful protest, thoughtful community activism, and the healing power of empathy?

15

CONFEDERATE MEMORIALS

CHOOSING FUTURES FOR OUR PAST: A VETERAN'S PERSPECTIVE

GEORGE W. McDANIEL

I n the autumn of 2017, I watched *The Vietnam War* on PBS, a film produced by Ken Burns and Lyn Novick, and I was pleased to see how they presented multiple points of view. I certainly have mine, and it is roughly divided into three parts: before I went to Vietnam; while I was in combat there; and when I returned home and reflected upon my experiences. The latter has changed over time, as the war has grown more distant, and the feelings less raw.

I am sure the documentary generated mixed feelings among Americans across the nation—among veterans, their families, those who lost a loved one, those who demonstrated against the war, and, perhaps the majority, those who went on living their lives and building careers or a family because the war was someone else's and "over there." For the millions born after the war, it may seem like "ancient history." For the Vietnamese who became refugees here and for those who remained in country, the war was seen quite differently. It was not "over there," or someone else's, but rather something that happened to their home and community, to them personally, whether they had wished it or not.

These different perspectives may inform us about war memorials in general and about Confederate memorials in particular. Over time, there have been attempts to reduce the memorials to a single interpretation. At the time of construction and for decades later in the South, the most popularized view among white civilians was that they were meant to honor our "glorious dead," who fought for what was perceived as a noble cause. While many African Americans and others may have thought otherwise, their opinions were discounted. In recent years this once dominant interpretation has been challenged. The depth of the offensiveness of these memorials has become more recognized, and their removal advocated. After the hateful violence and killing in Charlottesville, we saw a statue of a Confederate soldier in Durham, North Carolina, pulled down, kicked, and spat on. As a veteran, such actions toward any memorialized soldier disturb me, because I identify with soldiers myself. It is troubling when civil discussion becomes hard pressed, and the arguments on one side and the other all the more firmly entrenched.

The good news is that, even now, if museums, universities, and other organizations step up with vision and courage, these memorials can offer teachable moments for history and rare opportunities for them to get individuals engaged in their communities and to capitalize on this concern for history. They can show that discussions about history can be well facilitated and enriched by civil discourse, instead of diatribe or polemics, and can help people move from entrenched positions from which they fire away at opponents whom they stereotype and toward a deeper understanding of one another's heritage and culture and of how those factors shape point of view. I make this case for history education because we in the field of history, whether academic or public, have witnessed the study of history increasingly labeled as irrelevant, as evidenced by the work of national organizations addressing the issue.

We have seen the teaching of history diminished through less and less classroom time devoted to social studies and the hiring of fewer history teachers and professors in favor of those disciplines that lead to jobs, jobs, jobs. Recently, I heard a TV interview with former governors of South Carolina about education, and it was only after about fifteen minutes of focus solely on workforce readiness and job preparation that Governor Dick Riley mentioned the humanities as a subject important to America's future, and that was only in passing.[1] No one highlighted history, literature, civics, philosophy, foreign languages, or even writing. These recent public debates about memorials and the vitriol they have produced should, however, show how important humanities education, especially history, is. While we can't go back, we can look ahead and use recent tragedies in Charleston, Charlottesville, Orlando, and elsewhere as teachable moments to help us look at our history in order to enhance cross-cultural understanding, empathy, and tolerance, and prevent such bigoted tragedies from occurring again.

I would suggest that the Vietnam Memorial in Washington, DC, may be of help, for it tells us that monuments mean more than ideology and prompts us to look at them from different perspectives. On the one hand, the memorial is a monument to what many have concluded was a "mistake" and clearly a defeat. On the other hand, with my being a Vietnam veteran, the memorial meant that and more to me. When I came home in 1970 and was discharged immediately into civilian society, the world as I had known it before Vietnam was pretty shattered. While I may have seemed normal on the outside, I wasn't on the inside, especially at night. I felt alienated and alone. Memories lived, but I had no one to really share them with. I talked with shadows. I still see things differently. Just the other day I saw a billboard, "KIA for Sale." When I first saw it, I read it, not as an automobile for sale, but as K.I.A. (killed in action) for Sale. In a flash, I silently shouted to myself, "What the hell? Isn't anything sacred?"

For those reasons, more than a decade after my return, I went to Washington by myself for the dedication of the wall in 1982. I didn't know a soul. I was standing on the sidewalk of Constitution Avenue watching a "parade" of vets walking past, all in civilian clothes, when I saw a banner, "First Infantry Division, Big Red One." I walked out and joined the crowd and asked some of the guys what unit they had been with and when. As they were welcoming me and I was telling them, "First of the 18th, Alpha Company, 69-70," a guy yelled, "Mac!" It was my lieutenant, and we embraced on the spot. He hadn't known whether I had gotten home alive, nor did I know about him. When we ended up at the memorial, we heard speeches, but what was more special was that my memories of Vietnam were given a physical reality by the memorial. I could see it and touch it. Guys I knew were named on it. It was a deeply private and personal connection. A reporter from Kansas City interviewed me, and I explained that the dedication marked the first time I had saluted the flag since my return home not because I had to but because I wanted to. It was not patriotism, freedom, democracy, or my government I was saluting; it was my friends I had fought with, those dead and those alive. That is what we had been fighting for—our friends and to get home alive.

When I returned from Washington, I set about trying to contact the family of a friend in my platoon, Claude Giles, who had been killed on a mission by friendly fire. He was from Toccoa, Georgia. I had been reluctant to call his widow or mother when I returned in 1970 because I didn't know what the army had told his family about his death. Perhaps they'd been told he'd died a hero's death and not as a result of mistaken communications. During the dry season we had been sent into open rice fields and set up nighttime ambushes behind low dikes to protect a village from Viet Cong slipping in for food, money, or worse. Located in a position not far from mine, Claude had been killed by one of our snipers in another ambush position who was using a starlight scope and hadn't been informed of Claude's nighttime location. He put two rounds in Claude's chest. Immediately, muzzle flashes and tracer rounds lit the nighttime sky as Claude's squad opened fire across the open rice field, and the sniper's squad returned fire on Claude's. I was on my squad's radio, heard both squads calling for artillery support, and was expecting us to be hit by the Viet Cong soon and hard. Quickly, battalion headquarters recognized the mix-up and ordered the shooting to stop. However, it was too late for Claude. Upon my return from Washington, and deeply touched by my experience there, I decided to telephone Claude's mother. She was so glad to hear from me and to learn of my visit to the memorial. She had been told the truth, but what she wanted to hear again and again and again was that Claude's name *is* on the wall. I assured her that it is, and she wept. Her son had been remembered.

I recount this because when these memorials were going up from the 1880s to the 1920s or even later, veterans would still have been alive, though in diminishing numbers, along with parents and widows in earlier years, brothers and sisters, children, grandchildren, and friends. Most monuments were devoted to a symbolic soldier, one to whom many veterans would have connected. Others were to a revered leader like Ulysses S. Grant, Robert E. Lee, or Stonewall Jackson, which no doubt

Steve McCool and Claude Giles shortly before we were choppered out on a reconnaissance-in-force mission, First Infantry Division (Big Red One), ca. October–November 1969. We operated roughly between Saigon and Cambodia, often in the region between Lai Ke and the Song Be River, sometimes near the more famous Iron Triangle. Around this time, Claude received word of the birth of his daughter, about which he was elated. She was named Claudette, after him. A few months later, Claude was killed, so now, decades later, his daughter remembers her loss almost every time she signs her name. Photo by author.

sparked pride among veterans and their families, but veterans may have seen beyond the figure himself and felt that the monument gave tangible reality to a past war and meant their friends and lost ones had not been forgotten. In the South, they had not died in a "mistake." There was pride in their combat, in what they had gone through. They did not have the photographs, videos, audio recordings, or even letters to remember the dead by, the very things we take for granted today.

For Confederate and Union veterans, and their families as well, the monuments may have also stood for the wounded—physically and mentally—many of whom, given the carnage of that war, had been scarred in ways we can hardly understand since so much of it went

George W. McDaniel, First Infantry Division, autumn 1969, somewhere between Saigon and Lai Ke, before going out on a daytime patrol out from base camp. I can tell since I'm traveling pretty light with not much water and not carrying as much gear as Claude and Steve were. On my helmet liner, I'd written, "Fighting for peace is f-g for chastity." Photo by author.

undocumented. The fact that amputees were commonplace served as testimony to that carnage. It was only after Vietnam, and then only in spurts, that posttraumatic stress syndrome was seriously understood as a "wound," a wound with which many veterans and their wives and children had to cope for years on end. Also, for African American civilians and veterans in the South, Confederate memorials and their glorification may have generated deep anger and a sense of betrayal, which, in the South at that time, they had to keep in check; if not, they had to leave. As we discuss the future of monuments, theirs is a sentiment we should remember and take into account. For all veterans especially, both Confederate and Union, white and black, the monuments may have stood not just for the glories but also for the sacrifice and gore they saw on the battlefield and in the hospitals, things that the civilians around them could not imagine. What may have touched them was not so much the speeches but the memory of friendships. While politicians may have talked of our "glorious dead," veterans would have seen the reality of the latter, which was not pretty. The memorial may have helped them feel more connected to both the dead and the living—and, like Claude Giles's mother, to her son and to the future.

With all this in mind, I hope we can see that monuments, even Confederate ones, may mean different things to different people, and we reduce them to only one thing at our peril. As a result, I think we should proceed not by way of a "take it or leave it" choice, but look for "both/and" solutions and use them as teachable moments and ask: How might we capitalize on this heightened concern for history? Like we today, the people of that time did not act out of only one motive. For example, white supremacy was there, of course, and an awful force, but to conclude that was the one and only motive for erecting Confederate memorials is to be reductionist. We don't credit those people with the latitude we give ourselves.

I think we therefore need to give memorials the thought they deserve, even though it may make us feel uncomfortable, and to appreciate the complexity of those people just as we ask for understanding of our own. The key is to have civil discussions about their future, carefully strategized with museums, universities, and community organizations providing their vision, skills, and facilities. Such discussions should not be simply forums or town hall meetings, which can be dominated by a few, but rather gatherings broken down into small groups, ideally with each group deliberately mixed by race, background, or opinion and facilitated by trained persons. Respect should be one rule, with another being to listen and to learn and to speak from one's heart and mind, and not to debate or try to prove one's rightness. In Charleston, the Illumination Project, formed to sustain the racial healing efforts after the murders at Mother Emanuel AME, serves as an example of this approach.[2]

Such discussions can both enhance understanding and devise new solutions. If done fairly and with commitment, such discussions may mean giving up control, which can be hard to do, but they can lead to the achievement of two goals: the resolution of issues, and in the process, creation of a healthier community. The usefulness of such an approach was accented by F. Sheffield Hale, president and CEO of the Atlanta History Center, when he observed, "A top-down cleansing of the landscape of all Confederate monuments (even if that were practical or feasible) would not cleanse our personal or collective historical palates of their unpleasant taste. Indeed, mass removals may have the opposite effect. Those who defend the status quo on Confederate monuments would feel compelled to cling even harder to their uncompromising views."[3]

Given the high public interest and depth of feelings among citizens, especially in the South and among African Americans in particular, now is the time to act. If there's a will and a commitment to try, suggestions abound. Museums, universities, and historical organizations could lead the way. Results will vary, for one solution should not be expected to suit all, but we can learn from one another. For example, monuments, especially those in prominent locations that send an erroneous message about the community or arouse negative feelings among a significant portion of the community, may be moved to other sites and given a fuller interpretation. Providing an illustration is the University of Texas, for it has relocated a monument to Jefferson Davis, which commanded a prominent location on campus, to the Briscoe Center for American History in Austin and has interpreted it in a gallery as an educational rather than a commemorative exhibit. At the same time, some museums may not want the memorials or they may be too large to display, so what then? What opportunities does that provide?

If the decision is to leave the monument in place or if laws require such, what might be done? One answer is to develop a strategy and change the law. That takes leadership, alliances, funding, and time, but it should be a goal. A quicker answer is that while the monument may be left in place, plaques or other devices may be added to help to contextualize it. An informative illustration may be found at the University of Mississippi, where interpretive plaques were added to the statue of a Confederate soldier standing at the entrance to the campus, thanks to the Advisory Committee on History and Context consisting of alumni, students, and faculty members from different disciplines. Formed by Chancellor Jeffrey Vitter, its purpose is to address memorials, slavery, and other controversial issues in a thoughtful way, grounded in good scholarship and interpretation. In Charleston, South Carolina, Mayor John Tecklenburg created a History Commission of historians, museum and tourism professionals, artists, and laypeople to address memorials. Since South Carolina law prevents the removal of, and even major changes to, war memorials, the commission recommended plaques updating the interpretation and placing the monuments within the context of their own time and of ours today. For the towering statue of U.S. senator and proslavery proponent John C. Calhoun, located in Marion Square in the center of town, their reinterpretation stated in part:

> The statue remains standing today as a reminder that many South Carolinians once viewed Calhoun as worthy of memorialization even though his political positions included his support of race-based slavery, an institution repugnant to the core ideas and values of the United States of America. . . . Historic preservation, to which Charleston is dedicated, includes this monument as a lesson to future generations of the importance of historical context when examining individuals and events in our state's past.[4]

Some commission members preferred to characterize slavery as a "crime against humanity." Historian Bernard Powers declared, "If slavery's not a 'crime against humanity,' what is?" However, some realized that they needed the city's political approval, so they reached a compromise. While not everyone got everything they wanted, the language chosen was a decided improvement over what was there, and it will make a strong statement to residents and tourists alike. The problems with interpretive plaques arise from location, scale, and visibility. That is, controversial memorials, such as statues, are often sited in prominent locations in the public sphere, so plaques do little to mitigate that aspect. In scale, the statue often dwarfs the plaque and, by comparison, makes a statement about esteem, rank, and values. As for visibility, the plaque must be seen close up, while the memorial may be seen close up and far away. It may also be touched. The words on the plaque must also be read and often require a fairly high degree of historical literacy, which many children and adults may not have, in contrast to the memorial, which communicates in more simple and direct ways.

Even if words on plaques are easily understood, they may not register. A story told by former Charleston city police chief Greg Mullen illustrates this problem. A well-respected police officer was speaking in a workshop of community leaders about implicit bias, and after giving what he thought was a clear explanation, he asked for questions. An African American lady, known to have a PhD, responded, "What you said may have been fine, but as you were speaking, I want you to know that all I could see was a white man in a uniform with a gun." The officer was struck deeply by this statement, because he had been attuned only to his words, not the other messages his position and uniform gave. What we see matters. For example, it could have been a black man with long dreadlocks and pants low, "bustin' a sag," with a white lady responding. What we see triggers feelings that shape our perceptions more powerfully than words alone can do. So, too, with memorials.

With this in mind, communities may choose to add new monuments in counterpoint to controversial memorials. Such monuments may be figurative or symbolic, historical or contemporary in nature. The strength of this approach, in contrast to plaques, is that it addresses location, scale, and visibility. The same site can be shared by both monuments, and that very juxtaposition can make a compelling statement about history and values. The scale, design, and choice of material might be put to a commission of professionals and laypeople with community input given. A manageable and structured process could be devised, and this itself may help build a healthier community as different sectors come together to discuss, debate, and decide upon how to make their history tangible, visible, and engaging.

For example, next to a statue of a Confederate leader may be placed a statue of a leading African American political leader, or an educator, doctor, veteran, or civil rights leader. In South Carolina, since a state heritage law minimizes chances for removal of memorials, Democrat and Republican legislators are proposing to add a statue near Confederate memorials on the statehouse grounds commemorating Robert Smalls, an enslaved and skilled steamboat pilot who escaped with his family on a stolen Confederate ship to become a Civil War hero and, later, a congressman. Another proposal, also for statehouse grounds, is to add a statue of the Rev. Joseph A. De Laine, whose lawsuit against segregation, *Briggs v. Elliott*, was a legacy of the Civil War and Reconstruction and became the basis for the *Brown v. Board of Education* case. His opponent was Roderick Miles Elliott, the white superintendent of De Laine's county school district. Today that very proposal is being proposed by descendants of Elliot and De Laine, who have gotten to know one another in recent years. Their mutual efforts underscore the value of choosing outreach and civil discourse as a way to try to heal the wounds of prejudice and history. They could have chosen otherwise.

Also embarking on a racial healing project is the University of Mississippi, for it is taking its efforts regarding the Confederate statue a step further. Aimed at refurbishing and interpreting the Confederate cemetery on campus, it is now seeking to tell a more inclusive story. Specifically, this project will include a memorial to Union troops who were once buried in the cemetery on campus but were removed after the war, as well as a memorial to the U.S. Colored Troops from that area who fled slavery and fought for the Union Army. Such initiatives will help people see the Civil War from multiple points of view, not just those of the Confederates, and thereby add both breadth and depth to their understanding.

Digital technology may also provide new avenues toward reinterpretation of memorials. An illustration of this approach is in Charleston, where the History Commission is launching a mobile app project that will give "voice" to persons in memorials across the city, ranging from John C. Calhoun to civil rights leader Septima Clark. Scripts will be written and voiceovers will present the person's thoughts, values, and vision in ways that are more complete than a written plaque would allow. Other groups may choose a symbolic representation, say, of an idea or the struggle for freedom. At the National Military Park at Vicksburg, for example, Kansas chose not a figurative memorial but a symbolic sculpture of stone and wrought iron, simply designed, symbolizing union, disunion, and reunion.

Another option would be for communities to use the memorial and its setting for ongoing temporary or even traveling exhibits. Whether the memorials are left in place or moved, communities could use them as the inspiration for "digital memorials," ones that people create via art, verse, song, or video to express their ideas and feelings and then post them interactively on a website. One result could be a community of respondents, a dialogue with history, for one year, two years, or decades. As Vietnam veterans have done with the Vietnam Memorial, communities or museums might seize the moment and use it to raise funds for education and healing. In this case, it could be for K–12 programs about the history of the Civil War and its aftermath, including the legacy of slavery, war, white supremacy, and the struggle for freedom from different points of view. They might also raise funds to support public programs that use history to build bridges across entrenched factions.

I suggest these educational endeavors because as a combat veteran, I agree with General William T. Sherman, who observed that war is "terrible." It is no video game. Dead people don't get back up again. War is never quick and easy, as people too often think—our wars in Iraq and

Afghanistan being contemporary examples. Before the Civil War, leaders from the North and South thought that if a war came, it would be over quickly. As told in Robert Rosen's *Confederate Charleston*, former U.S. Senator James Chesnutt from South Carolina believed there would be no war and just a few days before the firing on Fort Sumter explained that if war came, "the man most averse to blood might safely drink every drop shed in establishing a Southern Confederacy."[5] The estimated total killed during those four years of the Civil War was—on the low end—620,000.[6] Chesnutt's naïve statement could be put to vivid demonstration through imaginative educational programs. If each death is measured as a pace of one yard, or three feet, the total would be 1,860,000 feet, or about 350 miles, approximately the same distance as if one walked, one pace at a time, from Richmond, Virginia, to New York City. While hard for us today to imagine, Civil War veterans and their relatives and friends experienced carnage of that scale. In the South, as in Vietnam, the war had been no abstraction. It had not happened "over there" but at home, to family after family after family. While deeply tragic, it had also resulted in freedom for millions of enslaved African Americans. For all Southerners, both white and black, history had happened to them.

I suggest these numerous and "both/and" approaches to thinking about memorials, instead of just a "take it or leave it" one, because the latter conveys a sense of finality. A war is never over. It is not over for us Vietnam vets, though it has been about fifty years. It is not over for the Civil War, though it has been for 150 years. The legacy continues to shape our society, politics, education, and race relations. While we've made progress in our nation and deserve to be proud of that, what we haven't done enough of as a people is to break bread together, to worship together, and just talk with one another, sharing our fears and aspirations. Our gatherings together should not be so much to debate or persuade one another of the rightness of our positions, but rather to develop mutual understanding, empathy, and tolerance.

The development of such should be the goal of history education. It may be reached in both the classroom and in the public realm, through lectures as well as in cross-racial and small-group discussions. As I have suggested, creative opportunities abound, if we but have the will to try and the vision of our common humanity, so that we might lessen the chances for war—for the things that veterans of all wars, including me, have experienced. If that becomes our goal, the question then becomes: How can we use these monuments to help us get there?

16

SPEECH UPON THE REMOVAL OF CONFEDERATE STATUES FROM NEW ORLEANS, MAY 19, 2017

MITCH LANDRIEU

Editor's note: Mitch Landrieu, the mayor of New Orleans, delivered a note-worthy speech about race and memory on May 19, 2017. Marking the removal of the last Confederate monuments from the city, Landrieu drew together history, community, memory, and the ongoing scourge of racism in this impassioned speech. It is reprinted in full here. Jeanie Riess published a thorough and insightful profile of Mitch Landrieu in the Oxford American *titled "Removal" that is also worth reading as a companion to this speech. (Issue 98, Fall 2017, September 5. See http://www.oxfordamerican. org/magazine/item/1284-removal.)*

My sincere thanks to the City of New Orleans Office of the Mayor for granting permission to reprint Landrieu's speech in this volume.

T hank you for coming.

The soul of our beloved City is deeply rooted in a history that has evolved over thousands of years; rooted in a diverse people who have been here together every step of the way—for both good and for ill. It is a history that holds in its heart the stories of Native Americans—the Choctaw, Houma Nation, the Chitimacha. Of Hernando De Soto, Robert Cavelier, Sieur de La Salle, the Acadians, the Islenos, the enslaved people from Senegambia, Free People of Colorix, the Haitians, the Germans, both the empires of France and Spain. The Italians, the Irish, the Cubans, the south and central Americans, the Vietnamese and so many more.

You see—New Orleans is truly a city of many nations, a melting pot, a bubbling caldron of many cultures. There is no other place quite like it in the world that so eloquently exemplifies the uniquely American motto: *e pluribus unum*—out of many we are one. But there are also other truths about our city that we must confront. New Orleans was America's largest slave market: a port where hundreds of thousands of souls were bought, sold and shipped up the Mississippi River to lives of forced labor of misery of rape, of torture. America was the place where nearly 4000 of our fellow citizens were lynched, 540 alone in Louisiana; where the courts enshrined "separate but equal"; where Freedom riders coming to New Orleans were beaten to a bloody pulp. So when people say to me that the monuments in question are history, well what I just described is real history as well, and it is the searing truth.

And it immediately begs the questions, why there are no slave ship monuments, no prominent markers on public land to remember the lynchings or the slave blocks; nothing to remember this long chapter of our lives; the pain, the sacrifice, the shame . . . all of it happening on the soil of New Orleans. So for those self-appointed defenders of history and the monuments, they are eerily silent on what amounts to this historical malfeasance, a lie by omission. There is a difference between remembrance of history and reverence of it.

For America and New Orleans, it has been a long, winding road, marked by great tragedy and great triumph. But we cannot be afraid of our truth. As President George W. Bush said at the dedication ceremony for the National Museum of African American History & Culture, "A great nation does not hide its history. It faces its flaws and corrects them."

So today I want to speak about why we chose to remove these four monuments to the Lost Cause of the Confederacy, but also how and why this process can move us towards healing and understanding of each other. So, let's start with the facts.

The historic record is clear, the Robert E. Lee, Jefferson Davis, and P. G. T. Beauregard statues were not erected just to honor these men, but as part of the movement which became known as The Cult of the Lost Cause. This "cult" had one goal—through monuments and through other means—to rewrite history to hide the truth, which is that the Confederacy was on the wrong side of humanity. First erected over 166 years after the founding of our city and 19 years after the end of the Civil War, the monuments that we took down were meant to rebrand the history of our city and the ideals of a defeated Confederacy. It is self-evident that these men did not fight for the United States of America. They fought against it. They may have been warriors, but in this cause they were not patriots. These statues are not just stone and metal. They are not just innocent remembrances of a benign history. These monuments purposefully celebrate a fictional, sanitized Confederacy; ignoring the death, ignoring the enslavement, and the terror that it actually stood for.

After the Civil War, these statues were a part of that terrorism as much as a burning cross on someone's lawn; they were erected purposefully to send a strong message to all who walked in their shadows about who was still in charge in this city. Should you have further doubt about the true goals of the Confederacy, in the very weeks before the war broke out, the Vice President of the Confederacy, Alexander Stephens, made it clear that the Confederate cause was about maintaining slavery and white supremacy. He said in his now famous "cornerstone speech" that the Confederacy's "cornerstone rests upon the great truth, that the negro is not equal to the white man; that slavery—subordination to the superior race—is his natural and normal condition. This, our new government, is the first, in the history of the world, based upon this great physical, philosophical, and moral truth."

Now, with these shocking words still ringing in your ears . . . I want to try to gently peel from your hands the grip on a false narrative of our history that I think weakens us. And make straight a wrong turn we made many years ago—we can more closely connect with integrity to the founding principles of our nation and forge a clearer and straighter path toward a better city and a more perfect union.

Last year, President Barack Obama echoed these sentiments about the need to contextualize and remember all our history. He recalled a piece of stone, a slave auction block engraved with a marker commemorating a single moment in 1830 when Andrew Jackson and Henry Clay stood and spoke from it. President Obama said, "Consider what this artifact tells us about history . . . on a stone where day after day for years, men and women . . . bound and bought and sold and bid like cattle on a stone worn down by the tragedy of over a thousand bare feet. For a long time the only thing we considered important, the singular thing we once chose to commemorate as history with a plaque were the unmemorable speeches of two powerful men."

A piece of stone—one stone. Both stories were history. One story told. One story forgotten or maybe even purposefully ignored. As clear as it is for me today . . . for a long time, even though I grew up in one of New Orleans' most diverse neighborhoods, even with my family's long proud history of fighting for civil rights . . . I must have passed by those monuments a million times without giving them a second thought. So I am not judging anybody, I am not judging people. We all take our own journey on race.

I just hope people listen like I did when my dear friend Wynton Marsalis helped me see the truth. He asked me to think about all the people who have left New Orleans because of our exclusionary attitudes. Another friend asked me to consider these four monuments from the perspective of an African American mother or father trying to explain to their fifth grade daughter who Robert E. Lee is and why he stands atop of our beautiful city. Can you do it? Can you look into that young girl's eyes and convince her that Robert E. Lee is there to encourage her? Do you think she will feel inspired and hopeful by that story? Do these monuments help her see a future with limitless potential? Have you ever thought that if her potential is limited, yours and mine are too? We all know the answer to these very simple questions. When you look into this child's eyes is the moment when the searing truth comes into focus for us. This is the moment when we know what is right and what we must do. We can't walk away from this truth.

And I knew that taking down the monuments was going to be tough, but you elected me to do the right thing, not the easy thing and this is what that looks like. So relocating these Confederate monuments is not about taking something away from someone else. This is not about politics, this is not about blame or retaliation. This is not a naïve quest to solve all our problems at once.

This is however about showing the whole world that we as a city and as a people are able to acknowledge, understand, reconcile and most importantly, choose a better future for ourselves making straight what has been crooked and making right what was wrong. Otherwise, we will continue to pay a price with discord, with division and yes with violence.

To literally put the Confederacy on a pedestal in our most prominent places of honor is an inaccurate recitation of our full past. It is an affront to our present, and it is a bad prescription for our future. History cannot be changed. It cannot be moved like a statue. What is done is done. The Civil War is over, and the Confederacy lost and we are better for it. Surely we are far enough removed from this dark time to acknowledge that the cause of the Confederacy was wrong.

And in the second decade of the 21st century, asking African Americans—or anyone else—to drive by property that they own; occupied by reverential statues of men who fought to destroy the country and deny that person's humanity seems perverse and absurd. Centuries old wounds are still raw because they never healed right in the first place. Here is the essential truth. We are better together than we are apart.

Indivisibility is our essence. Isn't this the gift that the people of New Orleans have given to the world? We radiate beauty and grace in our food, in our music, in our architecture, in our joy of life, in our celebration of death; in everything that we do. We gave the world this funky thing called jazz, the most uniquely American art form that is developed across the ages from different cultures. Think about second lines, think about Mardi Gras, think about muffaletta, think about the Saints, gumbo, red beans and rice. By God, just think.

All we hold dear is created by throwing everything in the pot; creating, producing something better; everything a product of our historic diversity. We are proof that out of many we are one—and better for it! Out of many we are one—and we really do love it! And yet, we still seem to find so many excuses for not doing the right thing. Again, remember President Bush's words, "A great nation does not hide its history. It faces its flaws and corrects them."

We forget, we deny how much we really depend on each other, how much we need each other. We justify our silence and inaction by manufacturing noble causes that marinate in historical denial. We still find a way to say "wait"/not so fast, but like Dr. Martin Luther King Jr. said, "wait has almost always meant never." We can't wait any longer. We need to change. And we need to change now.

No more waiting. This is not just about statues, this is about our attitudes and behavior as well. If we take these statues down and don't change to become a more open and inclusive society this would have all been in vain. While some have driven by these monuments every day and either revered their beauty or failed to see them at all, many of our neighbors and fellow Americans see them very clearly. Many are painfully aware of the long shadows their presence casts; not only literally but figuratively. And they clearly receive the message that the Confederacy and the cult of the lost cause intended to deliver.

Earlier this week, as the cult of the lost cause statue of P. G. T. Beauregard came down, world renowned musician Terence Blanchard stood watch, his wife Robin and their two beautiful daughters at their side. Terence went to a high school on the edge of City Park named after one of America's greatest heroes and patriots, John F. Kennedy. But to get there he had to pass by this monument to a man who fought to deny him his humanity.

He said, "I've never looked at them as a source of pride . . . it's always made me feel as if they were put there by people who don't respect us. This is something I never thought I'd see in my lifetime. It's a sign that the world is changing." Yes, Terence, it is and it is long overdue. Now is the time to send a new message to the next generation of New Orleanians who can follow in Terence and Robin's remarkable footsteps.

A message about the future, about the next 300 years and beyond; let us not miss this opportunity New Orleans and let us help the rest of the country do the same. Because now is the time for choosing. Now is the time to actually make this the City we always should have been, had we gotten it right in the first place.

We should stop for a moment and ask ourselves—at this point in our history—after Katrina, after Rita, after Ike, after Gustav, after the national recession, after the BP oil catastrophe and after the tornado—if presented with the opportunity to build monuments that told our story or to curate these particular spaces . . . would these monuments be what we want the world to see? Is this really our story?

We have not erased history; we are becoming part of the city's history by righting the wrong image these monuments represent and crafting a better, more complete future for all our children and for future generations. And unlike when these Confederate monuments were first erected as symbols of white supremacy, we now have a chance to create not only new symbols, but to do it together, as one people. In our blessed land we all come to the table of democracy as equals. We have to reaffirm our commitment to a future where each citizen is guaranteed the uniquely American gifts of life, liberty and the pursuit of happiness.

That is what really makes America great and today it is more important than ever to hold fast to these values and together say a self-evident truth that out of many we are one. That is why today we reclaim these spaces for the United States of America. Because we are one nation, not two; indivisible with liberty and justice for all . . . not some. We all are part of one nation, all pledging allegiance to one flag, the flag of the United States of America. And New Orleanians are in . . . all of the way. It is in this union and in this truth that real patriotism is rooted and flourishes. Instead of revering a 4-year brief historical aberration that was called the Confederacy we can celebrate all 300 years of our rich, diverse history as a place named New Orleans and set the tone for the next 300 years.

After decades of public debate, of anger, of anxiety, of anticipation, of humiliation and of frustration. After public hearings and approvals from three separate community led commissions. After two robust public hearings and a 6–1 vote by the duly elected New Orleans City Council. After review by 13 different federal and state judges. The full weight of the legislative, executive and judicial branches of government has been brought to bear and the monuments in accordance with the law have been removed. So now is the time to come together and heal and focus on our larger task. Not only building new symbols, but making this city a beautiful manifestation of what is possible and what we as a people can become.

Let us remember what the once exiled, imprisoned and now universally loved Nelson Mandela and what he said after the fall of apartheid. "If the pain has often been unbearable and the revelations shocking to all of us, it is because they indeed bring us the beginnings of a common understanding of what happened and a steady restoration of the nation's humanity." So before we part let us again state the truth clearly.

The Confederacy was on the wrong side of history and humanity. It sought to tear apart our nation and subjugate our fellow Americans to slavery. This is the history we should never forget and one that we should never again put on a pedestal to be revered. As a community, we must recognize the significance of removing New Orleans' Confederate monuments. It is our acknowledgment that now is the time to take stock of, and then move past, a painful part of our history.

Anything less would render generations of courageous struggle and soul-searching a truly lost cause. Anything less would fall short of the immortal words of our greatest President Abraham Lincoln, who with an open heart and clarity of purpose calls on us today to unite as one people when he said: "With malice toward none, with charity for all, with firmness in the right, as God gives us to see the right, let us strive on to finish the work we are in, to bind up the nation's wounds . . . to do all which may achieve and cherish—a just and lasting peace among ourselves and with all nations."

Thank you.

A REFLECTION OF US: *THE SIMPSONS* AND HEROES OF THE PAST

JOSE ZUNIGA

Historians know that there is one cliché that can apply to all peoples in all eras—the phrase "we sure do live in interesting times." That statement is true whether one is helping to build a pyramid or walking on the moon. Our present place and time in the story of humanity is no exception. One topic that has been on the forefront of our minds is the harsh schism that has emerged over the monuments and memorials erected by our ancestors. Reflecting attitudes and practices that we are beginning to acknowledge are hurtful or designed to encourage division, these statues have become touchstones for debate. Many voices have cried out against these monuments and others have come to their defense. Those of us tasked with preserving and teaching our collective history find ourselves pulled between the truths that we know through research, the truths that we believe in our hearts, and the truths that others expect us to give. How can we preserve history while also acting with empathy toward peoples who want their voices heard, their perspectives respected? Where do we turn in these challenging times for guidance? Why, to cartoons, of course!

In this chapter, I will explore the quintessential cartoon family of *The Simpsons* to illuminate controversial statues in a new way. In the almost thirty years that Homer, Marge, Bart, Lisa, and Maggie have been on the air, they—and the other fair citizens of Springfield—have commented on almost every aspect of American life in a deliciously satirical way. Fortunately for us, they have given us a window into the mind of the American public and also shared some delightful insights into how we and museum professionals can navigate controversy—and do so with smiles on our faces.

Way back in 1990, during the first season in which *The Simpsons* graced the small screen, there was an episode called "The Telltale Head."[1] The episode opens with Bart and Homer running through town carrying the severed head of a statue of the town's founder, Jebediah Springfield. Soon an angry mob appears—armed with clubs, pitchforks, and torches—and chases them to the center of town. Once cornered, Bart pleads with the townsfolk to allow him to share how he ended up in this situation, in the hope that his explanation might spare him their wrath. The enraged citizens reluctantly agree to hear him out.

The story then jumps back in time to the day before, when, after sitting through a mundane Sunday school class, Bart gets some money from his father to slink off and go see a movie. On the way, he encounters some of the town bad boys and they engage in various escapades.

After a hard day of hooligan shenanigans, the boys lie on a hill and look at clouds, picking out various gruesome shapes. After Bart remarks that one cloud looks like the statue with its head missing, the boys speculate on how wonderful it would be if someone actually removed the head of the Jebediah Springfield statue. They delight in the idea of the anguish it would cause the town. Bart is shocked and demurs, only to be driven away by his new friends with taunts of "we thought you were cool." Unsure about what to do, Bart turns to his father for advice. Homer, taking on the role of wise sage, informs him that being popular is the most important thing in the world.

Acting on his father's advice, Bart ninjas his way to the statue and under the cover of night beheads Jebediah. The following morning the town is shocked and devastated to learn of the vandalism. Bart stashes the head in his backpack and seeks out the delinquent boys to show them what he has done. However, before he can reveal the head, the

A worried Bart Simpson regrets beheading the statue of Jebediah Springfield, the town's founder. *The Simpsons*, "The Telltale Head," season 1, episode 8, originally aired February 25, 1990.

boys shock him by confessing that they, too, are deeply upset by the vandalism. Unsure of what to do, Bart finally succumbs to his conscience and reveals his crime to his family. Homer and Bart leave to return the head only to be confronted by the mob—bringing us full circle to the beginning of the story. After an emotional apology and plea for mercy, the mob comes around and decides to let them go. The chicanery ends, the statue's head is put back in place, and all is well.

There are two important lessons in this narrative that speak to us today about the way we treat our historic places, people, and monuments. The first is found in the pressure Bart feels to be popular. In the age of the internet and instant gratification, of video games and 3-D movies, many cultural institutions have found themselves searching for ways to keep up with the spirit of the times. Museums, libraries, and historical centers that once had quiet halls before the rise of smartphones find themselves under similar pressures to try to bring in as many visitors as they can. This has led to an emergence of many exciting experiential approaches and innovative programming. However, rushed solutions hurried into service without forethought can lead to even deeper struggles. In our interconnected age, small mistakes can be hugely magnified.

The second lesson to be found in this episode is perhaps one of the most humbling. After Bart steals the head, he was expecting many people to be upset. Just like Bart, committees, institutions, or curators are also prepared for the reaction of some citizens or interest groups concerning changes to monuments, statues, or structures. What Bart wasn't expecting was the reaction of the bullies to what he had done. Even though they had ridiculed him for defending the statue, they were upset after it had changed. Therein lies the potent reminder that oftentimes when discussing history—particularly controversial history—there is always going to be someone who is upset. We must be prepared to face the reality that we can never please everyone with the decisions that are made—and the people who end up taking umbrage may surprise us. This is perhaps best summed up in the ironic last line of the episode. Homer remarks, "Not all lynch mobs are this nice."

Bart's adventures with decapitation are not the only times that Jebediah Springfield has been a prominent figure in a *Simpsons* episode. Several years later in season seven, he was once again the focus of one of the Simpson children. This time it was Lisa who crossed paths with the town founder.

In the episode "Lisa the Iconoclast," the town of Springfield is getting ready to celebrate its bicentennial. Lisa is assigned to write an essay about the town founder, and, being the eager achiever she is, she goes to the Springfield historical society, where she meets the local historian Hollis Hurlbut, an expert on all things Jebediah.[2] He shows her to a case containing many of Jebediah's personal belongings. When she's left alone, Lisa attempts to play his fife only to discover a written confession on a piece of parchment hidden inside. Jebediah's writings reveal that he is none other than Hans Sprungfeld, notorious pirate and attempted murderer of George Washington. Lisa pursues her research and discovers that Sprungfeld was primarily remembered by history for having a prosthetic silver tongue.

Lisa attempts to spread the truth about Jebediah throughout town, only to be derided and dismissed wherever she goes. Finally, our desperate truth seeker confronts the town council. After much back and forth, the town leaders agree to exhume Jebediah's body to look for the

Lisa and Homer Simpson enjoy Springfield's historic festivities in "Lisa the Icono-clast." *The Simpsons*, season 7, episode 16, originally aired February 18, 1996.

infamous silver tongue. Lisa is shocked to discover that the tongue is nowhere to be found.

Certain that she was correct about the town founder, she has a dream that leads her to a revelation. The paper hidden in the fife was actually the bottom part of the famous Gilbert Stuart painting of Washington, which proved that Jebediah was actually Sprungfeld. When she confronts historian Hurlbut, he confesses to stealing the silver tongue out of the coffin before the town council could see it, terrified of what it would do to his career and his beloved institution.

After Hurlbut has a change of heart, Lisa and the historian run to the bicentennial events to tell the town the truth—dodging floats and marchers in the bicentennial parade. After convincing the town to listen to her, Lisa hesitates and ultimately decides not to reveal what she knows. In the end, she determines that in Springfield the myth is more important to the morale of the town than revealing the truth about who Sprungfeld actually was as a man.

There are many things in this episode that speak to us as guardians of culture and history. On the one hand, we can respect Lisa's commitment to the truth. Unlike everyone else in the town, she doesn't accept that the perception of Jebediah as a heroic town founder should make him immune from historical scholarship and inquiry. When she discovers his confession in the fife, she follows the evidence where it leads—even as it directs her to the revelation of a villainous con man who attacks a founding father while he sits for a portrait. Her passion for the truth is so strong that she does everything she can to share what she knows with her fellow townspeople.

On the other hand, she also confronts people with what she knows without the slightest thought as to how it will impact them. In her single-minded quest for the truth, she doesn't stop to think about trying a different approach to get more people on her side. She uses inflammatory language and is shocked when her attempts to confront people are met with hostility. She doesn't think about acting with empathy until the very end of the episode. We must also ask, was her choice to conceal the truth at the end the correct one?

Hurlbut is another dynamic character. He is a historian with deep pride in his work. He also has a strong personal passion for history and civic pride in his town. He has a sense of accomplishment in his work and a home in his museum, and you sense that he really enjoys sharing history with the townsfolk. However, his blinkered pride blinds him. When confronted with a source that contradicts his preferred narrative, he doesn't even bother to apply his expertise. He simply dismisses it out of hand. Then, when he is confronted with truth that he cannot ignore, he acts out of fear and tries to sabotage the pursuit of historical fact.

Truly *The Simpsons* is a mirror for the modern American dilemma. We see ourselves in its characters and their exploits. As we laugh at them, we are forced to confront our own prejudices, fears, and pride. Their satirical gaze leaves us with kernels of advice and puzzling conundrums. I wonder what historians of the future will think of this TV show featuring an animated family that we've adored over the years? Will the show be regarded as a diligent chronicler of pop culture? Will the various inside jokes and references confound future scholars after the slang terms, famous logos, and pop culture references are lost to time? When today's infamous Hollywood stars become tomorrow's forgotten detritus, will *The Simpsons* still resonate? Or perhaps these characters will be viewed like the people they reflect—human beings who live in very interesting times.

5

COMMUNITY RESPONSIVENESS AND HISTORICAL RECONTEXTUALIZATION

18

"THE STRUGGLE TO OVERCOME THE NEGATIVES OF THE PAST"

GERMANY'S *VERGANGENHEITS-BEWÄLTIGUNG* AND SOUTH AFRICA'S TRUTH AND RECONCILIATION PROGRAM

DAVID B. ALLISON

Statues and monuments are as old as antiquity. The human urge to create something lasting and remarkable is nearly universal. From the huge Moai heads standing in a sentinel ring around Rapa Nui (Easter Island) in the South Pacific[1] to the Ebenezer statue of remembrance raised by the prophet Samuel in the Bible, cultures across the world erect statues.[2] Thus far, this book has exclusively focused on American examples. But what can we learn from examples of controversial statues and memorialization in other countries? This chapter will provide a few key case studies—notably Germany's attempts to address its horrific Nazi era of the 1930s and early 1940s and South Africa's truth and reconciliation program stemming from that country's long history of apartheid and violence against non-whites—as a way to highlight how civic memory and memorialization can help salve the wounds of the past. Germany and South Africa have been on a journey to reconcile and heal. Healing often hurts; scabs form and pain flares up unexpectedly. When nations attempt healing, the process is the same—it is never perfectly smooth and painless and is often chock full of the inherent challenges of contested memory and historical misunderstanding.

Nazi Germany and the Post-World War II *Vergangenheitsbewältigung*

Adolf Hitler and the National Socialist (Nazi) Party consciously manipulated the visual markers of power as they violently took control of Germany in the 1930s.[3] Public displays of power became de rigueur during the Nazis' seizure of power and reign of terror over Germany.[4] Huge banners touting national socialism; parades of heavily armed, sharply dressed, and smartly marching soldiers; and monumental structures that hearkened back to ancient Roman imperial designs all conspired to evoke fervent nationalism, wide-eyed fear, and abject awe in spectators.[5] Indeed, the Third Reich intentionally sought to use both the symbols and the architecture of intimidation to align themselves with the perceived strength of the world's great empires of the past. For Nazis, Germany was destined for similar greatness. As such, their iconography needed to closely match this vision of their destiny.

As Germany broke treaties and escalated its militarism in the lead-up to World War II, the Nazi regime simultaneously stepped up its efforts to promulgate terror and death on any "non-Aryan" Germans.[6] When the Nazis overran Poland, France, and other European nations in 1939 and 1940, they brought with them their anti-Semitic, racially purifying

"Final Solution" to rid the planet of whomever they deemed undesirable. The resulting Holocaust cost the lives of at least six million Jews as well as many more individuals from other persecuted groups. These atrocities came hand-in-hand with Nazi rhetoric of righting the wrongs of the past—primarily the Treaty of Versailles—in the name of empire.[7] For Nazis, the symbols of power—monuments, parades, and propaganda posters—were inextricably tied to ethnic cleansing and strident nationalism and helped to propel their campaign of terror and genocide into the worldwide crisis that World War II became.

The symbols of Nazi power physically destroyed by the Allies during the war were not as easy to destroy in the minds and hearts of the German people. The sheer number and scale of the Holocaust concentration camps as well as the numerous battle sites across the country meant Germans could rarely escape visual reminders of this terrible past. In the war's immediate aftermath, Germans struggled to rebuild their guilt-stricken psyches nearly as much as they did to rebuild their nation.

By 1949, a divided Germany was left with two very different approaches to memorialization.[8] In West Germany (the Federal Republic of Germany) in the years immediately following the war, economic strength driven by capitalism and pan-European connectivity was valued highly. Therefore, memorialization in West Germany focused on realignment with neighbors and on demonstrating to the world that it had moved beyond the Nazi era.[9]

In East Germany (the German Democratic Republic), communism's grand narrative took center stage in the memory-making around Nazism. Fascism was viewed as a natural outgrowth of corrupt capitalism and thus the product of a historical process.[10] East Germany, then, celebrated antifascism as a blessing of communism, while not directly or openly addressing the memorialization of its devastating Nazi past.[11]

After German reunification in late 1989, *Vergangenheitsbewälti-gung*—a German word that means "the struggle to overcome the negatives of the past"—became a watchword. While the "negatives of the past" in this case initially focused on addressing Nazism and its atrocities head on, by the 1990s it also included overcoming the artificial division of Germany that occurred upon Germany's defeat in 1945. *Vergangen-heitsbewältigung* has been a continuing item of debate in German society and politics, as newer hard-right-wing politicians throughout Europe are often loath to apologize for Nazi complicity and rarely countenance open discussions of regret for the negatives of the past.[12]

German identity in the years since World War II has undergone many iterations.[13] The ways in which Germans have chosen to suppress the Nazi past, to create counter-memorials that urge citizens to "never forget," or (in some cases) to celebrate its repulsive past speak to a universally felt need to either face up to or reframe the crimes and horrors of a world-altering moment in history.[14] In Germany's case, *Vergangenheitsbewältigung* continues to be debated and reshaped as new generations of Germans see the world through circumstances that are quite distant from the Nazi reign of terror.[15] Germany's role as a host country for refugees from Syria's devastating civil war only draws into sharper relief the themes of redemption and reconciliation that often animate questions about overcoming a painful past. Might the welcome and human dignity granted to Syrians today help Germany to atone for the virulent anti-Semitism and racism of the Nazi regime? As always, this question is hotly contested, as economic and societal pressures push *Vergangenheitsbewältigung* into new and surprising places.[16]

Like Germany, Japan has also had a rocky relationship with the memorialization of its role in World War II—specifically as it has manifested itself in other countries. In September 2017, a statue went up in San Francisco's St. Mary's Square that featured three girls holding hands with a figure of a grandmother looking on. Erected to memorialize so-called comfort women—the girls and young women from thirteen occupied Asian-Pacific countries forced into sex slavery by the Japanese military during the war years—this statue has been a touchstone for controversy. The Japanese government vociferously opposed the statue (and others like it throughout the United States, Germany, Australia, and South Korea).[17] Like West Germany in the years after the war, Japan believes that its perception of itself as a commercial and cultural power in the world is threatened by statues that remind viewers of the atrocities of the Imperial Japan of the 1930s and early 1940s.[18] By seeking to quash construction of these memorials and by exerting soft power through diplomatic protests of the constructions of these memorials, the Japanese government attempts to control how its role in World War II is remembered. In doing so, it also engages with the past selectively. This is a familiar theme in memorialization that has clear parallels to experiences in the American South in the aftermath of the Civil War.

South Africa and Truth and Reconciliation

Perhaps no painful history and consequent efforts to memorialize the past are most vivid and similar to the experience of the United States than South Africa's. Many scholars have pointed to apartheid South Africa as analogous to what might have happened in the American South had the Confederacy won the war.[19] While the 2004 mockumentary *C.S.A.: The Confederate States of America* (2004) by director Kevin Willmott articulated a terrifying dystopian future in a clever, albeit fictionalized, way, the experience of South Africa as it loosened the grip of apartheid is an even clearer example of memorialization and difficult history that can be transposed atop the post–Civil War South.

South Africa's efforts to consciously unite the country through the construction of new monuments are fascinating and deserve attention, as they relate to how localities in the United States might replace their own controversial memorials. Most South African monuments built since the end of apartheid address head-on the country's painful past and the complex political maneuvering that kept black South Africans oppressed and disenfranchised.[20] In *Landscape of Memory*, historian Sabine Marschall documents this trend. "[South Africa's] new commemorative markers," she observes, "constitute a tangible manifestation of larger socio-political dynamics and state-promoted strategies of reconciliation and nation-building as they were defined during the immediate post-apartheid period."[21]

South Africa's colonial heritage did not fully become entrenched until 1948, when South Africa's Afrikaner-led regime began to institute a large-scale system of racial stratification—classifying people into the categories of white, black, colored, and Indian—as a way of separating black South Africans from the rest of society while simultaneously providing choice economic opportunities and land to whites.[22] The decades of oppression did not fully loosen their grip on the country until the election of Nelson Mandela as president in 1994. The reality and legacy of this oppression was (and is) a large proportion of black South Africans living in abject poverty and widespread international condemnation.[23] Labeled by many researchers as difficult history, sociologists Chana Teeger and Vered Vinitsky-Seroussi define the country's shared past as "an event that many (mostly the victims) wish to remember, many (mostly the perpetrators) wish to forget, and many wish that it had never have taken place."[24] As South Africa emerged from apartheid, its leaders attempted what they dubbed "Truth and Reconciliation"—a novel approach to healing the racial rifts and difficult history cleft by the pernicious influence of white supremacy.

As the government polity that initiated the court proceedings that attempted to bring restorative justice to victims of human rights abuses during apartheid, the Truth and Reconciliation Commission sought to open dialogue about the painful past and to bring to light the stories of the victims of violence.[25] Set up by the Government of National Unity, the Truth and Reconciliation Commission is organized into three separate committees—Human Rights Violations, Reparation and Rehabilitation, and Amnesty.[26] Black South Africans could use the program as a way to gain justice from those who perpetrated violence on them during apartheid. Unlike the Nuremberg trials of Nazi leaders after World War II that were focused on retributive justice, South Africa's Truth and Reconciliation Commission aimed to reconcile and to restore positivity and consensus to the era's historical interpretation for South Africans of all races.[27]

Some have argued that the Truth and Reconciliation Commission did not go far enough toward gaining justice for black South Africans. However, the intentional efforts placed toward building dialogue and toward forgiveness and redemption struck a hopeful and idealistic note in a country long under the cloud of systematic and rampant racism.[28] The ultimate effectiveness of South Africa's truth and reconciliation efforts are unlikely to be fully perceived for many years. Just like the reassertion of white supremacist and Lost Cause narratives of the early twentieth century in America, the sheer newness of the end of apartheid means that South Africa may eventually experience a similar backlash against its noble ideals of truth and reconciliation and, perhaps, an unfortunate revival of apartheid-era thinking. But one can hope that by honestly examining the past, in all its forms, South Africa may avoid this unfortunate outcome.

Other Examples of Memorialization from around the World

One can find contested history and controversial memorials nearly everywhere one encounters human beings. Ranging from the layers of meaning imbued upon the ancient sacred spaces of Jerusalem variously claimed and fought over for centuries by Islam, Christianity, and Judaism to the new Kigali Genocide Memorial in Rwanda and memorials to the Killing Fields of Pol Pot's regime in Cambodia, places that have been set apart for reflection and remembrance are integral to the public landscape of human habitations. As the meanings of these places are rewritten, they become palimpsests—places that have been altered or reused yet retain visible remnants of what once was. Layers of new meaning often obscure original intent. Ground that was once dusty with the mundane has been sown with the seeds of strife, of war, and of injustice and then of healing, of hope, and of the divine. Now these places bear the fruit of the culminating centuries, each successive generation altering the perception of the past to their own ends as the supremacy of their present rubs out the old palimpsest markings and adds new ones.[29]

Pondering the scope and scale of the past and the choices generations that preceded us made can quickly become overwhelming. Who are *we* to question the choices that *they* made? Does questioning their motivations and interpretation of the past actually move our society to become better, more egalitarian, or more just?

The examples of Germany and South Africa show that memorializing and remembering the painful past can indeed make a difference in the lives of those treated unjustly or whose families were riven apart by murder and violence. Difficult conversations prompted by the painful past can only be opened and discussed freely when they have been brought into the light.[30] Germany and South Africa both attempted (with mixed success) to unstintingly face the injustice and violence of their country's history. Justice. Reconciliation. Forgiveness. Healing. These are the goals when grappling with painfully difficult history. The methods Germany and South Africa employed differed greatly and were certainly tailored to the culture and place of each country. Yet both stand as exemplars to the simple act of thoughtful reflection.[31] We may all learn from their example.

The next section explores techniques for opening the critical conversations that can lead to change. Intentional and empathetic listening are the drivers for transformation. Dialogue and civic discourse are the tools that can create community buy-in for any sort of reinterpretation or removal of monuments, and the ways that community leaders and public historians approach this work will be vital for its future success.

"WE AS CITIZENS . . ."

APPROACHES TO MEMORIALIZATION BY SITES OF CONSCIENCE AROUND THE WORLD

LINDA NORRIS

One fall, on a rainy November day, I was walking down a street in Amsterdam, the Netherlands. Among the leaves plastered to the sidewalk I saw the gleam of brass squares. Those small brass squares are *Stolpersteine* (literally, stumbling blocks) that I have now seen in cities all over Europe: Berlin, Rome, Paris, and now Amsterdam. They never fail to cause me to stop, read the names, look up at the building, and try and imagine the lives of those who lived there.

The Stolpersteine are a project of German artist Gunter Demnig. According to his project website, his goal is to remember the victims of National Socialism (Nazism) with commemorative brass plaques

Stolpersteine are brass plaques commemorating victims of the Nazis that have been installed in front of their last known address. These are from the Netherlands. Photo by author.

installed in front of their last known address of choice—in other words, their last home. There are now 61,000 Stolpersteine in more than 610 locations in Germany as well as in Austria, Hungary, the Netherlands, Belgium, the Czech Republic, Norway, and Ukraine. The Stolpersteine in front of the buildings bring back to memory the people who once lived here. Each "stone" begins with "Here Lived . . ." and there is one stone for each person. One name. One person.

Demnig cites the Talmud in saying that "a person is only forgotten when his or her name is forgotten."[1] But it's not only those small brass blocks that encourage remembrance in public spaces. Remembrance is the initial motivation for every memorial and monument—that passersby should remember, not forget, whether it is the founder of a state, a victorious general, a beloved writer, or a victim of torture.

As the debate intensifies over the removal of memorials and monuments here in the United States, it may be illustrative to understand the work of putting up contemporary memorials around the world. In this brief overview, I'll share the memorialization work of several members of the International Coalition of Sites of Conscience ("the Coalition").

The Coalition is a network of more than 230 organizations—historic sites, museums, and memory initiatives—around the globe, in fifty-five countries, that connect past struggles to today's movements for human rights. The organizations, working individually and collectively, turn memory into action, working to build a more just future for all of us. Our members believe in four key principles:

- interpret history through site;
- engage in programs that stimulate dialogue on pressing social issues;
- promote humanitarian and democratic values as a primary function; and
- share opportunities for public involvement in issues raised at the site.

From Rwanda to Northern Ireland; from Argentina to the Czech Republic; from Nepal to the United States, Coalition members put those key principles into practice in their memorialization work.

The process of memorialization raises—and should raise—many questions. Yasmin Sooka, former commissioner of the South African Truth and Reconciliation Commission and a member of the Sierra Leone Truth and Reconciliation Commission, poses a host of vital questions for consideration in the Coalition's *From Memory to Action: A Toolkit for Memorialization in Post-Conflict Societies*. Among them:

- What role does memory play in the framing of contemporary debates in our society? Should it necessarily play a role?
- How can these memorials advance reconciliation and social reconstruction among former enemies?
- What memories do we seek to preserve and how?
- In whose name do we act?

- How much memory is useful, particularly in cases of mass murder and genocide?
- How can we limit the manipulation of public memory by political actors for their own interests?[2]

Many questions inevitably lead to many different solutions. Each group of people and each society must find their own way to a memorial. The answers are as varied as the circumstances, the specific event commemorated, and the cultures of each locality. A place of atrocity or human rights violations may be preserved as a site of memory with little intervention. Other times, a decision is made to commemorate a place by installing a physical memorial or monument. A museum can be created. In still other circumstances, the memorials are virtual ones, and in yet still other circumstances, they are personal, made for individuals or homes.

By sharing brief overviews of several Coalition members in creating memorials, it is my hope that those concerned with monument removal can frame their own critical questions in creating dialogue around the removal of existing controversial monuments and work with community members to find solutions.

A Site Untouched: Estadio Nacional, Memoria Nacional, Santiago, Chile

Estadio Nacional is Chile's national sports stadium. But in the early days after a coup in 1973, it was used as a center for detention, torture, and execution, with more than forty thousand people detained there at different times. The stadium has been newly renovated, but amid the renovations, a section of wooden bleachers always remains empty, to memorialize those who were detained there. The remaining wooden stands help to ensure that a memory is a part of everyday life. Even as football successes are celebrated, the empty seats remind us of those lost.

Remembering the Work Place: Hrant Dink Foundation, Istanbul, Turkey

Turkish Armenian editor, journalist, and activist Hrant Dink was assassinated in front of his office in Istanbul on January 19, 2007. There is a plaque out front of the building, but the Hrant Dink Foundation is thoughtfully working through a process to create a site of conscience. Importantly, however, the foundation members view the site not as the space in front of the building where he was killed, but rather his office— as the place where he worked—where his true legacy lives on. His office looks like you might expect—a desk, plaques, and photographs, the tools of everyday life. But the result of their planning will be something much more than just a historic site.

The foundation's goal is to create a living memorial, something that they are accomplishing through programmatic efforts including oral histories, fieldwork, collaborative partnerships, and a commitment to an active learning process for the staff and the organization, by connecting with Turkish and Armenian partners and with similar organizations around the world.

Letting the Landscape Speak: Fondazione Scuola di Pace di Monte Sole, Monte Sole, Italy

In 1944, Nazis roamed up and down a mountainous valley near Bologna, assassinating people in 115 different villages. Today, more than six thousand hectares make up a national park. There are small monuments throughout the park, but the entire region is largely depopulated and the visitor is encouraged to wander and explore, breathing in the natural beauty of the site as well as pondering the massacres that happened. This is a space for reflection.

In combination with the government, the Peace School of Monte Sole has chosen to enhance the deep meaning of the site by developing educational projects that not only explore the history of the site but also develop an understanding of ways to prevent future atrocities.

Building a Museum: Sierra Leone Peace Museum, Freetown, Sierra Leone

At the close of the Special Court for Sierra Leone, addressing that country's civil war, the Government of Sierra Leone requested that part of the court's facility be dedicated as a memorial. Rather than simply a memorial, it was decided to create a Peace Museum. Working with dozens of civil society groups, a team developed a museum that explores the conflict, but more important, provides a "physical and intellectual space to question the causes of the conflict and to discuss the nation's ongoing commitment to preventing future conflicts. It will strengthen people's understanding of the value of peace and monitor the ongoing process of reconciliation."[3] A museum, often combined with a memorial, provides a greater opportunity to share individual memories, to contextualize memories within a broader historical context, and to use the power of original objects as a tool for memorialization.

One-by-One Memories: Afghanistan Human Rights and Democracy Organization, Kabul, Afghanistan

Decades of ongoing conflict in Afghanistan have resulted in hundreds of thousands of victims. The Afghanistan Human Rights and Democracy Organization (AHRDO) drew inspiration from theorists such as Paolo Freire and Augusto Boal in designing the innovative memory box project. The goal of the project was to "aspire to make the victims of Afghanistan the main participants in the creation of public memory about the country's long history of violence."[4] The AHRDO held a series of workshops in which participants shared their stories, bringing specific objects and photographs that represented a family member now lost. They decorated boxes to contain those memories, and the collective boxes were shared both in an exhibition and in a publication. Individual memory begins to play a role in shaping public memory about the ongoing conflict when participants are empowered with the ability to contribute to memory-making in ways that are meaningful to them.

A Virtual Memorial: ACT for the Disappeared, Beirut, Lebanon

According to a police report published in 1991, 17,415 persons disappeared during the Lebanese Civil War (from 1975 to 1990). The government of Lebanon has never compiled a list of the missing, nor has it created a physical memorial to honor those missing and any other victims. As a result, ACT for the Disappeared established Fushat Amal (Space for Hope), an interactive website. Families of the missing can add a case or update information on individuals. The site includes photos, videos, and testimonies. Justine di Mayo, cofounder and director of ACT for the Disappeared, notes, "We, as citizens, can play an active role in giving voice to the families of the missing, recognizing the tragedy and in starting the investigation work to clarify the fate of the missing."[5]

For Sites of Conscience, the memorial, whether it be a site, physical structure, or a website, is only a part of a larger process of memory and reconciliation. The work of engaging communities and visitors in the work of memorialization—in the process, not just the result—and in ensuring that current and future generations use the memorial as a tool for learning are crucial. Sites of Conscience have created traveling and pop-up exhibitions, worked with young people to activate existing memorials to provide context, and developed web-based programming, to name just a few of their many activities around the world. Many members find particular importance in the work of engaging young people so that human rights abuses can be prevented in the future. These programmatic activities are often more critical than a physical structure itself. Through those activities, we begin to turn memory into action. Each of the sites builds on a strong commitment to victims, survivors, and the larger community, rather than solely responding to the desires of governments or political parties.

As the (sometimes heated) conversations about controversial monuments in the United States continues, returning to two of those framing questions may be key:

- What memories do we seek to preserve and how?
- In whose name do we act?

If we can begin to address those two questions, perhaps we can—together—begin to understand the ways in which memorialization can heal, rather than divide a society.

LISTENING AND RESPONDING TO COMMUNITY

A LONG VIEW

DAVID B. ALLISON

One of my first tasks when I bought my first home was eradicating a mold problem in the shower. Dust and debris piled at my feet as I removed the tiles. Satisfied with my work, I told my wife that the shower would be back to normal soon. I quickly discovered that my profound ignorance of even the most basic home repair techniques rendered my initial bravura premature upon the realization that I had neither the right tools nor the expertise to complete the task. My decided lack of skill and tools meant the shower stayed unusable until we could hire someone to fix it for us. The shower languished in partially destroyed uselessness. I learned that if I were to attempt a job of this magnitude in the future, I should be sure that I had the proper equipment and aptitude to carry it through to the end. The joy of demolishing moldy tiles gave way to the reality of the long, difficult—and pricy—process ahead.

This story illustrates some of the challenges that come with making connections in the community. It is easier to tear down and destroy than to build and repair. Without the proper tools and expertise for the job, the process can curdle quickly and become untenable. Quick solutions that have not been properly thought through are liable to derail when met with significant obstacles.

Similarly, working with community to attempt to heal and reconcile with the past is rarely simple. Feeble, half-baked solutions do not result in sustained success. Effective community work requires the right tools deployed at the right time to get the job done. As community leaders and public historians, our voices can echo resoundingly through the discourse of our times.[1] This chapter will explore not only *why* we must prepare ourselves to engage with our community but also *how* we can begin this important work.

Community Engagement as an Imperative for Museums and Historic Sites

Understanding museum origins and how these organizations framed themselves in relation to the public is helpful for us as we seek to sleuth out the role of community in museums today. Early European museums—which often served as guardians of "Western" culture and as temples to Enlightenment knowledge—inculcated a high culture–low culture dichotomy in the DNA of many museums. Wealthy collectors gathered their artifacts in exclusive galleries meant only for other rich people.

Collections set aside for the privileged eventually morphed into what we call museums. These museums became fixtures in European cultural centers and presented a sanitized vision of an orderly world. Obsessed with organizing and categorizing the human, plant, and animal inhabitants of the globe, eighteenth-century scientists sought to reinforce their belief in the perfectibility of a humanity that could make the natural world entirely cognizable.[2] Natural history museums were the most salient reflection of this perspective, as they built large cases and "curated" objects by size, importance, or taxonomic grouping.

Another strand of museum origins traces back to cabinets of curiosity, which sought merely to entertain and titillate—a thin vein of specious science and dubious historical artifacts providing the cover for a blatant money grab. The distance between low-brow entertainment—P. T. Barnum's huckster hawking a Fiji "mermaid"—and high-brow cultural transmission and guardianship—the cavernous, marbled halls of the Louvre—seems wide.[3] However, a closer examination shows that both strands of museum forebears had the same view of their patrons. The people who come to these museums were to be spectators and consumers, not active participants. The public needed to be educated and entertained and were to be totally in the thrall of the experts who curated exhibits—or promoted spectacle—for their benefit.

The heritage of these dual strands of museology continues to influence the perception of museums today. Researchers from IMPACTS (Intelligent Models to Predict Actionable Solutions) recently concluded, "People don't necessarily feel welcome or that they 'fit in' at cultural organizations . . . data shows that, on average, approximately four out of ten people in the U.S. don't feel comfortable at an art, science, or history museum—including science museums and historic sites."[4] Museums continue to be alienating for much of the public, despite their attempts to break down barriers for their audience.

Significant barriers to museum participation were well entrenched and pervasive until a widespread democratization of museums in the 1970s and 1980s. Learning theory and an increased focus on evaluation showed that participatory education and shared authority were more effective ways to engage the public than didactic, static exhibits, and presentations. In addition, museums increasingly sought to understand their role in communities. History museums founded as hagiographic paeans to the "great men" of the past began to tell alternative narratives from the perspectives of people who were not wealthy elites. Natural history museums turned away from trumpeting the ascendancy of white civilization in favor of championing an environmental ethos of shared responsibility for the earth. Art museums sought to showcase lesser-known and underrepresented artists to bring new stories to light.

Since the 1990s, many museums have striven to become integral parts of the day-to-day life of specific localities. These museums are storytellers that connect people to their past, rather than bastions for wealthy collectors to display the trappings of power and prestige. Robert Archibald gives voice to this perspective: "This is not the 'master narrative of old' that defined insiders and outsiders, but instead a process of story-making that creates room for the diverse and multiple perspectives that exist in consequence of our individuality."[5]

Museums are uniquely positioned to take up controversial issues in communities. Museums are trusted.[6] Numerous studies have shown that museums are viewed by the public as attractive leisure time destinations that provide both education and entertainment.[7] Museums are also viewed as mostly impartial and as trustworthy sources of information.[8] These advantages give museums a unique and powerful place in society. With this power, museums can take up the mantle as a trusted convener and as arbiter of difficult issues within a community.

Examples of museums holding forums, creating dialogue, and building shared experiences with the public can be found in communities across the world. Some examples are from the Missouri History Center, which Archibald ran for a number of years, and History Colorado. Elizabeth Pickard and JJ Lonsinger Rutherford, respectively, highlight these museums in case studies included in this volume.

In short, museums must listen to community. Museums that withdraw from the important dialogue of our times risk the slow death of irrelevance. Moreover, community is the barometer against which we can determine our value to the people who keep the doors open through their continued patronage. But how do we know when we are successful in meeting our community where they are and providing for their needs? What are the strategies that propel us toward becoming trusted partners and reliable forums for open dialogue?

Strategies for Working with Community

Community is a term that can be so vague as to lose all meaning. It is laden with multifarious definitions, tends to be overused, and is rarely applied consistently. Sheila Watson, in *Museums and Their Communities* (2007), attempts to fashion some solid toeholds for the term: "The essential defining factor of a community is the sense of belonging that comes to those who are part of it and that, through association with communities, individuals conceptualize identity."[9] In most contexts, this definition suffices. However, the word "community" can sometimes be used pejoratively, as one group of people define themselves in opposition to another group of people. Also, when museum professionals refer to community, a cynical view would say that they are instantaneously "othering" whomever they are talking about—these are people not like themselves who need to be reached in order to increase attendance, to drum up financial support, or to cultivate as a focus group for new initiatives.

This transactional view results in broken trust and a patronizing sensibility that reasserts the museum's power to exert control over narratives. Rather than cultivating community as "this for that," it must be approached from a place of humility and grace. Indeed, in the words of author Elizabeth Crooke, "Community is both a process and a product."[10] The process—how we approach relationships and build trust—is key to effecting change.

Audience data and evaluation help museums become embedded in their communities and better equipped to flex to the needs of their audiences. Community responsiveness is about more than mere lip service in the form of panels or community advisory boards—it needs to reflect an audience focus in all aspects of museum operations. Nina Simon has called for museums to become relevant in their communities.[11] In doing so, she called to the carpet stodgy museums that rely solely on their expertise to craft experiences. On a parallel track, design thinking as elucidated by the Stanford Design School introduced nonprofits to new ways of meeting community needs.

Sadly, neither a call to a return to relevance (an irretrievably empty buzzword) nor design thinking are the ultimate panaceas for what ails museums. Sweeping systemic change rarely emerges fully formed from a single theory applied blanket-style over problems. Instead, solutions for museum transformation must borrow from a wide range of sources and should be grounded in the expressed needs of their communities. Additionally, effective museum leaders draw from a variety of sources in an iterative and responsive give and take to ensure that their teams are constantly invigorated and question assumptions. Locking in to one leadership technique only serves to calcify business practices and strands organizations on shoals of inertia and decay.

Successful museums will also take on interesting partnerships in order to advance their mission and to build their cache in the community. Relationships built on a shared language of trust and respect can yield important insights as museums seek to design and develop new experiences and programs. An empathetic, conversational approach built on a foundation of shared authority with our audience is the best starting place.[12]

Sign spotted in a Denver-area classroom. The next image completes the statement. Photo by author.

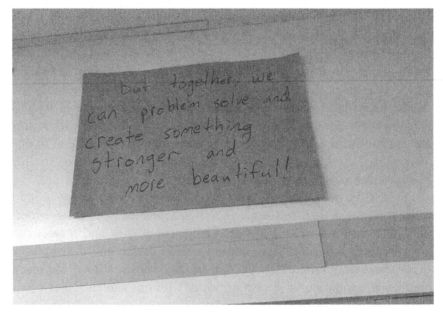

Second part of sign seen in a Denver-area classroom. Photo by author.

A number of my colleagues and I at the Denver Museum of Nature & Science were recently prototyping some new offsite programs at Swansea Elementary School in Denver in a fifth grade classroom. I happened to notice a couple of handwritten signs on the wall of the classroom that speak to the importance of persistence in relationships. One sign read, "All relationships have bad days . . . We might not be able to undo the harm that's done." The other sign finished the thought: ". . . but together, we can problem solve and create something stronger and more beautiful!"

Developing relationships is hard work. Even the simple act of reaching out to nontraditional museumgoers can be fraught. Diversity can be described as giving someone an invitation to the party. Inclusivity means that once they are at the party, you actually ask them to dance.[13] Efforts to include new voices in museums can come across as tokenism or as insincere if we do not listen carefully and take proactive action in response to what we hear.

When it is done well, the insights we gain from deep listening is an intensely humbling endeavor that drags our museums into new and uncomfortable places. Must we always preserve our "authority" as experts? What do we uniquely bring to the table when we meet on equal terms with community? Addressing these questions *before* we set out on the difficult journey of relationship building will set us up for success long into the future.

From appreciative inquiry (AI) to Stanford design thinking and other for-profit project management models, museums have a range of techniques from which to draw.[14] Which is right for you? The community in which you find yourself should determine what tools to use and how to blend techniques for maximal impact. As has been explained, for most museums, there will not be a single silver bullet that leads to success. Rather, a combination of approaches will yield results. Once a foundation of audience responsiveness and partnership has been built, community work can proceed in a number of intriguing directions.

Working hand-in-hand with community is even more important when addressing seemingly intractable historical situations. Mistrust spawned by years of racism, systemic poverty, and neighborhood neglect creates adversarial relationships between government officials and citizens. Seismically divergent ways of perceiving the world place wedges between citizens, and bureaucratic gridlock grinds change initiatives into useless dust. When difficulties creep in, how can museums and leaders within communities rise above the fray?

Museums' role as leisure-time options has sometimes resulted in a milquetoast retreat from difficult topics. Thinkwell's "2017 Guest Experience Trend Report" included a telling statement that is worth quoting in full:

> [Researchers] heard from patrons that they were coming to museums as a pleasurable escape and were put off by exhibits on challenging, topical content, such as global climate change or controversial historical periods. On the other, they also heard from patrons demanding just that type of content, feeling it's the role of a museum to tackle the "tough topics" like global warming or racism. Museums voiced that they felt stuck, and were unsure if it was a case of "a few loud voices" or if, really, the chasm was widening. The data informed Thinkwell's Trend Report that overall, people are going to these places for fun, entertainment, and to engage together as a family. "Escape" also ranked high. This doesn't mean people don't *also* want a deep and resonant experience, but it does mean that it isn't as strong a driver. Museums shouldn't shy away from tackling the hard stories, but they should keep in mind that visitors are still looking for a pleasurable time.[15]

Museums have the obligation to provide fun, entertaining diversions for the pleasure-seeking public, while also opening crucial conversations about the controversial topics of our day. The nuance required to maintain this sort of balance as civic passions are enflamed is substantial.

When Tempers Flare and Passions Rise, How Do We Mediate Effectively?

Some months ago, I found myself at a town hall–style forum about a new development project in Denver. Explosive growth in metro Denver recently has meant that longtime residents—often Latino and low income—have been marginalized and priced out of their neighborhoods by waves of gentrification. As community members, representatives from city government, and elected officials gathered, the tension and angst became palpable, and it seemed likely that we were in for a long night of vigorous debate.

After a string of polished presentations from city officials, community members began to share their opinions. Ranging from well reasoned and brief to rambling and interminable, participants' thin strands of patience began to fray as similar-sounding arguments and entrenched perspectives were repeated by one person after another. Becoming increasingly churlish, the participants began to withdraw from the dialogue. This seeming retreat from engagement only served to raise everyone's ire and to increase the surly atmosphere in the room.

The gray clouds continued to choke the proceedings, until one city councilman thanked the community members for being at the meeting and then shared his personal connection to the neighborhood and why he was excited about the project. The icy ill will that had built over the previous hours began to melt away as that individual's positivity shone through. Other community participants who had been silent were freshly emboldened to share their enthusiasm. Both city representatives and community members felt comfortable and ready to share their ideas and concerns from a place of respect. The meeting went from the clogged arteries of rancorous discord to the free-spirited gusto of true dialogue.

Crucial to this flipped situation was the bravery of one individual.[16] In this case, this person was able to make the proceedings less about the problems in the community and more about shared goals and common purpose. His personal story and good humor elevated everyone and gave new life to the discussion. He found common ground and showed empathy toward community members.

Museum professionals and community leaders must rely on empathy as a tool toward creating a shared understanding of how our communities might embark upon collective engagement with the past. When we perceive and share in the experiences of other people through genuinely seeking to listen to their ideas, needs, and values, we enhance our connectedness to each other.[17] This connectedness, in turn, enables us to see outside of ourselves and to envision a better future.

Ultimately, empathy, compassion, and deep listening are the tools that will allow us to value restorative justice and our shared humanity over narrowly defined self-interests and blindly followed personal peccadilloes.[18] When ignorance of history and reliance on tradition and power politics intrude upon community engagement, museum professionals and community leaders must band together as trusted conveners to initiate respectful, open dialogue. Finding our shared humanity and common purposes will enable us to be ready to not only address the difficult issues in our community but also do so with a grace and a willingness to change ourselves as we learn and grow with others.

Controversial monuments and memorials only remain controversial when our community is balkanized and divided by ideology. Dialogue and empathy provide a way out of the quagmire of divisiveness. Our communities will be ready to reinterpret, recontextualize, remove, or re-create the challenging past when we open our ears to listen and our hearts to transformation.

CONFEDERATE STATUES AT THE UNIVERSITY OF TEXAS AT AUSTIN

BEN WRIGHT

I n 1921, University of Texas at Austin president Robert Vinson sent Professor William Battle to Chicago with the task of reviewing several plaster models of Confederate leaders created by the Italian sculptor Pompeo Coppini. If approved, the statues would be finished and shipped to UT for use in a war memorial commissioned for campus. Battle was blunt in his criticism of the models. On one of Jefferson Davis, Battle wrote to Vinson, "In view of the fact that President Davis was a temperamental, excitable man, the serene thoughtfulness of the figure seems a misinterpretation." Vinson passed on Battle's extensive critique to Coppini. He was outraged, calling Battle a "snake, a mean rattler" in a letter to his friend, state senator Harry Hertzberg. Hertzberg replied, "To think of an artist having to have his work passed upon by a nincompoop of such dimensions."[1]

The exchange may seem comical to modern readers, but it illustrates how the university's Confederate statues were the source of hot tempers even before they were cast in bronze. The exchange also illustrates the potential that archival holdings have for creating a compelling and surprising historical context around Confederate monuments if they are relocated to a museum setting.

Until the summer of 2015, the University of Texas at Austin was home to four Confederate statues situated along the South Mall of the campus. Acts of vandalism and calls for their removal had gathered pace since 1990. Usually, these intermittent efforts sputtered out—students graduated, student leadership turned over, graffiti was white-washed, newspapermen and professors moved on to other things. The spring of 2015 saw yet another nascent student movement coalesce around opposition to the presence of the statues. However, things intensified dramatically after the racially motivated shooting of nine black churchgoers in Charleston, South Carolina, on June 9. Within three weeks, three thousand people signed an online petition, and social media was abuzz with images of the statues covered in graffiti—this time with slogans such as "DavisMustFall" and "Black Lives Matter."

On June 24, the university's president, Gregory Fenves, created a panel to investigate the statues and make recommendations about their future on campus. (This was the same day that South Carolina governor Nikki Haley called for the removal of the Confederate flag from the state capitol in Columbia, South Carolina.) The panel reported its findings in August. Soon after, Fenves decided to relocate the Davis statue to the Briscoe Center for American History (an archive and research center at UT), where it was eventually to be displayed in an exhibit. A lawsuit ensued, but on August 31, 2015, professional art handlers removed the Davis statue from the mall.

Over the next eighteen months, staff at the Briscoe Center conducted a research and curation process with a view to rehousing the statue in an educational setting. (The process could have been completed sooner, but the center was in the middle of a comprehensive renovation and the earliest the statue could be unveiled in an exhibit was April 2017.) Planning for the Davis statue exhibit was much aided by the fact that the center is home to the papers of the statue's benefactor, George Washington Littlefield (a Confederate general and university regent), the papers of the statue's sculptor (the Italian immigrant artist Pompeo Coppini), and the vast historical archive of the space in which the statue stood—namely, the university. What has emerged is a striking and surprising story that remains eerily relevant.

A Brief History of UT's Confederate Statues

Littlefield commissioned Coppini to create the Davis statue in 1919 along with several others intended for a memorial on campus honoring those who died in the Civil War and World War I. Coppini's concept for the memorial centered on a symbolic fountain—a statue of Columbia the goddess of liberty, flanked by American soldiers and sailors, all riding upon a ship propelled by wild seahorses of war (who in turn were barely restrained by demigods representing reason and learning). The fountain is an allegory of America joining World War I. Surrounding Coppini's fountain was to be a court of Southern (mostly Confederate) statesmen converging on two pillars that represented the North and South. In front of the Northern pillar: President Woodrow Wilson. In front of the Southern pillar: Jefferson Davis.

Coppini intended the memorial to symbolize the post–Civil War reconciliation of the North and the South, which, as Vinson termed it, "was not completed until the army and the navy of the United States crossed the Atlantic Ocean in the great war of 1917 and 1918."[2] According to Coppini, Littlefield bought into Coppini's idea for the memorial. (Littlefield had previously wanted a more overt tribute to the Confederacy.)

"Accepted Sketch" of the Littlefield Fountain, ca. 1919. Coppini-Tauch Papers. Courtesy of the Briscoe Center at University of Texas at Austin.

However, for Battle the memorial was subject to a "fatal objection . . . every single statue represents a southern man. How can a group composed of men from only one section stand for a united nation?"

The memorial was large, expensive, and much delayed. Littlefield died in November 1920, before it could be completed. The trustees of his will were left to finish the construction of the memorial. Over the course of the next decade, they clashed bitterly with Coppini, with the UT Board of Regents, and with each other over the memorial's financing, location, and design. Meanwhile, Coppini (who had been paid in installments on a statue-by-statue basis) kept sculpting and invoicing, despite calls to slow down. The Davis statue arrived in Austin in 1924, along with three other Confederate statues (Civil War generals Robert E. Lee and Albert Sidney Burleson and Davis's postmaster-general John H. Reagan). They were first displayed at the American National Bank at Sixth Street and Congress Avenue. The following year, they were moved to the rotunda of the state capitol.

Disputes about the memorial continued, and by 1929 the university's interest in the project had waned considerably. The Board of Regents attempted—unsuccessfully—to move the entire memorial to the east entrance of the campus. Eventually, Philadelphia-based architect Paul Cret brokered a compromise. He ditched the North/South pillars and installed the fountain at the base of the South Mall. He then distributed the portrait statues along the mall leading up to the Main Building.

With an agreement in place, the memorial was finally completed in the spring of 1933. Cret's solution addressed numerous aesthetic and practical dilemmas. However, the memorial's meaning—that concept of reconciliation between North and South—was fatally compromised. Instead of forming a court of honor applauding the World War I generation, the Confederate statues were now isolated from the fountain and each other. Coppini later criticized Cret's plan, calling it "a dismembered conception."

In 1955, the university added a statue of George Washington to the South Mall. For the next sixty years, the mall remained unchanged. As for the students, faculty, and staff who walked down it, they changed greatly, as did the culture they inhabited. While the fountain became a benign, even cherished feature of campus, the Davis statue in particular was increasingly the subject of protest, ire, and debate. Nevertheless, calls for its removal remained sporadic. Between 1960 and 1990,

Contrast between Coppini and Littlefield's original concept and Paul Cret's 1930 redesign. Courtesy of the Briscoe Center at University of Texas at Austin.

students mostly ignored or ridiculed UT's Confederate statues. However, from 1990 onward, calls for their removal steadily grew. At the same time, efforts to diversify the symbolic message of campus architecture were successful. Statues of Martin Luther King Jr. (1999), Cesar Chavez (2007), and Barbara Jordan (2009) were all unveiled. Even so, a pattern had emerged—whenever the university's record on integration and inclusivity was questioned, Confederate statuary came back into focus. This was the situation in which the university found itself again in 2015 after the Charleston shooting.

The Briscoe Center's Approach to Exhibiting the Davis Statue

The Briscoe Center is the fourth location the Davis statue has been publicly displayed in the city of Austin. Sculpted in Chicago (by an immigrant), bronze cast in Brooklyn (by Yankees), the Davis statue was shipped to Galveston and then freighted to Austin, where university officials quietly plotted against it. At first displayed in a bank and then at the state capitol, the statue was hoisted into position on campus by African American workers. Such details point to the uncanny mobility of monuments (despite the myth of permanency they exude) and the surprising cast of characters behind the politics of commemoration. Teasing out details like these from the historical record was an important goal of the research and curation process.

The finished Littlefield memorial, 1933. The main building was replaced in 1937 with UT's iconic tower. Coppini-Tauch Papers. Courtesy of the Briscoe Center at University of Texas at Austin.

The result of that process was *From Commemoration to Education: Pompeo Coppini's Statue of Jefferson Davis*, an exhibit on display since April 2017 in the Briscoe Center's exhibit hall. The title points to the historical journey the statue has made—from its controversial presence in a place of honor to its display in a place of study. It also underlines the fact that the exhibit focuses not on Davis and the Confederacy, nor on the current debate surrounding race in America, but on the history of the statue itself.

This is a point worth reiterating: *From Commemoration to Education* is an exhibit about the history of an object. As such, it emphasizes archival material (historical evidence) over current issues and interpretations, historical facts (as embedded in historical material) over historiography, and the history of commemoration and symbolism over the history of Davis or the Confederacy.

This choice—to let the archival objects and materials do the talking—has not been without criticism. For some, it feels like an attempt to bypass the obvious radioactivity around the Confederacy, as well as other discussions related to race, privilege, and policing that need to happen. For others, an exhibit that focuses on a statue of Davis but doesn't delve into his life and legacy (which the exhibit doesn't) is misguided. Intriguingly, this is a criticism received from both ends of the political spectrum: from conservatives who wanted the exhibit to include content that discussed Davis's service in the U.S. military and U.S. Senate, and from liberals who lamented the lack of content around Davis's racism and role in an abortive rebellion.

These criticisms are not without validity. Confederate commemoration is an emotional, controversial subject that is difficult enough to discuss in the public sphere, let alone comprehensively capture in an exhibit. A more thematic, contemporary approach is certainly possible and could create room for comparison with controversial memorialization elsewhere in the world—including Soviet statues in Estonia, statues of Cecil Rhodes in South Africa, and Chiang Kai-shek statues in Taiwan. Furthermore, the historical consensus (at least at the academic level) about the causes and horrors of the Civil War (and indeed of the Jim Crow era) is stable enough to envision an exhibit that casts a wider net— one that gets into other historical subjects such as Davis's treason, the centrality of slavery to the Civil War, or the shameful legacy of Jim Crow laws in the post-Reconstruction United States.

However, doing so would have been at the expense of the uniquely comprehensive historical record (archived at the Briscoe Center) that speaks to UT's Confederate statues. Though rich, archival records seldom contain "smoking gun" documents, where historical actors clearly articulate their ulterior or subliminal motives. (For example, at no point does Littlefield cite "white supremacy" as a reason for wanting to commemorate the Civil War.) With this in mind, prescribing contemporary political conclusions from the documents on display seemed inappropriate. Instead, it was always the goal of the exhibit to guide visitors through an examination of historical evidence, and to furnish them with the means of drawing their own conclusions to the questions raised by the material. Though the exhibit focuses on the history of the Davis statue, discussions of white supremacy, race relations, police brutality, campus diversity, and culture wars invariably accompany visitor reactions, class tours, and media coverage. The material on display inspires rather than dictates dialogue on these matters.

Exhibiting the Davis Statue: Interpretation

After the research phase of the curation process, staff set about using the vast sum of documents and photographs unearthed to answer the following questions:

- Why was this statue placed at UT in the first place?
- How did it remain on campus while the world around it changed?
- Why is it now at the Briscoe Center?

We determined that these questions could be addressed through a chronological rather than thematic presentation of the statue's history. Such an approach suited the space we had at our disposal for the exhibit: a 14-foot-by-60-foot-wide hallway that lends itself to a linear approach. The statues chronology was broken into four sections: Commission and Creation; Delays and Disputes; Compromise and Construction; and the statue's recent history. Two thematic sections (How the Statues Were Made, and Inscriptions and Interpretations) were included as well.

The statue's recent history section (1955–2015) posed an interesting quandary. The closer the story gets to 2015, the more digital in nature the primary sources become. In fact, the vast majority of primary sources from 2015 are solely digital—tweets, Facebook posts, pdfs, digital videos from public forums, digital photographs of statues covered in graffiti, and so on. Our solution was to house this section in an interactive touch-screen panel, rather than in a traditional exhibit case.

While it can seem strange, even twee, to talk about social posts as primary sources, they often contain a surprising amount of historical information. For example, the tweet on page 213 is ostensibly a photograph of the vandalized Davis statue with a timestamp. However, upon closer inspection, one can perceive a host of historically relevant information embedded within the image. First, it was posted by a student and retweeted by a local reporter (Mose Buchele). Second, the image is enveloped with textual commentary that allows researchers to map the author's sentiments onto a larger historical context. For example, the use of a fist emoticon evokes the Black Power movement of the 1960s and 1970s, as well as John Dominis's iconic image of Tommie Smith and John Carlos from the 1968 Mexico Olympics.[3] The hashtag #blacklivesmatter mirrors the graffiti and links the demand for removal of Confederate statues to wider debates in American society about police conduct and race relations.

Within this structure—four chronological sections and two thematic ones—staff mapped out the content for space planning, revising as exhibit design and object selection developed. The research text was also

Mose Buchele Retweeted

Thomas Fawcett @revgetdown · 23 Jun 2015
Jeff Davis had another bad night. #blacklivesmatter👊👊 #bumpthechump
#byefelicia #utaustin

Re: jefferson davi

Social media post, June 23, 2015. Note the use of hashtags (which mirror the graffiti) and emoticons (fists). The author, a white student, uses these functions of the platform to link his own sentiments with wider historical movements (such as Black Lives Matter and Black Power). Courtesy of the Briscoe Center at University of Texas at Austin.

adapted with this structure in mind. Text reviewers included outside editors; the center's director, Dr. Don Carleton; and the university's provost, Dr. Mauri McInnis. The design work was performed by outside vendors, as was the refurbishment of the statue itself. Primary source selections for the exhibit were at first document heavy, which risked making it dry and overly textual. A second round of archival research uncovered a number of photographs, newspaper clippings, and material culture items that helped to diversify the selection.

Exhibiting the Davis Statue: Design

The physical design of the exhibit had to accommodate certain constraints, including relationships with other spaces in the building. The exhibit gallery is the de facto path for anyone accessing the reading room (which is the majority of visitors to the center), so the statue's size (nine feet tall) and its potential to dominate the space had to be taken into account. We wanted to ensure that the statue was not the first and most dominant architectural element of the hall gallery upon entry, so we added a wing wall into the space that created a niche for the sculpture itself, ensuring that the various sightlines to the statue from other parts of the hallway were always interrupted with interpretive content. Additionally, we placed a large super graphic behind the statue and an interpretative panel adjacent to it, the point being to underline how the statue is now an object in an exhibit, not the centerpiece of a public memorial, with all that that implies. The super graphic—a large-scale rendering of the 1919 Coppini design that Littlefield had approved—also added historic context, giving viewers an idea of how the memorial had been originally intended.

Exhibit cases are stacked along the hallway at right angles to the hall's exterior wall. Visitors navigate the cases before passing by the wing wall and encountering the statue itself. The setup encourages visitors to interact with the selected historical materials (which provide a rich context of the statue) before interacting with the statue itself. This also allows for a visual layering of the primary source evidence in a linear fashion—from case to case—enforcing the chronological approach we had opted for. Adjacent to the statue is the interactive panel, which again serves to anchor the statue as a teaching asset rather than as something to be honored.

Finally, it was also important for the design to reflect the statue's ties to campus. This was supported through a color palette that drew

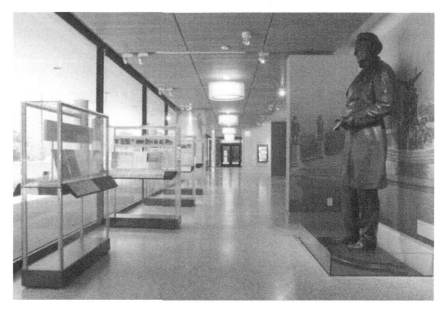

The Briscoe Center's exhibit, *From Commemoration to Education*. Courtesy of the Briscoe Center at University of Texas at Austin.

inspiration from the evergreen live oak trees visible through the floor-to-ceiling windows that run along the exterior wall of the exhibit hall. We utilized historical photographs in three ways: in the cases, as super graphics, and on fabric scrims. They further emphasized the statue's ties to the university and provide visually engaging historical context.

Exhibiting the Davis Statue: Launch

The exhibit was opened in April 2017. Several classes were invited to preview the exhibit two days before the official opening. Not only did this seem appropriate (given that everything that happens on a campus must naturally link back to the university's teaching mission), but it also enabled us to create important media assets—photographs of students in the exhibit space that we could distribute to media immediately upon opening.

We made preparations for anticipated media questions in collaboration with the university's central communications team. In addition to answering questions, it was important to emphasize a positive message—that the university was actively taking the lead on a difficult and controversial matter. Local media covered the exhibit's opening, as did several national press outfits. Media availability (on the day before the opening) was utilized in particular by local TV news crews, which involved having the center's director, Dr. Don Carleton, speaking with eight different reporters in the space of two hours—a somewhat intense and grueling schedule. National media outlets did not show the same interest in the exhibit's opening as they had done in the original statue controversy. (Controversies make for better news stories than solutions to controversies!) Preparations for potential vandalism of the exhibit—both from those who wanted it put back on the South Mall and from those who wanted it melted down—were made with the campus police department. Fortunately, the exhibit has not been subjected to vandalism or protest, despite criticism.

The opening of the Davis statue exhibit was successful, but it was not the end of the story. Reacting to the disturbing events in Charlottesville in August 2017, President Fenves decided to remove UT's remaining Confederate statues from the South Mall. Those three statues will become part of the center's artifact collection. However, there is no mandate and no plan to put them on public display in a museum setting. Instead, a policy will be formulated to make them available to scholars on a by-appointment basis. Additionally, they can be digitized using 3-D scanning techniques for use in teaching and research. It is plausible that in the future the Davis statue exhibit will be updated to tell a slightly wider story about all of the university's Confederate statues.

Answering Common Questions and Concerns

The removal and relocation of the Davis statue underlines the powerful role that monuments and symbols continue to play in American culture. They are silent, still, and heavy; yet they are in fact communicative and dynamic—contestable, controversial, and indeed movable. Resting on stone plinths, their legitimacy is contingent on cultural foundations. As those foundations shift, so does the legitimacy of the monument atop them. As Americans continue to debate the removal of Confederate monuments, three arguments continue to emerge. The first is that such monuments do very little, if any, harm when left alone; second, that removing them is tantamount to erasing or white-washing history;

and third, that removing them sets a dangerous precedent. Each of these arguments is flawed.

Regardless of past intentions (for example, Coppini and Littlefield's attempt at reconciliatory symbolism), Confederate statues now convey a disturbing and offensive message to the general public, and particularly to minority communities. By moving them to museums, archival holdings, and other educational settings, they can be preserved as historical evidence as well as original works of art. The historical evidence encoded within their very bronze is useful to scholars, teachers, and students. But their ability to educate is compromised by their presence in public commemorative spaces.

Monuments are designed to emit cultural, political, and historical messages to the public. Confederate monuments symbolize worldviews, historical viewpoints, and cultural assumptions (for example, assumptions about race) that are unacceptable today. Their presence in public spaces implies endorsement of those worldviews, viewpoints, and assumptions. For example, UT's statue of Davis portrays him not as a rebel or a traitor, or even as a retired curmudgeon, but as a Christian statesman. The statue's very pose implies legitimacy of not just his personal characteristics but also his racial views and rebellious actions.

Within educated circles, there is no credible debate about whether Confederate leaders have a positive legacy for modern America. This is for good reason. They were men who violated their oaths of allegiance to the United States and led a tragic rebellion against a democratically elected government in order to preserve slavery. They do not—and cannot—represent American civil society in a democracy in the twenty-first century.

Furthermore, Confederate monuments were designed to aggressively assert a specific view of the Civil War (the Lost Cause) that was based on alternative facts (such as the war really being about tariffs and states' rights rather than slavery). Such monuments also pay tribute to a menacing vision of white supremacy. To quote Director Carleton, "The message to African Americans was clear: 'Reconstruction is over and the old sheriff is back in town.' That message was underscored by Jim Crow laws and brutal lynchings." More recently, Confederate symbols have become central to an increasingly ugly debate over what America is really about that whirs at light speed in our social media age. Events like

Charlottesville show that such symbols have undergone a process—from *The Dukes of Hazzard* to David Duke—that has made them once more the focus of a dark vision of America. The use of Confederate statues and flags by such people points to the enduring appeal of hate symbols to new generations of racists. Previously, perhaps these monuments could be ignored or taken with a pinch of salt. That appears to be implausible now. We—and they—have lost our innocence.

But despite these sensitivities, isn't removing statues an attempt to erase the past rather than to deal with it? No. First, those who gain their knowledge of history from historic statuary rather than scholarship have a very limited understanding of the discipline. History (the critical analysis of past events and people based on historical evidence) and commemoration (the glorification or remembrance of the past) are very different things. If someone destroys the evidence of the past—for example, by burning books or deleting emails—they are certainly assailing history and compromising the ability of the public and the academy to understand it. However, if evidence of the past is simply moved from one location to another—which is what happens when a Confederate statue is relocated to a museum setting—the historical information remains both intact and accessible.

Often with the ensuing debates about the past that take place during a statue removal (not to mention the resulting exhibits), history ends up being elaborated upon rather than erased. What changes is that a community finds a more appropriate platform from which to grapple with the past. To be clear, something is being erased and assailed. But it isn't history—just a false view of it. The relocation of a statue underlines the fact that Confederate leaders, as well as their ideas and actions, are no longer commemorated or endorsed.

Finally, numerous commentators, including President Donald Trump, have expressed concern for the fate of other statues, such as those depicting George Washington and Thomas Jefferson. After all, both were slaveholders, like Lee and Davis. "Where will this all end?" has therefore become a common refrain, with the implication being that statues of the Founding Fathers are now also vulnerable to the whims of liberal cities, seminaries, and other institutions.

While some non-Confederate statues may indeed be vulnerable (perhaps Christopher Columbus, for example), ultimately the fear that the floodgates have been opened appears misguided. While Washington and Jefferson certainly have mixed legacies, they were democratically elected presidents who peacefully relinquished power, passing it on to their political rivals. Davis, Lee, and other Confederate leaders can hardly make the same boast. More important, Jefferson and Washington aren't presently used as hate symbols. As observed in Charlottesville and Charleston, Confederate statues and symbols have become so.

Finally, the intentions of those who erected Confederate monuments were often very questionable. Many of these monuments were built in the early twentieth century—a time of great transition and anxiety in America. Immigration and industry were in full swing, undermining America's rural white traditions and creating a more urban, multicultural nation. Confederate monuments—often funded by wealthy, elderly benefactors—were reactionary, aiming to put both minorities and progress in their place. In this sense, they were anchors as much as they were monuments, thrown overboard in order to ground culture identity despite racial progress and economic change.

A comprehensive response to these three arguments could easily be elaborated. No doubt they will be employed again in future controversies around Confederate statues. It is important to remember that at the heart of these questions are often the sincere concerns of ordinary Americans. They are therefore worthy of repeated discussion. Unlike scholars and museum professionals, most people do not spend their days thinking about the cultural, philosophical, and historical questions that monuments and statues pose. Therefore, there remains need to walk local communities through decisions and discussions that open up these historical discourses. This should be done without any sanctimonious eye-rolling by those who believe they have it all figured out. After all, shouldn't we be glad that people value history enough to worry that it's being erased, even if it isn't?

Moving forward, three different questions will also be central to the discussion about public statuary:

- What is the historical legacy of those being memorialized?
- What were the motivations of those who built the monuments to them?
- Is the presence of these memorials useful to present-day racists?

Undoubtedly, there are more questions that need answering, too. However, these three are vital—both to decisions about whether to remove statues and to curators and researchers tasked with recontextualizing them in educational settings. Finally, it is worth noting that an educational setting doesn't necessarily mean a museum setting. It also could mean archival storage with scholarly access, or online access through 3-D scanning and digital curation. There likely are perhaps a thousand Confederate statues still standing in America.[4] It seems unfeasibly arduous and expensive to house them all in museum settings. Many of them are not original pieces of artwork but sheet metal–pressed factory reproductions. Designed to weather the elements, most will not require intensive archival preservation. Due to the way that the public mood appears to have shifted between Charleston and Charlottesville, nonmuseum settings seem more of a feasible option than perhaps they were before.

Final Thoughts

Housed at the Briscoe Center, in one of Coppini's early notebooks, is a sketch of a proposed war memorial titled "Charity in War." It shows two male figures, presumably soldiers, one picking up the other from the battlefield. It is not clear whether they are comrades or enemies. If such a memorial had ever been created, it would have abstracted the Confederacy to a certain extent, emphasizing instead the comradeship of veterans caught up in historical forces beyond their control. (Incidentally, this is the approach to commemoration taken by a number of Vietnam War memorials.) Coppini's sketch contrasts jarringly with the Littlefield memorial, both as it was planned and as it was executed. The finished memorial was almost braggadocio in its commemoration of the Confederacy and the Civil War, celebrating its political and military leaders, and by extension, the ideas and prejudices they stood for (and which cost so many ordinary Americans their lives).

Since the integration of American life began to gather pace in the 1950s and 1960s, Confederate statues have stood as a stern nod to views not only unacceptable today (particularly to people of color) but also unacceptable to millions of Americans who lived through the Civil War era (particularly those who were in bondage).

Coppini's "Charity in War" points to a form of commemoration that was largely left untried during the Jim Crow era—a form of remembrance

Coppini's "Charity in War" notebook sketch, ca. 1920. Coppini-Tauch Papers. Courtesy of the Briscoe Center at University of Texas at Austin.

for those caught up in the Civil War but that didn't pay homage to the Confederacy. Such a distinction was of no concern to men like Littlefield. Instead, their monuments were much more likely to be what John Hope Franklin called an attempt to "win with the pen what they had failed to win with the sword."[5] An aggressive defense of the slaveholding South— cast in bronze and set in stone—was part of the Lost Cause mind-set. Therefore, moving Confederate statues—from commemorative contexts to educational ones—isn't about erasing history or enforcing political correctness. It is about challenging false narratives by downgrading objects of honor to archival material. By doing so, the hope is that such statues cease to be pillars in a fabricated, divisive, and dangerous history. Instead, they become assets in an accurate, evidence-based history that is of use to those who value the past and who strive to work for a more perfect union.

22

HONORING
EL MOVIMIENTO

THE CHICANO MOVEMENT
IN COLORADO

JJ LONSINGER RUTHERFORD

On September 27, 2017, the History Colorado Center in Denver opened a new core exhibit on the history of Colorado's Chicano movement. This exhibit is part of the museum's permanent *Colorado Stories* exhibit, which looks at ten different communities over place and time that help to shed light on who we are as Coloradans, today. Nearly five hundred veterans of the Chicano movement,[1] community leaders, elders, and family members attended the opening. Following brief introductory remarks, the group marched out singing "Yo Soy Chicano"—an anthem of the movement.[2] Later, we shared refreshments and memories as we listened to a band play songs of the movement. *Latin Life Denver* wrote, "Chicano pride filled the room September 27 at the Colorado History Museum [*sic*] as long time Chicano activists, supporters, and leaders from throughout Colorado came together to celebrate the installation of the *El Movimiento* (*The Movement*) as a permanent and core exhibit at the museum."[3] What was most incredible for the institution and the community was that neither the exhibition nor the opening was a product of the museum. Everything about it—the speakers, the entertainment, and most important, the exhibit itself—derived from the community.

As the lead exhibit developer for *El Movimiento: The Chicano Movement in Colorado*, I was truly overwhelmed by the response. It was a night I couldn't have even dreamed of when this collaboration began three years earlier. The evening left me in tears, understanding anew the tremendous power museums have in their communities and how validating it is for communities to tell a story in "the Museum."

While I felt the gratitude and excitement of the community acutely, just as tangible to me was the pain a history of exclusion had wrought on participants. History Colorado, my place of work for nearly twelve years and a museum I love dearly, had historically not been as welcoming to this community as it should have been. We had failed to connect to the Hispanic, Latino/a, and Chicano/a community of Colorado and we had sent a message, albeit unintentionally, that we valued the contributions of Anglo people over those of Chicano/a or Latino/a descent. Our success in this endeavor was a result of the museum learning to better listen to the community we were serving and invest in relationships in a new and deeper way. We needed to afford the project time to blossom. Most important, we needed to relinquish authority over the final product.

Though its roots predate Colorado statehood, History Colorado (née the Colorado Historical Society) was formally chartered in 1879. For much of its first 150 years, the institution's exhibitions, programs, and collections focused on traditional Anglo-Western history themes: mining, railroads, cowboys, homesteaders, fur trappers, explorers, and the like. Colorado's state museum was like many other state museums. We were not particularly bad, nor did we perceive our exclusivity as being egregious (although marginalized communities would perceive otherwise). Much of what we offered was what was expected and reflected a national Western history narrative.

In 2012, the state government gave the Colorado Historical Society the chance to create a completely new museum from the ground up. Having been housed in a small, historic building for many years, a new space would provide the museum with opportunities to tackle different stories and to serve visitors more effectively. With the new building, the institution had the opportunity to reimagine itself: whose stories it would reflect, whom it would truly be representative of, how it would authentically connect with audiences, and how to weave in inclusive stories of Colorado's past and its citizenry. One of our most important visible steps was to drop the word "society" from our name, for it evoked a sense of exclusion.[4] We also tried to focus on inclusivity by creating core exhibits on Japanese internment during World War II, on prejudice toward African Americans and segregation in Colorado in the era of Jim Crow, and on the state's contested borderlands.

The *Borderlands* Exhibit

Despite what we felt were very sincere attempts at inclusion, the results—as measured through audience surveys and anecdotal responses—still didn't make everyone feel as valued and welcome as intended. We had made concerted, honest attempts to connect to our Chicano/a, Hispanic, and Latino/a audiences. To reach these communities, we hired an outside evaluator, held focus groups, engaged in intercept interviews, conducted storyline testing and phone interviews—we just hadn't succeeded. In response, our institution looked inward. We accepted the results that clearly showed our shortcomings. Ultimately, we determined to be open to discovering new ways to be inclusive, by following the lead of members of the community we hoped to better serve.

One day in 2013, a little more than a year after the museum opened, I met with well-known members of Colorado's Chicano community working with AARP. They reached out to me to share their disappointment in the new History Colorado Center, particularly noting that we had failed to honor Colorado's Hispano, Chicano/a, and Latino/a history. While we truly intended the *Borderlands* exhibit we had spent so much time creating to reflect the story they sought to be told, they had barely noticed it. It just didn't resonate—perhaps, we thought, because it was light on material culture and heavy on technology. Whatever the reason, they believed that a vitally important chapter in Colorado history needed to be told in the museum: the story of the national Chicano movement and Colorado's major role within it.

Then, heeding their admonitions, we dove headfirst into efforts to be more inclusive with Colorado's Hispano, Chicano/a, and Latino/a

Entry to History Colorado's *Borderlands* exhibit. Photo by author.

communities.[5] We asked the community members who had initiated the meeting with me to take the lead on what we would do. Their initial idea was an evening honoring the history of the Chicano movement in conjunction with AARP's advisory committee, El Comit.

As the director of education and an exhibit developer at History Colorado, I was fortunate to have the opportunity to be project lead for the entire collaboration that resulted. I listened carefully to their concerns, accepted responsibility for History Colorado's past shortcomings, and got to work. To be honest, if I had thought at that point about trying to create a new permanent exhibit on the history of the Chicano movement with no collections, no community connections (in fact, we had a negative reputation within the Latino/a community), no money, no exhibit space, and no dedicated staff, I might have given up. Fortunately, we approached inclusion with the community incrementally. As we opened doors at History Colorado, each one led to another door with more opportunity behind it. We took small steps, documented successes, and leveraged it to create something bigger.

First, in 2013, as mentioned above, History Colorado worked with AARP's advisory committee, El Comit, to put together an evening at the History Colorado Center honoring the legacy of the Chicano movement. For a year, I went to El Comit meetings and listened and learned. The meetings were as much social—merely getting to know each other as people—as they were productive. We made progress slowly, fueled by an endless stream of coffee. The entire project was driven by process, which was atypical for a deadline-driven institution. Our main focus was just being a good partner and getting smarter about a very important and deeply personal story that we didn't know very much about.

Our initial idea for a single evening event morphed into a small weeklong community-curated exhibit on the Chicano movement. Small tables around the atrium explored different aspects of El Movimiento—land grants, the farm and labor movements, the Crusade for Justice, student activism, the Vietnam War, arts and culture, and people of the movement. Our pop-up exhibit was in the voice of our partners, personal, and moving.

This unpolished pop-up exhibit sparked a response from the local Chicano/a, Hispanic, and Latino/a community. The response was immediate and incredible. Though the evening was free, we sold out—five hundred tickets in twenty-four hours. We had opened the first door.

We used the success of that evening to ask for more from both the museum's leadership and our community partners. We got permission from History Colorado's executive team to put together a small, temporary exhibit on the history of the Chicano movement in Colorado to coincide with *1968*, a major traveling exhibit we had previously scheduled to host. This provided an opportunity to shine a light on what was going on in Colorado as the Chicano movement gained steam in the late 1960s while also localizing the exhibition. History Colorado coordinated this project, though we never usurped control of its content. We organized exhibit meetings and facilitated the exhibit design, object acquisition, and technical support. We invited AARP's El Comit and others to serve in an advisory capacity. The group, History Colorado's Chicano Advisory Committee, met monthly to plan the exhibit.

The people who served on our Chicano Advisory Committee inspired me beyond belief. They came from as far away as Pueblo and Greeley, both more than an hour from Denver, for our monthly meetings. Deborah Espinosa, who had been the director of History Colorado's El Pueblo

Museum for more than twenty years and had recently retired, came out of retirement to serve as the exhibit codeveloper. As veterans of the El Movimiento, our community advisors came with deeply personal attachments to the history. They were the ones who actually stood up and said "¡Ya Basta!" ("Enough already!") to discrimination and harassment; who embraced the pejorative "Chicano" as a symbol of pride; and who endured racism, profiling, arrests, intimidation, and (in some cases) violence to move American society toward justice and equality for Chicanos.

We welcomed anyone to participate in our meetings, and the group size fluctuated a bit as a consequence. We ended up with a core group of about twenty people who came consistently. We were very intentional about accounting for and acknowledging everyone's suggestions and diligent about taking and disseminating meeting minutes—a significant step toward transparency. After a year, we opened our temporary exhibit in February 2014. It was another successfully opened door for History Colorado.

We originally intended to keep *El Movimiento* open six months but ultimately kept it open for nearly two years. Eduardo Diaz, director of the Smithsonian Latino Center, attended the exhibit's opening reception and wrote about it in the *Huffington Post*. "With *El Movimiento*," he said, "History Colorado shifts the paradigm of a historical society, a reference framework that usually embraces the 'official story,' often excluding the histories of 'the other.' In initiating the *El Movimiento* project, History Colorado begins the process of centering the margin by including Colorado Chicanos and their histories."[6]

In addition to an exhibit, our work on *El Movimiento* also created opportunities for History Colorado staff to develop and deliver programming about the Chicano movement. Labor activist Dolores Huerta came to discuss the movement with teachers and students, using the exhibit as her classroom. Dr. Jose Angel Gutierrez, founding member and past president of La Raza Unida, lectured about his own life and experience with El Movimiento.

Hundreds of students visited *El Movimiento* for tours led by members of the Chicano Advisory Committee. They reported leaving the exhibit inspired, proud, and validated. Toward the end, the exhibit invited visitors to add names to a wall that said "El Movimiento is . . ." Every week our wall exploded with names, comments, and Chicano Power drawings on sticky notes. Photos of public programs showed engagement in real

Dolores Huerta at the
El Movimiento exhibit.
Photo by author.

time. We created an exhibit impact statement and captured everything we could think of.

When I reflect on our efforts, I believe the most important thing that happened is that the community gave History Colorado a second chance (actually, it was more like a third or fourth chance). Even though Colorado Historical Society had not been the most inclusive, welcoming historical society or museum for much of its history, when a door was opened and we genuinely asked for help, community members responded. Despite initial impressions, people for whom I hold the highest respect and who literally fought to make the world more just and equitable didn't write us off as hopeless. They certainly could have.

A few things stand out to me. When our Chicano Advisory Committee designed the temporary exhibit, we spent a lot of time thinking about how to create the context of the movement. "What led to this explosion in the 1960s and 1970s?" we asked. We talked about disempowerment and

Note from Dolores Huerta found at the *El Movimiento* exhibit. Photo by author.

tried to find a symbol that would represent it. We chose a photo of uniden-tified workers of Mexican descent working in a field in Northern Colo-rado, stooped over and using short-handled hoes (a farming implement that was, in time, outlawed because of its brutal effects on stoop laborers) to weed sugar beets. Exhibit codeveloper Deborah Espinosa wrote what we portrayed over the image: "As colonized people we were invisible. We were not there; we weren't in the history books. . . . We were not considered."

These men whose names were lost to history stood for thousands of nameless workers in Colorado's sugar beet fields. Yet, as a result of this exhibit, members of the community (in one case, direct descendants) identified and named all three. We were able to restore agency, honor, and legacy to three theretofore unidentified men whose families still reside in Colorado today.

There is more to the work. We created traveling versions of the exhibit for the cities of Pueblo and Greeley. With a grant from the Institute for

Students are fully engaged at the *El Movimiento* exhibit as a community member shares her story. Photo by author.

Museums and Library Services, we created an online exhibition for *El Movimiento* and awarded digital badges for students and teachers who explored the exhibit. We've also begun to build our collections and partner with other organizations to digitize collections related to the Chicano movement.

Here are some of the main lessons we learned:

- You can start small and see where things lead. You don't have to start with a huge ambitious project.
- Listen first and talk second (or third, or fourth, or last, or not at all!). Listen!
- Be honest about what you don't know. You don't need to be the authority. In fact, unless you are part of the community you are working with, you are most definitely not the authority.
- Act and follow up. Without action, you will lose trust.
- Say *yes* first. Have a good reason for saying no.
- Use your power to do good. That power might not be creating a new permanent exhibit. It might be giving free room rental to a

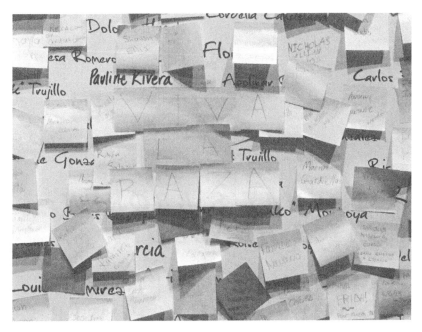

Viva la Raza note discovered at *El Movimiento* exhibit. Photo by author.

community group. Yes, you will probably have to come in on Saturday morning and welcome the group and work, but if this is the power that you have, use it for good.

- Seek to make real change in your organization, but acknowledge and be honest about what you are *not* able to do.
- Take small steps, document every success, and use it to ask for more from your institution and your community.
- Invest your time in relationships and people. Don't always go in with the end result in mind. Relationships take time to build and are far more important and more durable than "the schedule."

While it is important for museums to act quickly and be responsive to current events, we must acknowledge the historical role museums have played in perpetuating an Anglo-oriented story, however unintentionally. It takes time to build authentic relationships and build trust to shift that narrative, and it isn't always a fast process. History Colorado didn't have much of a foundation to build on, and we've come a long way in three years. There is so much more to be done, but we're on the right path.

NOT WHAT'S BROKEN; WHAT'S HEALED

WOMEN IN EL BARRIO AND THE HEALING POWER OF COMMUNITY

VANESSA CUERVO FORERO

Not What's Broken; *What's Healed* was a series of happenings and community engagements focused on the civil and reproductive rights of women of color in East Harlem. Taking the controversial statue of J. Marion Sims (the presumed father of gynecology who experimented on enslaved black women) as point of departure, *Not What's Broken; What's Healed* looked critically at issues of historic preservation, violence against women, and the importance of building community through civic engagement as modes of resistance. The project was a celebration of the women of East Harlem and served as a platform for sharing their stories of resilience and empowerment through art and community building.

What Was the Motivation for Gathering Community Together?

As part of the Create Change Fellowship in Harlem, four fellows from the Laundromat Project[1]—Rahviance Beme, Vanessa Cuervo (the author of this piece), Autumn Robinson, and Terence Trouillot decided to work closely with the community of East Harlem to address issues concerning women of color. In partnership with the local organizations: Violence Intervention Program (VIP), East Harlem Preservation (EHP), El Museo del Barrio, and performance artist Francheska Alcantara, we organized a series of events and workshops to augment the continued efforts of the East Harlem community to eulogize and celebrate the strength and courage of women of color.

Why Did We Choose to Focus Our Efforts on the Sims Statue?

In 1894, German artist Ferdinand Freiherr von Miller designed the first statue depicting Dr. James Marion Sims. Erected in Bryant Park, New York City, this monument was meant to honor a physician who is often called the "father of modern gynecology." The statue was later moved to Central Park, facing the New York Academy of Medicine, at the corner of Fifth Ave and 103rd Street. The existence of this statue in East Harlem—a predominantly Latino and African American neighborhood—raises many questions.

Dr. Marion Sims has been credited with developing some of the earliest forms of gynecologic instruments, such as the speculum. His most significant work was to develop a surgical technique for the repair of vesicovaginal fistula, a severe complication of obstructed childbirth that affected many young women.[2] Although he is continually praised by academics for this surgical breakthrough, it is rarely acknowledged that Sims's success came as a result of his experimentation on enslaved African American women. Sims operated on these women dozens of times without their consent and without anesthesia. These procedures were unethical and have been described as "a prime example of progress in the medical profession made at the expense of a vulnerable population."[3]

His journals show records of how Dr. Sims would buy these enslaved women specifically for the purpose of operating and experimenting on them.[4] This is how we know the names of three of these women: Anarcha, Betsy, and Lucy. In her book *Medical Apartheid* (2006), Harriet Washington explains that the historical silence and absence of record about Sims's victims illuminates the uncredited and unrecognized role that black bodies have in the medical and scientific landscape. Despite historians' revelation of these unethical and grotesque experiments, Sims's techniques are often defended by white medical professionals as the "practices of the time."[5]

Because slavery was so embedded in the landscape and culture of the Confederate states of the South, a legacy of silencing black voices is still reflected in their monuments and continues to be at the center of many debates about memorialization. However, northern states have not done nearly as much examination of their troubling racist legacy, although there is also much to grapple with. New York City is the most diverse city in the world; yet studies have pointed out that communities within the city are still largely segregated along racial and ethnic lines.[6]

As historians continue to uncover the deplorable intersection of medicine, race, and experimentation, these issues become more visible, and so does the pushback and rejection of the positive commemoration of controversial individuals and events. The presence of Marion Sims's statue reflects the prolonged complexity of race within the public landscape of a city as diverse and important as New York City.

In 2011, after consulting with members of the community, our partners at East Harlem Preservation requested that the statue be removed. New York City Parks Department bluntly responded that it was not the policy of the city to *"remove art retroactively on the basis of content."* The solution they proposed was to add language that would recognize the controversial nature of Dr. Sims's legacy. This response seemed to directly ignore that the statue is a symbol of a history of violation of human rights that persist even today, affecting every day the communities that inhabit this neighborhood.

In the series of workshops that we facilitated for a group of predominantly Latina women from VIP Mujeres—an organization that supports victims of sexual and domestic violence—the statue proved to be a point of departure to discover how women's sexual and reproductive rights continue to be violated in the present. In order to build and strengthen a support network for these women from Central and South America and the Caribbean, we held creative workshops centered on healing and celebrating new opportunities. These workshops included theater, crafts, and plenty of story sharing that allowed the participants to process their trauma and experience in several ways. One of the central themes was their role as mothers and experiencing maternity away from their home, far from their families, and within a health system that continues to be very violent. As women shared their stories, we started noticing a clear pattern in which a vast majority of these women, who had survived violence at home, also had a story about bad experiences with doctors and medical institutions in the United States. Many of them talked about doctors claiming that their babies were not moving enough and suggesting abortions; some were diagnosed as carrying babies with a malformation or with Down syndrome and also advised to terminate their pregnancies, only to find out, once their babies were born, that they were actually healthy. One of them, who had seven children, shared with the group how her doctor even expressed that "she already had enough children, and that it wouldn't be wise to have the one she was pregnant with." With assenting reactions and head nodding, many women were surprised to find out how common and collective an experience that they battled with in isolation and were ashamed to share could be. We did not consider these stories as mere coincidences, but rather as reaffirmations of how in the contemporary United States, women's reproductive rights continue to be violated, and systematic population control policies continue to target women of color, especially immigrants.

Actions in the Community to Protest the Sims statue

After working closely with and deeply listening to the community, going to meetings, holding workshops, and attending local events, we decided to hold a speak-out against the J. Marion Sims monument called "NOT OUR STATUE: Speak Out in Solidarity for the Reproductive Rights of Women of Color." The speak-out was led by Marina Ortiz, founder and president of East Harlem Preservation. The event aimed to bring public attention to the history of this controversial figure and to broadcast the community's continued effort to speak out against the statue. As a monument that does not reflect the identity and culture of East Harlem, but one that represents a constant reminder of the atrocities of slavery and a legacy of violence against women of color, the Sims statue was an apt target for this event. Throughout the speak-out, Francheska Alcantara commemorated the unknown and known women (we only know the names of three of the women who were experimented on by J. Marion Sims—Anarcha, Betsy, and Lucy) through an engaging performance.[7]

We also hosted a quilt-making workshop with the women of Violence Intervention Program (VIP) at El Museo del Barrio. As part of VIP's continued collaboration with Monument Quilt Project, the workshop promoted a space for healing and for remembering those who have been impacted by sexual and domestic violence. The space also exhibited part of the existing quilt made previously by the women of VIP and other artworks by VIP Mujeres created through the series of workshops facilitated in preparation for this event. This was also intended to serve as a space to share women's stories and celebrate the community of East Harlem.

This experience confirmed that community work is most effective when those engaging in it are truly committed and connected to the community, in a way that builds real, strong, and healthy relationships. This can only happen over time and requires a lot of base building and "sweat" equity, which means hours of sharing activities that are quotidian and informal. Superficial quantitative research and mapping can never be as effective as this sort of deep engagement with community.

The value of feeling empowered in public spaces and the importance of taking over a physical space—especially in these hyperdigital times—tends to be exceedingly underestimated. It is one thing to share your story and create an artwork among those close to you, but when stories and art are brought into a public light and shared with a large general audience, the effect it has on those who created it is profoundly transformative. Seeing the VIP Mujeres and other community members participating at the speak-out was a reminder that social change does not always have to involve dramatic revictimization and political rhetoric—sometimes an honest, live, and bright celebration of resilience is more effective for everyone involved.

A monument or a statue can be the gateway to promote education and continued discussion on issues including racialized health disparities, consent, reproductive health, memory, and the rectification of the erasure and elision of historical injustices. This project aimed at promoting gender and racial healing, dialogue, and understanding in East Harlem. The debate about Dr. Sims's statue is one example among many sites of controversial memorialization, and this was our way of exploring the ways in which communities can come together to solve complex issues. Although each context is different, we hope this example can open new pathways to deal with other community issues.

About Our Partners

East Harlem Preservation

East Harlem Preservation (EHP) is a volunteer advocacy organization founded in 2005 to preserve and promote the neighborhood's history and culture. EHP provides news and updates on large-scale development, displacement, and other issues of public concern to residents and stakeholders in East Harlem/El Barrio and surrounding areas. EHP first became involved in the campaign to remove the statue in 2007 when it learned of a hand petition that was being circulated in Harlem by Viola Plummer soon after the publication of Harriet Washington's book, *Medical Apartheid*. EHP endorsed the campaign immediately because it agreed that the statue was an affront to the predominantly black and Latino community of East Harlem. African Americans and Puerto Ricans, in particular, have historically been subjected to medical experiments without permission and regard for their health.[8] Notable examples include the Tuskegee experiments[9] and the forced sterilization of Puerto Rican women.[10] The heinous repercussions of the eugenics movement of the early twentieth century fell most heavily on women, individuals with disabilities, and racial minorities in the United States.[11]

As a part of its continual efforts to highlight East Harlem's unique cultural history, EHP regularly conducts educational walking tours, public forums, and film screenings. Their core of volunteers include local artists, photographers, filmmakers, writers, and community organizers. Working in a predominantly Latino and African American neighborhood, EHP also aims to focus on the important contributions these groups have made to the cultural and political landscape of the neighborhood and New York City as a whole. The organization also maintains an electronic library of photographs and documents relating to East Harlem that is used by educators and other institutions.

East Harlem Preservation has been a partner in several community events including the Annual Brides March to draw attention to victims of domestic violence, the renaming of East 111th Street as Young Lords Way to honor the Puerto Rican nationalist group, and an ongoing campaign to preserve the historic murals on East Harlem streets.

VIP Mujeres

Since 1984, Violence Intervention Program (VIP) has helped women lead healthy, safe, and productive lives while advocating for systems and policies that protect all victims of abuse and violence. VIP believes that access to culturally competent services that support self-determination empower survivors to meet any challenge ahead. Its mission is to lead Latina victims of domestic abuse to safety, to empower them to live violence-free lives, and to help them reach and sustain their full potential. VIP pursues this mission by raising community awareness, engaging in activism, and providing culturally competent services.

El Museo del Barrio

El Museo del Barrio was founded forty-five years ago by artist and educator Raphael Montañez Ortiz and a coalition of parents, educators, artists, and activists who noted that mainstream museums largely ignored Latino artists. Since its inception, El Museo has been committed to celebrating and promoting Latino culture, thus becoming a cornerstone of El Barrio and a valuable resource for New York City. Through its extensive collections, varied exhibitions and publications, bilingual public programs, educational activities, festivals, and special events, El Museo educates its diverse public in the richness of Caribbean and Latin American arts and cultural history.

TELLING THE WHOLE STORY

EDUCATION AND INTERPRETATION IN SUPPORT OF *#1 IN CIVIL RIGHTS: THE AFRICAN AMERICAN FREEDOM STRUGGLE IN ST. LOUIS*

ELIZABETH PICKARD

> Some of our history is problematic, some of our history is troubling, some of it causes elation and is very positive. But it's all history. And I think you have to tell the story. You have to tell the whole story—the good, the bad, the ugly.
>
> —Gwen Moore, curator for Missouri History Center's *#1 in Civil Rights* exhibit

magine, if you will, a man on a horse. It is almost always a man, and he is certainly white. It is a statue of a white man on a horse carved in stone or cast in bronze, much larger than life size, commanding the landscape from on top of the plinth upon which it has been positioned for the better part of a century. He fought and lost a war that was over long before his monument was raised. His name may no longer even be familiar, but the very bulk and presence of the monument says to the viewer, "Look at this! This is what matters! This is what happened! This is what is important!"

Of course, no single statue, no one monument can contain the whole story of a person or of a moment in time. The story of the man on the horse is inherently incomplete. Who put him there and why? Who wanted him there and who did not? During his life, who shod the horse and mucked out its stall? Who did the work, and what were the conditions of the society that allowed that man to rise to horse ownership, wealth, education, and prominence? Who carried on the work at home while he was horsing around? Whom did he kill? Who marched in the mud and heat and cold at his command? Who followed his orders? Who did not? Who stood against him? Whom does he still inspire? Who resisted, endured, persisted, and thrived in spite of his best efforts?

These questions and the stories that help provide answers are essential to understanding our past and our present. History museums have the great good fortune to be able to ask these questions, to explore the answers from multiple perspectives, and to do so in greater depth than a statue allows. We have the opportunity to bring long-overshadowed stories to light. Those of us who work in museum education and interpretation are especially well positioned to do this critical work because we do not necessarily have to wait for an exhibition to change to begin interpreting this history. This is especially critical in matters of racism and white supremacy, where the white supremacists have the statues and those whom they oppressed go largely unmemorialized.

#1 in Civil Rights: The African American Freedom Struggle in St. Louis

There are, of course, challenges inherent in bringing such narratives forward. We encountered several of these in the development of the Missouri History Museum's *#1 in Civil Rights: The African American Freedom*

Struggle in St. Louis exhibit and its accompanying educational and inter-pretive programming.

First, the incredibly rich and important history of struggle in St. Louis had been largely unrecognized and its scope has not been perceived, even by knowledgeable visitors. Second, while the Missouri Historical Society (which operates the museum) was founded in 1866, its collecting of artifacts linked to African American history has largely been a recent effort. Many of the artifacts that are in the collection are two-dimensional documents and oral histories or have been very recently accessioned as part of the Ferguson Collecting Initiative. This collecting initiative began after an unarmed black teenager named Michael Brown was killed by a white police officer in Ferguson, Missouri, in 2014—sparking months of protests locally and around the country.[1] The sheer volume of Ferguson artifacts and the controversy surrounding the events themselves posed a third challenge.

Ferguson forced a reimagining of the scope of the exhibit, which had been under development since 2013 and had initially been intended to end chronologically with the year 1968. After Ferguson, however, it was clear to the exhibit team that the museum had to include those events in *#1 in Civil Rights*. This posed a unique set of interpretive and educational challenges. How might we interpret history that is still unfolding?

While the Ferguson initiative brought in a flood of artifacts, many earlier moments in the African American freedom struggle were unrep-resented by three-dimensional artifacts because of the Missouri Histori-cal Society's earlier collecting choices. This created a risk of imbalance in the exhibit, which contains fewer than twenty three-dimensional objects in a 3,000-square-foot exhibition. Yet the exhibit's narrative and the his-tory it encompasses is remarkable and complex—it begins with a pro-test opposing the Missouri Compromise in 1819. Then it moves through freedom suits, the Dred Scott decision, successful streetcar boycotts and integration in the 1870s, the March on Washington movement in the 1940s, lunch counter sit-ins beginning in 1944, the *Shelley v. Kraemer* housing discrimination Supreme Court case in 1948, employment pro-tests at Jefferson Bank in 1963—and much more. Despite the wealth of stories and important incidents regarding St. Louis's connection to civil rights, because of a dearth of three-dimensional objects, the museum struggled to determine how to convey the importance of these efforts in the exhibit.

The interpretation and weighting of the exhibit was further complicated by how little known this essential history was in the region. Curator Gwen Moore often encountered the statement "I didn't think St. Louis had a civil rights movement" when giving talks in the community. It was also not uncommon to hear this viewpoint expressed by pundits on the national news during the height of events in Ferguson. The leaders of the struggle in St. Louis, with few notable exceptions, were not household names. How might we honor our region's leaders in the struggle for equality and put their work in a national context?

The museum addressed these challenges and questions through innovative creation and use of exhibit content, interpretive strategies, educational methods, and incorporation of community voices. The next section will explore how these techniques combined to bring the story of civil rights in St. Louis all the way up to the present.

Art, Media, and Museum Theater

> The Negro knocks at America's door and cries, "Let me come in and sit by the fire. I helped build the house."
>
> —George L. Vaughn, oral arguments
> before the U.S. Supreme Court, 1948

In dealing with the challenge of a lack of three-dimensional artifacts and how to honor St. Louis's leaders, the museum used audio/video resources, artwork, and museum theater to give attention to people and events with no artifacts associated with them. The exhibit makes strong use of recorded material. To interpret leaders from the nineteenth century, actors excerpted, read, and recorded written documents. Actors represented twentieth-century leaders mostly through audio recordings. In a few cases, the museum had recent audio/video recordings and collected some new ones as well. Thus, listening stations were present throughout the exhibition, not just in the most recent sections, giving voice to centuries of struggle. Second, the museum commissioned local African American artists to paint portraits and create multimedia pieces honoring many of the leaders and events featured in the exhibit. This includes a large mural commemorating collective struggle. Much of the artwork will eventually become part of the collection of the Missouri Historical Society.

Museum theater also plays an integral part in the exhibit experience. The exhibit portrays a living, breathing movement. What could be more suitable than doing so with living, breathing people? Thanks to a major grant from the Institute of Museum and Library Services,[2] the ACTivists Project allows the museum to staff the gallery with actor-interpreters for most of its open hours, a major expansion of the museum theater program. The actor-interpreters perform short, five- to seven-minute plays about twentieth-century leaders. These portrayals include such luminaries as George L. Vaughn, the lawyer who argued the *Shelley v. Kraemer* case at the U.S. Supreme Court; Margaret Bush Wilson, the first African American woman to lead the NAACP; David Grant, a leader in the March on Washington movement during World War II; Pearl Maddox, who spearheaded lunch counter sit-ins in 1944; Kathryn Johnson, who traveled to St. Louis in 1916 to organize the local NAACP; and Billie Teneau, who in 1948 helped found St. Louis's CORE chapter.[3] These characterizations both celebrate St. Louis's leaders and link our community's history to the national story through recognizable national events like World War II and the Double Victory campaign, or

Peggy Harris portraying Margaret Bush Wilson for an adult group. Courtesy of the Missouri History Museum.

Linda Kennedy portraying Pearl Maddox next to a portrait of Pearl Maddox commissioned for the exhibit. Courtesy of the Missouri History Museum.

the later, but better-known, sit-ins to protest segregation in Greensboro and elsewhere.[4]

Visitors are visibly, emotionally moved when they hear the ACTivists' stories "first hand," in real time. Theater provokes emotional responses in a way that few other interpretive techniques can and for a few minutes brings the past to the presence of the audience. One visitor said, "I've lived in St. Louis most of my life, but the history depicted here was hardly taught. I am white—saw the discrimination first hand—but wasn't schooled to understand the poison of racism—the real brutality of it. This is a powerful exhibit—and the actor was a wonderful addition. We're not in a postracial America—it's critically important that these messages continue to be shared."

For school groups on field trips, the ACTivists perform the *Imagine Play*. This piece invites students to learn songs sung at the Jefferson Bank protests for fair employment practices in 1963. From this performance, students get a strong sense of how the songs united protesters, helped them to hold firm, and to feel less alone in their struggle. Remarkably, even the most reluctant or shy students prove willing to sing, and the fact that young people continued the protests when the older leaders were arrested clearly resonates with them.

The ACTivists also perform outreach visits to local classrooms. For these visits, the performers deliver a forty-five-minute lesson. The experience includes a twenty-minute performance in which they introduce nineteenth-century civil rights leaders. Women portray Lucy Delaney, who won a freedom suit as a teenage girl, and men portray Charlton Tandy, who in the 1870s successfully integrated St. Louis's public transit system through a combination of court action, boycott, protest, and direct action that would be familiar to civil rights strategists a century later.[5] The museum developed these visits to be a pre–field trip activity. Since St. Louis's civil rights history has been scarcely acknowledged, the outreach lesson plan goes deep. It begins by introducing the idea of what civil rights are, how individuals can stand up for what they believe in, and explores the fact that the civil rights movement did not begin and end with Dr. Martin Luther King Jr., but rather is a long and important chain of events, linking the distant past to the present moment. Students who have an ACTivist visit prior to coming to the museum for a field trip demonstrate good recall of the performance. One student was even able to pick out Charlton Tandy on a timeline and then sing the song the actor sings during the play. The ACTivists outreach visit has also expanded the effectiveness of the exhibit by reaching students whose districts have no field trip funding. In one district, the ACTivists performed for nearly one thousand students who would have otherwise had no access to the exhibit content with their classes due to barriers to visiting the museum such as bus availability and cost.

Educational Strategies

The museum's K–12 Education team saw the lack of three-dimensional artifacts in the *#1 in Civil Rights* exhibit as an opportunity to ask students to examine a museum's choices over time. One of the three big ideas for the K–12 guided tour says, "Different artifacts hold different perspectives about historical events; it is the job of a historian to use many different kinds of artifacts to piece together the whole story." We ask students to record the kinds of artifacts they see in the Ferguson section of the exhibit and to start thinking about what stories are told by the artifact, and what stories are left out. We ask older students to consider why there are more and different kinds of artifacts for Ferguson than for other parts of the exhibit.

In order to situate St. Louis's civil rights history in the national narrative, the K–12 team and the ACTivists outreach visit include a simple but very effective timeline. At the top are "landmark" national events like the American Civil War, the Great Depression, World War II, and Barack Obama's inauguration, an event that some of our K–12 students are too young to remember but still can connect to because they remember President Obama. In the middle are the "greatest hits" of the national civil rights movement: *Brown v. Board of Education of Topeka* in 1954; the Montgomery Boycott in 1955; the "I Have a Dream" speech at the March on Washington in 1963; and the passage of the Civil Rights Act in 1964. At the bottom are St. Louis's civil rights landmarks from 1819 to the present day. Most of our students do recognize and remember Ferguson. With just a few minutes of looking at it, the timeline explodes the idea that the civil rights movement started in 1954 and ended in 1968, or that it existed only in the Deep South.

Dialogue is also an essential piece of the exhibit experience and educational programs. The entire approach to Ferguson in the exhibit is fueled by asking visitors what it means to them, whether they see it as a movement or as a moment, and by inviting them to leave their thoughts on a response wall. As part of the museum's interpretive training, the ACTivists and museum educators received in-depth information and strategies for cultivating dialogic interpretation from the International Coalition of Sites of Conscience prior to the exhibit's opening. The emphasis on action in the dialogic arc was particularly helpful. For K–12 programs, we give students examples of ways ACTivist historical figures stood up for themselves—by speaking out, sharing their stories, staying strong, or asking for help. We then invite students to think about a situation they want to address in their own communities and to brainstorm how they can use these same approaches. Adult tours are also based on dialogue and the desire to privilege the voices in the exhibition over

Peggy Harris performing the *Imagine Play* at the Missouri History Museum. Courtesy of the Missouri History Museum.

those of our guides. Adults are asked how the stories in the exhibit call to them, what they will leave thinking about, and what they would tell others about their experiences.

Community Voices

As has been well documented by Melanie Adams in her essay titled "Working to Address Community Needs" published in *Positioning Your Museum as a Critical Community Asset: A Practical Guide*, the Missouri History Museum's work with community organizations around issues of race and equity goes back several years through its Community Collaborators program (formerly called the Community Partners program).[6] This strong foundation meant that the museum became a space for difficult dialogue when the region was thrust into months of protests following the killing of Michael Brown. Happily, the programming around the *#1 in Civil Rights* exhibit has continued that work.

We drew some of the members of the exhibit's advisory committee from our preexisting community collaborator group. Community programs on race, policing, equity, and activism have been integral to the offerings at the museum during the exhibit's run, and they will continue long after its close as part of the museum's commitment to bringing these essential conversations to the fore.

The museum is also fortunate to have as part of its staff a group of talented local students in the Teens Make History program who bring the voice of the teen community to the table. The Teens Make History Players have researched, written, and performed dozens of plays in conjunction with the museum's exhibitions over the ten years of the program's existence. Many of the plays have focused on African American and civil rights history. As part of the gallery programming in *#1 in Civil Rights*, they are performing examples from this body of work every Saturday. Teens in the program wrote one of the plays—*#NextHashtag*—at the time of Michael Brown's death. The play focused on their own fears and concerns, and on what they wished others understood about being an African American teen in St. Louis in 2014. When the Teens Make History Players first performed the play, it ran thirteen minutes but often sparked conversations that ran for forty-five minutes. It brought a seldom-heard voice at that time into the light. The play's central question was "Will I be the next #hashtag?" In other words, will I be the next unarmed teen shot and killed? The teens performed *#NextHashtag* in *#1 in Civil Rights* both as representative of that moment in time, written as it was in August 2014, and as an example of how the question of policing in black communities and the struggle against violence continues.

The teens also drew strong connections between themselves and a group of activist artists who worked in St. Louis in the 1960s and 1970s in their play *BAG Then/BAG Now.* The Black Artists' Group, or BAG, promoted black artists, protested horrific living conditions in the city's Pruitt Igoe housing project, and supported Black Power.[7] The teens wrote a play that drew comparisons between the present and the past, and celebrated both—and described themselves as the next BAG. One audience member said they would leave the play thinking about "how youth can reach across generations without offending, but instead [can] open communication." This is often just what happens when the teens perform. Opening such dialogue is critical to the success of the exhibition and the programs that will continue beyond its run.

> This is our history, and this is our legacy and it is something we can be proud of. And I don't think it should be ignored anymore.
>
> —Gwen Moore

No doubt there are challenges for cultural institutions in illuminating histories that have been overshadowed, minimized, or ignored for too long. It is essential that we do the work to address underrepresentation and rise to those challenges with creativity and innovation. By listening and making room for voices that have been too long unheard, we can truly tell the whole story.

PROJECT SAY SOMETHING'S *WHOSE MONUMENT* PROJECT

NOT TEARING DOWN HISTORY, BUT BUILDING UP HOPE

BRIAN MURPHY

Like many cities in the U.S. South, Florence, Alabama, is reluctant to discuss its history of racial inequality. In fact, the Tennessee River Valley prides itself on a history of interracial cooperation that coalesces around its music history: black and white musicians famously recorded together in the early 1960s at FAME music studio.[1] Yet this narrative tends to stifle meaningful dialogue about race and racism in an area that also experienced slavery and segregation and that continues to struggle with racial disparities in the present. When rioting and racial unrest rocked Ferguson, Missouri, in 2015, Camille Goldston Bennett created Project Say Something (PSS) to begin a community conversation about the legacy of racial injustice in Florence. Project Say Something's mission is to "unify, educate, heal, and empower communities in the mid-south to realize social justice through non-violent communication and direct action against racism, poverty and related forms of oppression." Since 2015, the organization has held numerous panel discussions and documentary screenings, has organized vigils around national tragedies, instituted a police citizens' advisory council, and has been awarded several grants for its history initiatives.

The process has been difficult in Florence, a city that prefers to avoid conflict by sweeping it under the rug. "Nothing happened here" is a familiar refrain that both white and black residents repeat about the civil rights movement—or lack thereof—in Florence. Residents are happy to distinguish themselves from the violence and chaos that characterized Birmingham and Montgomery during the civil rights movement, although reluctant to discuss the price of peace. PSS regularly urges the community to engage in dialogues about race that are awakening yet painful, frustrating yet productive. These conversations set the foundation for PSS's Confederate monument campaign, which has begun a prickly community dialogue about Civil War memory culminating in a monument that all community members could be proud of. PSS hopes that the monument campaign can be a blueprint for similar cities across the South to engage in meaningful dialogue about their memorialized past and, most important, the vision for the future they wish to leave for the next generation.

The Confederate monument that stands in front of the Lauderdale County courthouse in downtown Florence is an exemplary model of Lost Cause nostalgia. Carved on the base of the statue are the words "*Deo Vindice,*" the motto of the Confederate States of America, Latin for "God will vindicate." Below this are the words "*In Memory of the Confederate dead from Lauderdale County, Florence, Alabama.*" Further below are the following inscriptions: "*The manner of their death was the crowning glory of their lives,*" and "*Glory stands beside our grief.*" The statue guards the courthouse and serves as a reminder of Florence's power structure. The city, settled in 1818, has an African American population of 20 percent. The first African American city department head (out of forty-one total) was appointed just three years ago. Few of the city's police officers, and none of its judges and lawyers, are African American. Black citizens rarely patronize thriving Court Street, the main downtown commercial corridor. African Americans make up 93 percent of the West Florence neighborhood, where the poverty rate is a staggering 77 percent. The Confederate monument outside the building charged with upholding justice is a symbolic representation of the power imbalance in Lauderdale County.

In digging into Florence's racial history, PSS members noted the lack of African American heritage represented in both the physical landscape and the city's written narrative. To address this issue, PSS applied for and was awarded a community grant from the Muscle Shoals National Heritage Area. The grant, in which Project Say Something partnered with the Florence-Lauderdale Public Library, with help from the University of North Alabama's Public History program, collects pieces of local African American history in the Shoals area. Community members donate artifacts such as photographs, documents, and oral histories, which are then digitized, curated, and included on a website hosted by the public library. Other outcomes of the project include an educator's resource packet, a public presentation, and the incorporation of local artifacts into the city's bicentennial celebration and timeline in 2018.

While PSS was trying to write African Americans back into the historical narrative of Florence, the state of Alabama was cementing the legacy of the Confederacy to its landscape. In May 2017, the Alabama state legislature passed the Alabama Memorial Preservation Act, effectively banning the removal of all monuments on public property more than forty years old. PSS began to explore ways to address the legislation protecting a memorial that undermines the narrative of racial cooperation on which northwest Alabama tends to pride itself.

In the wake of this legislation, Project Say Something began to conceive of a year-long campaign to educate residents about the existing monument, collaborate with community members on seeking to provide context to the monument, and, ultimately, raise money to place a new, inclusive monument in front of the Lauderdale County Courthouse opposite the Confederate memorial. PSS applied for and was awarded an "art for justice" grant from the Fringe Foundation to launch the Confederate memorial reimagining campaign in June 2017. The campaign would engage the residents of Florence in a conversation about its racial past, present, and future.

Spurred also into action by the violence at Charlottesville in August 2017, PSS struggled over how to unveil the campaign and what it should achieve. Should the new monument address the Confederate monument? Should it represent a single historical figure? Should it be an African American? To help gain broader community input, I approached Dr.

Brian Dempsey at the Public History Center (PHC) at the University of North Alabama (UNA). Dr. Dempsey, director of the PHC, along with graduate assistants Sarah Harbin and Stephanie Vickers, designed the anonymous "Florence Community Confederate Monument Survey" as another research method to access and engage with diverse perspectives and to generate data that academics and community organizations may use for better-informed community outreach and dialogue. The survey is administered via Qualtrics, a digital survey platform, and consists of basic questions that assess Florence community perceptions of the Confederate monument. The PHC launched this project to work in parallel with Project Say Something here in the Shoals, but it can also be replicated for community dialogue in other places. As a tool for public historians seeking to gain more specific data related to individual perception of monuments, anonymous online surveys that reach individuals may yield vital information not otherwise accessible through public contexts alone. The surveys themselves also served as community conversation starters.

PSS debated how to address the Confederate monument's indebtedness to white supremacy. Local research uncovered the dedication speech that was read at the unveiling of the monument. The keynote speaker, Dr. H. A. Moody, a local physician, extols the virtues of the Lost Cause triumphalist hero-making of the Confederate soldier before launching into a diatribe against the North's notions of racial equality. The speaker claimed the North "looks upon a Negro as a white man with a colored skin and believe[s] education to be the one thing needful. We of the south know better. No other people know him so well or love him so well, but nowhere here is he accorded social equality." These words were spoken moments before thirteen white schoolchildren, each representing a state that fought for the Confederacy, pulled down the white veil covering the statue of a Confederate soldier in front of nearly five thousand people at the courthouse—the newspaper described it as a "moment of enthusiastic rejoicing."[2]

The speech provided a powerful launching pad for the campaign. PSS filmed a short video with community members—white and black, male and female, young and old—each reciting a line of this speech, ending with a call to participate in a town hall meeting.[3] The video accomplished its goal of starting a dialogue about the monument. Our vision was to open a wound in our community's past with the ultimate purpose of healing. We sought to create a process of reconciliation through which the community could envision a new monument together. White community members reported via social media that they believed the speech was somehow taken "out of context." African American community members felt that it proved what they had suspected all along: Confederate monuments justify and perpetuate white supremacy. The conversation had begun.

The video was deliberately provocative, but no matter how unifying the outcome, detractors were inevitable. The Florence newspaper ran a story about the project in which invited panelists were quoted extensively.[4] The article also captured the feelings of the local chapter of the Sons of Confederate Veterans. Responses to the article on social media were mixed. Many of the members on the PSS Facebook page expressed excitement over the project. Others responded to the article on the newspaper's Facebook page with overwhelmingly negative comments. A local heritage group launched a counter-video, featuring a montage of Confederate monuments across the South, displayed over the Confederate flag while the song "Dixie" played in the background. Many still seemed to think that the campaign wanted to take the statue down. The debate over Confederate monuments is so divisive that we often presume all dialogue surrounding Confederate monuments entails removal.

The town hall event was standing-room only because of the buzz generated by the video and the newspaper article. Panelists included a white female history professor, an African American female business owner, an African American male pastor, and myself, a white male graduate student in public history (and PSS board member). PSS founder Camille Bennett served as moderator. Each panelist spoke about the Confederate monument, contextualizing the era in which it was built, opining on why it was built, and speaking to what it represents to African American community members. Afterward, discussion was opened to the audience for questions and comments. Audience members were respectful and civil, following the tone set by the panelists and moderator. There was some dissension over the meaning of the monument from several local historians. White community members listened to their black neighbors' concerns over the Confederate monument. This shift in power was important; white citizens are rarely obligated to listen to the concerns of black citizens in a public forum.

The most important takeaway PSS gained from the first town hall event was that the history of slavery, the Civil War, and Reconstruction were not being taught effectively in many local schools. Several educators raised concerns over the inadequacy of school textbooks, the avoidance of slavery as a cause of the war, and the prevalence of Lost Cause rhetoric that exists in Alabama classrooms. This lack of education has dangerous consequences. Much of the fallout from the first event proved mild, but threats were directed at the black female panelist and moderator, both of whom dared to question the statue's purpose. Both women claimed it was erected to intimidate African Americans, though neither advocated for its removal. One of the female panelists suggested a statue to an African American congressman from Florence. She later received a letter threatening violence if a statue "to a black" should be erected in front of the courthouse. Merely questioning the memorial landscape of the Confederacy can lead to vehement, anonymous, and threatening rebuttals.

PSS decided to hold an additional meeting in an African American church to allow community members to voice their ideas about what belongs in the space next to the Confederate memorial. While the first town hall was heavy on panelists, the second meeting was geared toward letting the community speak as much as possible, especially the black community. The second event had a lower turnout, and despite inviting the congregations from two prominent African American churches, the demographics of the event reflected the demographics of the community: about 20 percent African American. From the beginning, the atmosphere of the event was uneasy. Two hostile white men entered the church and, without speaking or making eye contact with other community members, sat in the back of the room and recorded the entire event on their phones, sometimes thrusting their phones into the faces of those speaking. While some community members threw out ideas for the monument, others questioned the project's goals—namely, why Confederate monuments were offensive in the first place. PSS did not do a great job of explaining what exactly its mission was. Some board members wanted to build a monument to justice; others wanted to contextualize the Confederate monument; still others wanted a monument to a prominent African American statesman.

As a public historian and board member, I was in a position to both provide guidance for the project and help solicit community support. Nothing is more important than listening during these public conversations. I heard the defensiveness of white people who did not want to be told that their ancestors may have been racist; I heard African Americans frustrated with the lack of historical accountability. I watched as our community grappled with race in a very public way that seemed like unchartered territory for Florence. As the project goes forward, the next event is planned as a community roundtable to hash out ideas about the new monument and gather support from local leaders, followed by an artist's gathering in which we will solicit and display various renderings of a new monument sketched by local artists.

Most informative were the varied, confusing, and virulently defensive responses we received from white southerners, including those who self-identified as "progressive." Some sought to deflect from the very racial conversation PSS was pursuing: "the north was racist, too"; "Reconstruction was awful"; "my ancestors never owned slaves." Other responses minimized or denied racial inequality altogether: "the war was not about slavery"; "slavery was already waning"; "the cause was noble to them [Confederates]"; "it's not fair that we can't have southern heroes"; "we cannot judge our ancestors." Still others were purely emotional: "you're calling my ancestors racist"; "my property was destroyed in the war"; "we revere our ancestors here." Embedded within these emotional responses was a regionalized and racialized tribalism that expressly ignored the equally impassioned sentiments expressed by our black Southern panelists: "you're not from here, it's not your blood; you can't possibly understand." Each of these justifications motions toward the same imperative, which also functions as a thinly veiled threat: as one retired history professor opined in a newspaper editorial on our town hall gathering, "quit messing with history." The responses we received within a project that proposed building a new monument did not differ from the national responses surrounding monument removal. We have learned that any framing of Confederate monuments as incomplete or insufficient representations of history results in the same series of defensive reactions; hence these reactions that are dressed as arguments against removal, objections to the erasure of history, are really objections to any interrogation of white supremacy.

The monument project is forcing the city of Florence to confront its silence about past and contemporary racial inequality. The community struggles to admit that its past was based on white supremacy; African Americans continue to assert that the present is not too much different from the past. Citizens of Florence continue to argue about the meaning of the Civil War and the place of African Americans in the current era. As we move forward with these questions, it is imperative that PSS remains open to rational dissension, facilitates meaningful dialogue, and pushes community members toward an empathetic understanding of each other and their shared history.

CONCLUSION

C**ontroversial statues** are much more than the stone or metal that they are made of. They are etched with layers of meaning and carved with the deep cuts of transient passions. Their creators and progenitor champions conceive of them with hopes of controlling the story of the past. The people who built the statues chose heroes and crafted their narratives—and their faces—out of the seemingly lasting materials with which they are constructed. Some of these statues may once have been controversial, but they lose relevance over time and fade to obscurity, gradually corroding and wearing away. Others seem to grow in power with the march of time, as they come to symbolize ideas and concepts that become culturally repugnant or politically untenable.

Statues constructed during a time of broad consensus may take years to become controversial. Driven by deep-set grievances that have long festered under powerful systems of cultural and social oppression, strong advocacy against controversial statues usually arises during times of profound change or humiliated disillusionment. Perhaps now is such a time in these United States?

Consider the multitude of conflicts and discord that now intrude upon our lives: We sow divisions wrought by blinkered faith in our own moral rectitude. We cling to the belief that the "other" side is intent on remaking the ship of state into a badly programmed self-driving car, bound to crash into the median of societal ruin and international irrelevance. Our will to listen to each other face-to-face is sapped by the blaring, incessant grind of anonymous social media run amok. Bifurcated news reports cater solely to audiences who trust them to the exclusion of all else, and their self-reinforcing messages allow us to lounge in the comfortable womb of news stories that strengthen our preexisting schemas.[1] Politicians coddled by moneyed elites and corporate bigwigs natter and preen while the people they were elected to serve suffer.

Does all of this mean that a national dialogue and long-overdue reckoning with our troubled past will never materialize? Before we find ourselves in hand-wringing worry and succumb to the inevitability of entropy, we should ask whether the vitriol and ennui is unique to our time. A glance at the past shows that fierce debate and rampant political malfeasance is not, in fact, exceptional. Rancorous politics are nothing new in the United States. A small example from the tumultuous years prior to the Civil War is illustrative.

In May 1856, Charles Sumner, an antislavery Republican senator from Massachusetts, issued a strongly worded diatribe against bringing Kansas into the Union as a slave state. Railing against slavery and those in the Senate who would accommodate it, he took personal aim at two of his fellow senators. Stephen Douglas from Illinois and South Carolina's Andrew Butler became the focus of Sumner's ire as he ridiculed and disparaged both men. Butler's South Carolinian relative Preston Brooks took exception to this affront to his kinsman's honor and viciously attacked Sumner on the floor of the Senate chamber with a metal-topped cane. Bloody and nearly unconscious, Sumner spent months afterward convalescing.[2]

Maybe it's not surprising that this most notorious incident of violence in the halls of government was touched off by a debate about slavery. Chattel slavery in the United States was brutal and violent. Africans were forcibly taken from their homes, separated from all they had ever known, packed into slave ships, and debased and dehumanized in unspeakably gruesome ways.[3] Violence begets more violence and the deep wounds of oppression and the triumphs of resistance to that oppression remain ever present in the United States. White supremacy and racism are millstones that continue to thwart national reconciliation and healing.

The past is rarely truly behind us. It lives on because we refuse to live unmoored from the world we know and the trusted (or reviled) voices of

The brutal caning of Charles Sumner on the floor of the Senate during the tense years leading up to the Civil War revealed both the acrimony of politics and the deep divisions between antislavery and proslavery advocates. John Henry Bufford and Winslow Homer. *Argument of the Chivalry*, 1856. Courtesy of the Library of Congress.

our forebearers. The prerogatives and passions of our predecessors have left us with a landscape changed and molded to what they perceived to be important and worthy of commemoration. This is as it should be. The tragedy of forgetting is that when our memories fade, we lose our connections to that which we love and value. For an individual with Alzheimer's disease, the world becomes a haze of disconnected experiences, blurred memories, and confused moments divorced from reality. Likewise, our world is thrown into disarray and chaos when the ascendant present and our nightmares of a dystopian future cause us to forget and suppress instead of to remember and reflect.

This book has explored the many ways that remembrance and reflection can draw us closer to healing and true reconciliation with the past.

- We heard from Modupe Labode about how the triumvirate concerns of race, power, and history that animate discussions about controversial monuments should be the spur for museums to open difficult discussions in their communities.
- The article reprinted from *Civil War Times*—"Empty Pedestals: What Should Be Done with Civic Monuments to the Confederacy and Its

Leaders?"—shared a wide range of opinions about what to do with Confederate statues. From this article, we learn that there are no simple answers for the final destiny of these contested monuments.

• New Orleans mayor Mitch Landrieu's speech from May 2017 brought an alternative approach to civic pride that hearkens to the pluralism and shared cultural traits of residents of the Crescent City as a basis for combating the history of white supremacy and slavery that Confederate statues represent.

• W. Todd Groce called for a reintegration of history and the humanities as vital to contextualizing STEM education in our schools. He also provided a valiant defense of historical revisionism.

• Gerard Baker shared how new stories and perspectives coupled with bold leadership focused on building bridges transformed the historical narratives at the Little Bighorn Battlefield National Monument.

• Elizabeth Pickard highlighted the Missouri History Museum's ACTivists and their community work in response to Ferguson to show how museums can be relevant to the societal issues that concern our world today. She explained how critical partnerships were the ballast that kept activism steady in the face of competing pressures and influences.

• Benjamin Wright related the story of a reinterpretation of Confederate statues through an exhibit at the Briscoe Center at University of Texas and how new stories have the chance to emerge when they are given room in the dialogue-enhancing halls of museums.

• Linda Norris brought international intentionality to her case study as a way to emphasize the many ways that sensitive historic sites can seek to promote national healing.

• Jill Ogline Titus's chapter about monuments at Gettysburg uncovered the close tie between the civil rights movement and statues to the Confederacy. She also explored how Cold War politics drove a reimaging of the memorials at that battlefield.

• F. Sheffield Hale provided a detailed recounting of how the Atlanta History Center threw its weight behind a comprehensive effort to explore how white supremacy has provided enduring power to Confederate statues in Georgia.

• Using History Colorado as a case study, JJ Lonsinger Rutherford discussed the benefits derived from deep community engagement around difficult history that results in exhibits that not only honor but also celebrate the people involved in momentous historical events.

- Art as activism enlivened Vanessa Cuervo Forero's chapter about the Laundromat Project's work in partnership with a variety of organizations to share alternative perspectives from a community in opposition to dominant historical narratives embodied in a statue of J. Marion Sims.

- Jose Zuniga delved into *The Simpsons* to reveal the ways that popular culture can lay bare our own self-seriousness and desire for approbation and the many ways that history and tradition can be used as a cudgel to beat our communities into submission to a single, narrow narrative about the past.

- George W. McDaniel used his experiences as a veteran of the Vietnam War to show how changing cultural values can warp and distort the comradery and patriotism of brothers in arms.

- The border state of Kentucky received a thorough exploration of its Confederate history from Stuart Sanders, and the case study he shared about the fates of two statues in Lexington provided an example of a path to removal for communities across the south.

- William Walker's glance at Theodore Roosevelt's life and legacy illuminated the multiplicity of strong opinions and contested interpretation that has made the equestrian statue of Roosevelt outside the American Museum of Natural History so contentious in New York City.

- Julian C. Chambliss sketched the borders of Confederate iconography and proposed radical new ways to use art to thwart symbols of oppression.

- Brian Murphy explored how Project Say Something's community conversations in Alabama focused on access to services, economic inequality, and social justice through the lens of historical recontextualization and with the strong engagement of public historians.

- Thomas Seabrook's chapter about monument-building and the United Daughters of the Confederacy in Virginia during the World War I era showcased the intricate layers of gender, politics, and race that motivated the construction of these statues honoring Confederate leaders and soldiers.

As these case studies and essays have shown, museums and historic sites can be at the forefront of the work of reconciliation and healing in partnership with community. And, of course, museums and historic sites would not function without the efforts of the individuals who have committed their time and energy to them. We must start by transforming *ourselves*—you'll notice that I am not calling for some vague, impersonal concept of institutional or organizational change—to be open to partaking in deep community engagement. We must meet expressed community needs, instead of forcing community to hew to our own image.[4] We must carefully and cogently contextualize the past to illuminate new paths forward built on a solid foundation of trust.

When we stop to listen and shed our preconceived ideas, we discover what truly matters and can get to the difficult task of positively building into the lives of others through our work and avocations. Each of us—whether we are honchos in the board rooms, front-line staff meeting and greeting guests on a daily basis, or community activists pushing for change—can give the gift of time and active listening to clear out the noisome angst of clamorous, ill-informed opinions and subjective judgments harshly rendered. Having an opinion is easy. It is much harder—and more rewarding—to truly listen to someone else's opinion and to subsume one's self into the experiences and hopes of another person. Personal transformation of this sort is in short supply. Our beliefs calcify with age and our circle of friends tightens as we seek out people who march in lockstep with our own philosophical cadence. Breaking through the comfort of tradition and into new realms of experience and relationship creates within us the fortitude and wisdom to lead change from a place of empathy and humility.

Then, when these silent, cold monuments kindle passions and stir up hate, we will be prepared to wade into the riptide, confident that we are trusted and valued by our community and will not be swept away into an open sea of ignorance and indifference. The tragedy of Heather Heyer's death at Charlottesville in August 2017 draws into sharp focus the gravity and significance of historically informed community activism. Blind anger, self-righteous bigotry, and calloused racism will not go away. Nationalistic warmongering and bloviating disregard for life are not likely to fade. We cannot conform the world to an enlightened (yet entirely unattainable) vision of a hope-filled utopia of the future.

Instead, we must root out the quiescent, lazy parts of ourselves that have stopped asking questions, forgotten how to be curious, and neglected to love those around us.

In Shakespeare's play *King Lear*, Edgar says to the Earl of Gloucester, "Thy life is a miracle. Speak yet again."[5] Life is truly wondrous in its variety and beauty. Relationships and shared dreams are part of that miracle.[6] Museum professionals, public historians, and community leaders have the obligation to share the centrality of human stories in relatable, actionable ways to show how the miracles of our lives and the lives of the humans of the past can fuel a purpose that transcends corporeal divisiveness and parochial tribalism. Only then will statues take their rightful places in a past properly aligned with our human destiny.

NOTES

Introduction

1. N. Oliver, K. Burnell Evans, Vanessa Remmers, and Robert Zullo, "How the Disaster in Charlottesville Unfolded, as Told by the People Who Were There," *Richmond Times-Dispatch*, August 18, 2017, http://www.richmond.com/news/virginia/how-the-disaster-in-charlottesville-unfolded-as-told-by-the/article_34838b2c-df44-5018-92e3-14e983ff00ee.html.

2. An independent inquest into the actions of the Charlottesville Police Department and the Virginia State Police in response to the rallies revealed that they were poorly planned and coordinated and that the police departments were ill prepared and equipped for the events that transpired (Joe Heim, "Charlottesville Response to White Supremacist Rally Sharply Criticized in New Report," *Washington Post*, December 1, 2017, https://www.washingtonpost.com/local/charlottesville-response-to-white-supremacist-rally-sharply-criticized-in-new-report/2017/12/01/9c59fe98-d6a3-11e7-a986-d0a9770d9a3e_story.html?utm_term=.fdb6c5f16286).

3. See Tony Horwitz's excellent 1998 book *Confederates in the Attic: Dispatches from the Unfinished Civil War* (New York: Vintage Departures) for a deep dive into the ways that the Civil War is still ever-present in the lives and memories of many citizens of the United States.

4. Oliver et al., "How the Disaster in Charlottesville Unfolded." This speech at the Lincoln Memorial occurred on June 25, 2017.

5. Ibid. The park in Charlottesville is now named Emancipation Park instead of Lee Park, as of June 2017.

6. "Charlottesville Vice Mayor Wes Bellamy Reacts to White Nationalist Rally," NPR, *All Things Considered* interview, August 13, 2017, http://www.npr.org/2017/08/13/543259506/charlottesville-vice-mayor-wes-bellamy-reacts-to-white-nationalist-rally.

7. This musing owes a debt to Chuck Klosterman, whose book *But What If We're Wrong: Thinking about the Present as If It Were the Past* (2016) convincingly argues that what we currently value and consider important will not be valued or thought about in the same way in the future. Thus, our present interpretation of the value or importance of political events (will anyone care about the impact of Brexit in 2120?), pop culture (what musical artists from the 2010s will actually stand the test of time? My guess is maybe only Kanye West, Janelle Monae, and possibly Radiohead), and scientific breakthroughs (string theory may replace traditionally held Newtonian theories of gravity sooner rather than later) will be superseded by what people in the future deem important. After all, that is their prerogative. We did the same thing to our ancestors.

8. See Charles B. Dew, *Apostles of Disunion* (Charlottesville: University of Virginia Press, 2002). Five Southern states—South Carolina, Georgia, Mississippi, Texas, and Virginia—expressly mentioned the preservation of slavery in their declarations of cause for secession.

9. John Lewis Gaddis, *The Landscape of History: How Historians Map the Past* (Oxford: Oxford University Press, 2002).

10. Eric Castillo, "Expressions of Another Center: Borderlands Visual Theory & the Art of Luis Jimenez" (University of New Mexico American Studies thesis, 2011), 64.

11. Ibid.

12. See Jason Horowitz, Nick Corasaniti, and Ashley Southall, "Nine Killed in Shooting at Black Church in Charleston," *New York Times*, June 17, 2015, for more information about Dylann Roof's white supremacy beliefs and the shooting at the Emmanuel AME Church in Charleston, South Carolina.

13. See John Coski's *The Confederate Battle Flag: America's Most Embattled Emblem* (Boston: Harvard University Press, 2005).

14. Statistics on numbers of Confederate statues in the United States are drawn from the Southern Poverty Law Center website. See "Whose Heritage? Community Action Guide," accessed November 27, 2017, https://www.splcenter.org/20160421/whose-heritage-community-action-guide.

15. Or Riker's box schemas, if you prefer that method of preserving entomological collections of preexisting dogma to Schmidt's boxes.

16. STEM stands for "science, technology, engineering, and mathematics" and is a widely adopted integrative approach to emphasizing the critical technical and scientific skills that are needed for success in the twenty-first century. More recently, many educators and scholars have called for adding an "A" for the arts to STEM to ensure that artistic, creative endeavors are granted the importance that they deserve alongside science, technology, engineering, and math.

I have sometimes posited (only partially joking, of course) that it really should be SCHTEAM, which stands for science, culture, humanities, technology, art, and mathematics. At which point, you might as well just say that everything is important, grab E. O. Wilson's fatuous and reductive book *Consilience: The Unity of Knowledge* (New York: Alfred A. Knopf, 1998), and call it a day. For my money, however, Wendell Berry's brilliant takedown of Wilson's conception of consilience is a far better and more hopeful read. See *Life Is a Miracle: An Essay against Modern Superstition* (Berkeley, CA: Counterpoint Press, 2001).

17. "Charlottesville Vice Mayor Wes Bellamy Reacts to White Nationalist Rally."

18. "Read President Obama's Speech on the Charleston Church Shooting," *Time Online*, June 18, 2015, http://time.com/3926839/president-obama-charleston -transcript/. Barack Obama gave this eulogy for Reverend Clementa Pinckney on June 18, 2015.

Chapter 1

1. David Glassberg, *Sense of History: The Place of the Past in American Life* (Amherst: University of Massachusetts Press, 2001), 9.

2. Ibid., 10.

3. In *Beyond 1492: Encounters in Colonial North America* (Oxford: Oxford University Press, 1992), James Axtell writes, "For the past is filled with the lives and struggles of countless 'others,' from whom we may learn to extend the possibilities of our own limited humanity" (264).

4. David Lowenthal, *The Past Is a Foreign Country* (Cambridge: Cambridge University Press, 1985), 26.

5. Michael Wallace, *Mickey Mouse History and Other Essays on American Memory* (Philadelphia: Temple University Press, 1996), 10.

6. *Downton Abbey*, 2010–2015. Julian Fellowes, PBS Masterpiece Classic.

7. *Mad Men*, 2007–2015. Matthew Weiner, Lionsgate Television.

8. *Stranger Things*, 2016–. Matt and Ross Duffer, Netflix.

9. See Jose Zuniga's chapter, "A Reflection of Us," later in this book for a close examination of a great example of monuments and contested history of statues in popular culture.

10. In L. P. Hartley's 1953 novel *The Go-Between*, one character remarks, "The past is a foreign country: they do things differently there."

11. At publication, Ancestry.com reported more than four million customers.

12. Institute for Museum and Library Services, "Government Doubles Official Estimate: There Are 35,000 Active Museums in the U.S.," May 19, 2014, accessed November 7, 2017, https://www.imls.gov/news-events/news-releases/ government-doubles-official-estimate-there-are-35000-active-museums-us.

13. Phillip Bump, "Historians Respond to John Kelly's Civil War Remarks: 'Strange,' 'Sad,' and 'Wrong,'" *Washington Post*, October 31, 2017, accessed

November 3, 2017, https://www.washingtonpost.com/news/politics/wp/2017/10/
31/historians-respond-to-john-kellys-civil-war-remarks-strange-sad-wrong/
?utm_term=.c0c01c21e31b.

14. I throw around the word "epistemological" not only to convey that historians have a theory of knowledge but also as a way to elevate our knowledge of lexicon. And of course the footnote to this endnote would define lexicon in a similarly witty way, if footnotes to endnotes were allowable and (perhaps most important) not obnoxiously pretentious.

15. Kevin Walsh, *The Representation of the Past: Museums and Heritage in the Post-Modern World* (Abingdon: Routledge, 2002), 7.

16. Data-driven predictive analyses are becoming increasingly fashionable in popular discourse. Having been applied to all sorts of businesses, "big data" seems to be transforming society in ways that elevate it beyond a merely trendy buzzword. Nate Silver's *The Signal and the Noise: Why So Many Predictions Fail—But Some Don't* (New York: Penguin, 2012) is a particularly fascinating dissection of how canny quantitative questioning and assumptions feed predictions in all manner of fields of study and corners of our world.

17. Note the chapter by W. Todd Groce later in this section that explores the concept and popular perceptions of revisionism within the context of Civil War memorialization.

18. James West Davidson and Mark Hamilton Lytle, *After the Fact: The Art of Historical Detection* (New York: McGraw-Hill, 1992), 70.

19. Ibid., 74.

20. A much more thorough discussion of living history museums is found in my book *Living History: Effective Costumed Interpretation and Enactment at Museums and Historic Sites* (Lanham, MD: Rowman & Littlefield, 2016).

21. See Sten Rentzhog, *Open Air Museums: The History and Future of a Visionary Idea* (Kristianstad, Sweden: Carlssons and Jamtli Press, 2007).

22. Consensus historians had sought to use history as a way to affirm values that supposedly uniquely united Americans in order to provide a bulwark against the threats of communism. See Thomas Schlereth, "It Wasn't That Simple," *Museum News* 56 (January–February 1978): 36–41.

23. See "Enacting Nationhood: An Afterpiece," by Scott Magelsson, in *Enacting Nationhood: Identity, Ideology and the Theatre, 1855–1899*, Scott R. Irelan, ed. (Newcastle on Tyne: Cambridge Scholars Publishing, 2014).

24. John H. Falk and Lynn D. Dierking, *The Museum Experience Revisited* (New York: Routledge, 2016).

25. The British Museum in London used VR to give guests a more visceral experience of the Bronze Age, and the Salvador Dali Museum has used VR to give guests the experience of stepping into one of Dali's surrealist paintings. See "How Virtual Reality Is Being Used in Museums," *Education* (May 2016), accessed October 30, 2016, https://unimersiv.com/virtual-reality-used-museums/. The British

Museum partnered with Samsung to realize its vision for its Bronze Age VR experience, and the museum leaders approached the use of VR from a pragmatic, functional perspective. That is, they were not interested in using VR if it did not match the expressed needs and interests of their visitors. For the British Museum, VR was not just a trendy addition to its normal exhibits. Rather, it was absolutely essential to realizing the goal for the exhibit—to get people to truly *feel* and *understand* what life might have been like in Bronze Age Britain.

Chapter 2

1. University of North Carolina at Chapel Hill Library, Documenting the American South, *Commemorative Landscapes of North Carolina*, http://docsouth. unc.edu/commland/; Kenneth E. Foote, *Shadowed Ground: America's Landscapes of Violence and Tragedy*, rev. ed. (Austin: University of Texas Press, 2003).

2. Southern Poverty Law Center, *Whose Heritage: Public Symbols of the Confederacy*, April 21, 2016, https://www.splcenter.org/20160421/whose -heritage-public-symbols-confederacy.

3. For a discussion of the Confederate battle flag in U.S. history, see John M. Coski, *The Confederate Battle Flag: America's Most Embattled Emblem* (Cambridge, MA: Belknap Press of Harvard University Press, 2005).

4. Karen L. Cox, *Dixie's Daughters. The United Daughters of the Confederacy and the Preservation of Confederate Culture* (Gainesville: University Press of Florida, 2003); Jonathan Leib and Gerald Webster, "On Remembering John Winberry and the Study of Confederate Monuments on the Southern Landscape," *Southeastern Geographer* 55, no. 1 (Spring 2015): 8–18; Kirk Savage, *Standing Soldiers, Kneeling Slaves: Race, War, and Monument in Nineteenth-Century America* (Princeton: Princeton University Press, 1997).

5. This was one of the monuments that the city of New Orleans removed from public view in 2017.

6. Angelina Ray Johnston and Robinson Wise, "Commemorating Faithful Slaves, Mammies, and Black Confederates," in *Commemorative Landscapes of North Carolina* (2013), http://docsouth.unc.edu/commland/features/essays/ray_ wise/. Natchitoches removed this statue, often called "Uncle Jack," from public view in the 1960s, and the Louisiana State University Rural Life Museum eventually acquired it. Over the years, the museum has struggled with where to place the object and how to interpret it. See "Uncle Jack Statue," Louisiana Regional Folklife Program, https://folklife.nsula.edu/civilwartocivilrights/02Statue.html; Adam Duvernay, "Statue of Black Man Has History of Controversy," *LSU Now*, October 6, 2009; Fiona Handley, "Memorializing Race in the Deep South: The 'Good Darkie' Statue, Louisiana, USA," *Public Archaeology* 6, no. 2 (2007): 98–115.

7. Coski, *The Confederate Battle Flag*, 237. Mississippi had already incorporated the Confederate battle flag into its state flag in the 1890s.

8. Jenny Jarvie, "As Monuments to the Confederacy Are Removed from Public Squares, New Ones Are Quietly Being Erected," *Los Angeles Times*, October 22, 2017, http://beta.latimes.com/nation/la-na-new-confederate-memorials-20171020-story .html; Kyle Munson, "'Stupid Liberals' vs. White Privilege: Iowa Caught Up in Confederate Monuments Debate," *Des Moines Register*, August 25, 2017, https://www .desmoinesregister.com/story/news/local/columnists/kyle-munson/2017/08/25/ americas-civil-war-over-confederate-monuments-takes-root-iowa/588650001/.

9. Dell Upton, *What Can and Can't Be Said: Race, Uplift, and Monument Building in the Contemporary South* (New Haven, CT: Yale University Press, 2015). For efforts to commemorate the 1918 lynching of Mary Turner, see Julie Buckner Armstrong, *Mary Turner and the Memory of Lynching* (Athens: University of Georgia Press, 2011); Mary Turner Project, www.maryturner.org; and the Georgia Historical Society marker commemorating the site where Turner was murdered, http://georgiahistory.com/ghmi_marker_updated/mary-turner -and-the-lynching-rampage-of-1918/.

10. Dell Upton, "Confederate Monuments and Civic Values in the Wake of Charlottesville," SAH [Society of Architectural Historians] blog, September 13, 2017, http://www.sah.org/publications-and-research/sah-blog/sah-blog/2017/09/ 13/confederate-monuments-and-civic-values-in-the-wake-of-charlottesville.

11. Paul A. Shackel, *Memory in Black and White: Race, Commemoration, and the Post-Bellum Landscape* (Walnut Creek: AltaMira Press, 2003); Joan Marie Johnson, "'Ye Gave Them a Stone': African American Women's Clubs, the Frederick Douglass Home, and the Black Mammy Monument," *Journal of Women's History* 17, no. 1 (2005): 62–86.

12. Derek H. Alderman and Owen J. Dwyer, "A Primer on the Geography of Memory: The Site and Situation of Commemorative Landscapes," from *Commemorative Landscapes of North Carolina*, http://docsouth.unc.edu/commland/ features/essays/alderman_two/; Christy S. Coleman, "Among the Ruins: Creating and Interpreting the American Civil War in Richmond," in *Interpreting the Civil War at Museums and Historic Sites*, ed. Kevin M. Levin (Lanham, MD: Rowman & Littlefield, 2017), 7.

13. Owen Dwyer and Derek Alderman, *Civil Rights Memorials and the Geography of Memory* (Chicago: Center for American Places at Columbia College, 2008).

14. "58 Maury Civil War Soldiers Added to Monument," *The Daily Herald* (Columbia, Tennessee), October 19, 2013, http://www.columbiadailyherald.com/ sections/news/local-news/58-maury-civil-war-soldiers-added-monument.html. Thank you to Martha Norkunas for bringing this project to my attention in 2015.

15. For example, in 2007, two white boys spray-painted the dates of the Nat Turner rebellion on a monument in Montgomery, Alabama. Dell Upton, *What Can and Can't Be Said*, 25–26. See also Sarah Beetham, "From Spray Cans to Minivans: Contesting the Legacy of Confederate Soldier Monuments in the Era of 'Black Lives Matter,'" *Public Art Dialogue* 6, no. 1 (2016): 9–33.

16. Simon Romero, "Statue's Stolen Foot Reflects Divisions over Symbols of Conquest," *New York Times*, September 30, 2017, https://www.nytimes.com/2017/09/30/us/statue-foot-new-mexico.html?_r=0.

17. Kenneth E. Foote, "Editing Memory and Automobility and Race: Two Learning Activities on Contested Heritage and Place," *Southeastern Geographer* 53, no. 4 (Winter 2012): 384–97; Ari Kelman, "For Liberty and Empire: Remembering Sand Creek, Rethinking the Civil War," *Common-Place* 14, no. 2 (Winter 2014), http://www.common-place-archives.org/vol-14/no-02/kelman/#.Wh1cF0qnGUk; Danika Worthington, "A History of Racism, the KKK and Crimes against American Indians: Colorado's Struggle with Divisive Monuments Started Long Ago," *Denver Post*, August 18, 2017, http://www.denverpost.com/2017/08/18/confederate-monuments-statues-kkk-racism-charlottesville-colorado/. For an argument in favor of retaining and interpreting monuments, see Michele Bogart, "In Defense of 'Racist' Monuments: These Are Works of Public Art with Complex and Specific Histories," *New York Daily News*, August 24, 2017, http://www.nydailynews.com/opinion/defense-racist-monuments-article-1.3436672.

18. Upton, *What Can and Can't Be Said*.

19. Richard H. Schein, "A Methodological Framework for Interpreting Ordinary Landscapes: Lexington, Kentucky's Courthouse Square," *Geographical Review* 99, no. 3 (July 2009): 377–402.

20. For example, Blue Ribbon Commission on Race, Memorials and Public Spaces (Charlottesville, Virginia), 2016, http://www.charlottesville.org/departments-and-services/boards-and-commissions/blue-ribbon-commission-on-race-memorials-and-public-spaces; Special Commission to Review Baltimore's Public Confederate Monuments, 2016, https://mayor.baltimorecity.gov/news/featured-headlines/2016–09–13-baltimore%E2%80%99s-public-confederate-monuments-report. Christy Coleman, CEO of the American Civil War Museum, chairs the commission in Richmond, Virginia (https://www.monumentavenuecommission.org/).

21. For cities debating monuments, see Christopher Guinn, "Lakeland City Commission: Leave Confederate Monument in Munn Park," *Lakeland Ledger* (Florida), November 6, 2017, http://www.theledger.com/news/20171103/lakeland-city-commission-leave-confederate-monument-in-munn-park; Lex Talamo, "Split Caddo Commission Votes to Move Confederate Monument," *Shreveport Times* (Louisiana), October 19, 2017, http://www.shreveporttimes.com/story/news/2017/10/19/split-caddo-commission-votes-move-confederate-monument/782449001/; Sheldon Gardner, "St. Augustine's Confederate Monument Context Group Is Developing, and So Are Plans for Protest," *St. Augustine Record* (Florida), November 30, 2017, http://staugustine.com/local-news/news/2017-11-30/st-augustine-s-confederate-monument-context-group-developing-and-so-are.

22. Alderman and Dwyer, "A Primer on the Geography of Memory"; Aleia Brown, "The Confederate Flag Doesn't Belong in a Museum," *Slate*, June 25, 2015, http://www.slate.com/articles/news_and_politics/history/2015/06/confederate_

flag_it_doesn_t_belong_at_the_south_carolina_capitol_it_doesn.html; Kirk Savage, "What to Do with Confederate Monuments," November 15, 2015, http://www.kirksavage.pitt.edu/?p=545.

23. Brown, "The Confederate Flag Doesn't Belong in a Museum"; Alderman and Dwyer, "A Primer on the Geography of Memory"; Savage, "What to Do with Confederate Monuments."

24. Julia Rose, *Interpreting Difficult History at Museums and Historic Sites* (Lanham, MD: Rowman & Littlefield, 2016).

Chapter 3

1. "U.S. Students Remain Poor at History, Test Show," *New York Times*, June 14, 2011; "Survey: Students and Adults Ignorant of Basic U.S. History," *The Trumpet*, January 27, 2010.

2. "White Support for the Confederate Flag Really Is about Racism, Not Southern Heritage," *Washington Post*, July 1, 2015.

3. David Blight, "Historians and Memory," *Common-Place* 2:3 (April 2002).

4. Brook D. Simpson, Stephen Sears, and Aaron Sheehan-Dean, eds., *The Civil War: The First Year Told by Those Who Lived It* (New York: The Library of America, 2002), 1.

5. James W. Loewen and Edward H. Sebasta, eds., *The Confederate and Neo-Confederate Reader: The "Great Truth" about the "Lost Cause"* (Jackson: The University of Mississippi Press, 2010), 127.

6. Ibid., 149–52.

7. Ibid., 187–90.

8. The literature on the growth and development of the Lost Cause is extensive. Among the best works is Charles Reagan Wilson, *Baptized in Blood: The Religion of the Lost Cause* (Athens: The University of Georgia Press, 1980); Gaines M. Foster, *Ghosts of the Confederacy: Defeat, the Lost Cause, and the Emergence of the New South* (New York: Oxford University Press, 1987); and David Goldfield, *Still Fighting the Civil War: The American South and Southern History* (Baton Rouge: Louisiana State University Press, 2002).

9. The domino theory held that if one country fell to communism (such as Vietnam), others would soon follow in a domino-style knockdown. See Frank Ninkovich, *Modernity and Power: A History of the Domino Theory in the Twentieth Century* (University of Chicago Press, 1994).

10. "STEM Education Is Vital—But Not at the Expense of the Humanities," *Scientific American*, October 1, 2016; "Study Finds Chinese Students Excel at Critical Thinking—Until College," *New York Times*, July 30, 2016; "Chinese Students at Top Universities 'Less Creative Than Others,'" *Times Higher Education*, September 28, 2016; "Chinese Educators Look to American Classrooms," *New York Times*, September 2, 2013; "Why America's Obsession with STEM Education Is Dangerous," *Washington Post*, March 26, 2015.

11. For an examination of Jobs's "faith in the liberal arts," see Jonah Lehrer, "Steve Jobs: 'Technology Alone Is Not Enough,'" *The New Yorker*, October 7, 2011. For an intriguing look at Turner's liberal arts education and the pressure he received from his family to switch majors from the classics to business, see Ted Turner, *Call Me Ted* (New York: Grand Central Publishing, 2008), 33–36. On Edison's extensive humanities background, see Jim Powell, "The Education of Thomas Edison," *Foundation for Economic Education*, February 1, 1995.

Chapter 4

1. Robert Penn Warren, *The Legacy of the Civil War: Meditations on the Centennial* (New York: Random House, 1961), 3.

2. The name of the book about arms and equipment of the Civil War was aptly *Arms and Equipment of the Civil War* by Jack Coggins (Garden City, NJ: Doubleday, 1962).

3. Bruce Catton, *Civil War: Three Volumes in One* (New York: The Fairfax Press, 1984). The three volumes in this book are *Mr. Lincoln's Army*, *Glory Road*, and *A Stillness at Appomattox*.

4. Ibid., 415.

5. All Civil War buffs are prone to the malaise of oversharing. We love to regale anyone who will listen with tidbits about the war. I am no exception. One of my former coworkers referred to this insatiable helpful fact-dispensing as having a subscription to "Modern Know-It-All Quarterly" and "Wisenheimer Windbag Weekly."

6. Jonathan Haidt, *The Righteous Mind: Why Good People Are Divided by Politics and Religion* (New York: Vintage, 2013), 61.

7. The irony that I referred to my re-creation of a battle in my mind (which soldiers during the Civil War called "seeing the elephant") as being driven by the elephant part of my brain is not lost on me. Pachyderm paralysis, I suppose.

8. See Charles B. Dew, *Apostles of Disunion* (Charlottesville: University of Virginia Press, 2002).

9. Richard H. Sewell, *A House Divided: Sectionalism and the Civil War, 1848–1865* (Baltimore: Johns Hopkins University Press, 1988), 81.

10. Ibid., 85. Northern abolitionists were most interested in the destruction of the south's system of chattel slavery. Westerners often were more interested in reopening trade with the south on the Mississippi, and others simply desired a restoration of peace so that profitable business could recommence.

11. Ibid., 86. It is also noteworthy that the planter class in the South was so intimately tied to slavery that they were willing to compromise their fealty to the Confederacy. Sewell writes, "Most planters gave primary allegiance not to the Confederacy, which they viewed as simply a means, but to the end it had been designed to serve: plantation slavery" (120). An interesting tangent that may be

worth exploring in the future would focus on issues of class, wealth, and social status with regard to the interpretation and history of statues to Confederate generals, leaders, and common soldiers.

12. Please note that white northerners should not be absolved from their complicity in perpetuating oppression of African Americans. In her article, "The Long Civil Rights Movement and the Political Uses of the Past," Jacquelyn Dowd Hall writes, "This . . . broader narrative undermines the trope of the South as the nation's 'opposite other,' an image that southernizes racism and shields from scrutiny both the economic dimensions of southern white supremacy and the institutionalized patterns of exploitation, segregation, and discrimination in other regions of the country—patterns that survived the civil rights movement and now define the South's racial landscape as well" (*Journal of American History* 91, no. 4 [March 2005]: 1233–63).

13. Gail Bederman, *Manliness and Civilization: A Cultural History of Gender and Race in the United States, 1880–1917* (Chicago: The University of Chicago Press, 1995). Bederman asserts that "during the Civil War, 180,000 black men enlisted in the Union Army, despite unequal and offensive treatment, because they understood that enlisting was their most potent tool to claim that they were men and should have the same rights and privileges as all American men" (21). As in the note above, an interesting "side road" to this discussion about monuments and memorials could explore gendered interpretations of statues throughout American history.

14. David W. Blight, *Race and Reunion: The Civil War in American Memory* (Cambridge, MA: Belknap Press of Harvard University Press, 2001).

15. Ibid.

16. Leon F. Litwack, *Been in the Storm So Long: The Aftermath of Slavery* (New York: Alfred A. Knopf, 1979).

17. Bederman, *Manliness*, 30.

18. Janice D. Hamlet, "Fannie Lou Hamer: The Unquenchable Spirit of the Civil Rights Movement," *Journal of Black Studies* 26, no. 5 (1996): 560–76.

19. Robert J. Cook, *Troubled Commemoration: The American Civil War Centennial, 1961–1965* (Baton Rouge: Louisiana State University Press, 2007), 41.

20. Ibid., 273.

Chapter 5

1. Christine Vendel, "Armed 'Patriot' Accidentally Shoots Self in Leg at Gettysburg Battlefield," *Penn Live*, July 1, 2017, accessed December 8, 2017, http://www.pennlive.com/news/2017/07/patriot_shot_in_leg_gettysburg.html.

2. Maggie Astor, Christina Caron, and Daniel Victor, "A Guide to the Charlottesville Aftermath," *New York Times*, August 13, 2017, accessed December 8, 2017, https://www.nytimes.com/2017/08/13/us/charlottesville-virginia-overview.html.

3. Jaweed Kaleem, "After Violence in Charlottesville, Cities Rush to Take Down Monuments, as White Supremacists Gear Up to Fight," *LA Times*, August 14, 2017, accessed December 8, 2017, http://beta.latimes.com/nation/la-na -charlottesville-causes-20170814-story.html; Scott Hancock, "In Gettysburg, the Confederacy Won," *CityLab*, August 24, 2017, accessed December 8, 2017, https:// www.citylab.com/life/2017/08/in-gettysburg-the-confederacy-won/537756/; Bill Broun, "Why Confederate Monuments Should Be Removed from Gettysburg," *The Morning Call*, August 20, 2017, accessed December 8, 2017, http://www.mcall .com/opinion/yourview/mc-confederate-monuments-gettysburg-broun-yv-0818 -20170819-story.html.

4. Aleia Brown, "The Confederate Flag Doesn't Belong in a Museum," *Slate*, June 25, 2015, accessed December 8, 2017, http://www.slate.com/articles/news_ and_politics/history/2015/06/confederate_flag_it_doesn_t_belong_at_the_ south_carolina_capitol_it_doesn.html.

5. Jennifer Murray, *On a Great Battlefield: The Making, Management, and Memory of Gettysburg National Military Park* (Knoxville: University of Tennessee Press, 2014), 13; Jim Weeks, *Gettysburg: Memory, Market, and an American Shrine* (Princeton, NJ: Princeton University Press, 2003), 21–22, 63–64; "Veterans, Monuments, and Memory: An Introduction to the Monumentation of Gettysburg," *Hallowed Ground*, Gettysburg 150 Commemorative Issue (2013), accessed July 22, 2016, http://www.civilwar.org/hallowed-ground-magazine/gettysburg-2013/ veterans-monuments-and.html?referrer=https://www.google.com/.

6. James B. Myers, Superintendent, Gettysburg National Military Park, Letter to Payne Williams, February 15, 1963, Vertical Files Collection, Drawer 17, Folder 63, Gettysburg National Military Park Library; Ronald F. Lee, Regional Director, National Park Service, Memo to NPS Director, April 11, 1963.

7. "S.C. Monument Dedicated by Gov. Russell," *Gettysburg Times*, July 3, 1963.

8. Columbia SC 63, Our Story Matters, "Civil Rights Timeline," accessed July 22, 2016, http://www.columbiasc63.com/civil-rights-timeline/.

9. "S.C. Monument Dedicated by Gov. Russell"; Robert Cook, "(Un)Furl That Banner: The Response of White Southerners to the Civil War Centennial of 1961–1965," *Journal of Southern History* 68, no. 4 (November 2002): 908–9; Brian Matthew Jordan, "We Stand on the Same Battlefield: The Gettysburg Centenary and the Shadow of Race," *Pennsylvania Magazine of History and Biography* 135, no. 4 (October 2011): 500–502.

10. Cook, "(Un)Furl That Banner," 908–9.

11. Kittridge A. Wing, Superintendent, Gettysburg National Military Park, Memo to Regional Director, Northeast Region, NPS, June 10, 1963, Vertical Files Collection, Drawer 17, Folder 43, Gettysburg National Military Park Library.

12. A rich body of literature on the relationship between the Cold War and the American civil rights movement has developed over the past twenty years. See Penny von Eschen, *Race against Empire: Black Americans and Anticolonialism, 1937–1957* (Ithaca, NY: Cornell University Press, 1997); Mary Dudziak, *Cold War*

Civil Rights: Race and the Image of American Democracy (Princeton: Princeton University Press, 2000); and Jonathan Rosenberg, *How Far the Promised Land? World Affairs and the American Civil Rights Movement from the First World War to Vietnam* (Princeton: Princeton University Press, 2006), among many others.

13. Transcript, Florida Gettysburg Memorial Commission Monument Dedication Ceremonies, July 3, 1963, Vertical Files Collection, Drawer 17, Folder 43, Gettysburg National Military Park Library.

14. Hancock, "In Gettysburg the Confederacy Won"; Broun, "Why Confederate Monuments Should Be Removed from Gettysburg."

15. Daniel Vermilya, "The Florida Monument at Gettysburg: The Complicated Legacies of the Civil War," *From the Fields of Gettysburg: The Blog of Gettysburg National Military Park*, September 19, 2017, accessed December 8, 2017, https://npsgnmp.wordpress.com/2017/09/19/the-florida-monument-at-gettysburg-the-complicated-legacies-of-the-civil-war/; Christopher Gwinn, "The Lee Controversy of 1903," *From the Fields of Gettysburg: The Blog of Gettysburg National Military Park*, December 19, 2013, accessed December 8, 2017, https://npsgnmp.wordpress.com/2013/12/19/the-lee-controversy-of-1903/.

16. For a full definition of "counter-monuments," see James Young, "Memory and Counter-Memory: The End of the Monument in Germany," *Harvard Design Magazine*, no. 9 (Fall 1999), 3.

17. Christopher Phelps, "Removing Racist Symbols Isn't a Denial of History," *Chronicle of Higher Education*, January 8, 2016, accessed July 25, 2016, http://chronicle.com/article/Removing-Racist-Symbols/234862/.

Chapter 6

1. "My privilege is this, ladies and gentlemen: To declare this chapter in the history of the United States closed and ended, and I bid you turn with me with your faces to the future, quickened by the memories of the past, but with nothing to do with the contests of the past, knowing, as we have shed our blood upon opposite sides, we now face and admire one another." "Address of President Wilson Accepting the Monument in Memory of the Confederate Dead at Arlington National Cemetery, June 4, 1914," Frances Crane Leatherbee, *Addresses of President Wilson, 1913–1917* (1918).

2. Thomas J. Brown, *The Public Art of Civil War Commemoration: A Brief History with Documents* (New York: Bedford/St. Martin's, 2004), 24.

3. "2,500 Witness Unveiling of Hanover's Monument 'To Her Confederate Soldiers and to Her Noble Women Who Loved Them,'" *Hanover Progress*, August 28, 1914; Mary Grundman Vial, "Hanover Confederate Soldiers Monument: Hanover Court House, Virginia," *UDC Magazine*, March 2012, 20–21.

4. This urge to vindicate the Confederacy grew out of the reconciliation of North and South in the five decades after the Civil War. The destruction of slavery

enabled white men and women on both sides to look past their old differences and reunite on the basis of shared whiteness. Reconciliation on Southern terms— ignoring the role of slavery in the Civil War and the Union's avowed support of emancipated slaves during Reconstruction—was essentially complete by the Spanish-American War in 1898. The triumph of the Lost Cause was not tenable without continued efforts, however. Having proved their military virtue in 1898, Southerners next had to prove the virtues of their hierarchical culture. Their selective emulation of the Confederate legacy glossed over the unpleasant aspects of the war, including slavery and the extreme violence of the conflict, to create a brand of Southern identity that fit neatly into existing American identities. See David Blight, *Race and Reunion: The Civil War in American Memory* (Cambridge, MA: The Belknap Press of Harvard University Press, 2001).

5. "The Confederate Monument," *Hanover Progress*, August 28, 1914.

6. Virginia, along with most of the former Confederacy, had one of the highest desertion rates in the country during World War I. See Jeanette Keith, *Rich Man's War, Poor Man's Fight: Race, Class, and Power in the Rural South during the First World War* (Chapel Hill: The University of North Carolina Press, 2004), 5.

7. "Addresses at Spotsylvania," *Daily Star* (Fredericksburg, VA), May 31, 1918. Spotsylvania's memorial is a soldier on a large base, standing in the middle of the Confederate cemetery near the Spotsylvania County courthouse. The inscription on the front of the monument provides background: "*Erected and dedicated May 12, 1918 by the Spotsylvania Chapter United Daughters of the Confederacy, Confederated Southern Memorial Association and Citizens of Spotsylvania County to commemorate and perpetuate the valor and patriotism of the sons of Spotsylvania County, Virginia, and other Confederate soldiers who repose in this cemetery.*" The inscription on the back of the monument base is taken from the poem "March of the Deathless Dead" by Father Abram J. Ryan, a Catholic priest and Confederate sympathizer. It reads, "*We have gathered the sacred dust of warriors tried and true who bore the flag of our nation's trust and fell in the cause 'tho lost, still just, and died for me and you.*" On the two sides are simple inscriptions, common throughout the South: "*Love makes memory eternal*," the motto of the United Daughters of the Confederacy, and "*Lest we forget*," taken from Rudyard Kipling's poem "Recessional." Young and well equipped, Spotsylvania's soldier keeps watch over the graves of almost six hundred Confederate soldiers. *Confederate Monument*, Spotsylvania Courthouse, Virginia, 1918.

8. "Confederate Unveiling of Monument at Monterey, Virginia, Friday, July 4, 1919," Highland Historical Society, McDowell, VA.

9. *Confederate Soldiers Monument*, Monterey, Virginia, 1919.

10. See Stephanie McCurry, *Confederate Reckoning: Power and Politics in the Civil War South* (Cambridge, MA: Harvard University Press, 2010). To be sure, not all Virginian (or Southern) women shared the same opinions about their place in society and the changes on the horizon. Women's suffrage had its proponents

in the Old Dominion and the other states of the former Confederacy, a result of the "second wave" of suffrage organization in the South between 1910 and 1920. As the New South continued to industrialize, many women began pushing for increased voting rights. While women in Virginia were divided on the issue of equal suffrage, however, the voice of the antisuffrage faction was often louder due to the elevated status of its members.

11. Elna C. Green, *Southern Strategies: Southern Women and the Woman Suffrage Question* (Chapel Hill: University of North Carolina Press, 1997), xv, 71, 84.

12. Ibid., 71.

13. Count taken from Benjamin J. Hillman, *Monuments to Memories: Virginia's Civil War Heritage in Bronze and Stone* (Richmond: Virginia Civil War Commission, 1965). A total of thirty-six Confederate monuments honoring Virginians were built in the commonwealth over the course of the 1910s. Twenty of those were sponsored at least primarily by the UDC. The UDC total does not include other women's groups—the "Ladies of Lunenburg County," for example, helped erect Victoria's monument in 1916 without any official UDC involvement. The monument in Bristol, Virginia, was given to the local UDC by a private male donor (1920); *Confederate Monument*, Hanover Courthouse, Virginia, 1914.

14. *Confederate Monument*, Spotsylvania Courthouse, Virginia, 1918.

15. *Minutes of the Sixteenth Annual Convention of the United Daughters of the Confederacy* (Opelika, AL: Post Publishing Company, 1909), 301. The current motto of the UDC is "Think, Love, Pray, Dare, Live," which also appeared on some UDC material as early as the 1910s. "Emblem and Motto," *United Daughters of the Confederacy*, 2013, http://www.hqudc.org/about_udc/index.htm#Emblem.

16. "Victoria Has Biggest Day," *Lunenburg Call*, August 17, 1916.

17. Drewry brought the women he was addressing into the fold at the end of his speech, saying, "This monument will remain forever to the world as a memorial to the memory of the Confederate soldier, but it will also stand as a memorial to the faithful constancy and devotion of the women of Lunenburg, who helped to make possible this tribute of your citizens builded in the imperishable granite." "Victoria Has Biggest Day," *Lunenburg Call*, August 17, 1916.

18. See McCurry, *Confederate Reckoning*, 4. To this day, one objective of the United Daughters of the Confederacy is "to record the part played during the War by Southern women, including their patient endurance of hardship, their patriotic devotion during the struggle, and their untiring efforts during the post-War reconstruction of the South." "Object of the UDC," *United Daughters of the Confederacy*, 2013, http://www.hqudc.org/about_udc/index.htm#Emblem. Throughout Virginia, female memorialists honored the ideal of Southern womanhood alongside the Confederate soldier with monuments such as the ones at Prince George, Spotsylvania Courthouse, Goochland Courthouse, and Monterey, all of which bear the

name of the United Daughters of the Confederacy among their inscriptions. The presence of the UDC "brand" kept viewers in mind of the driving force behind the monuments—that is, women.

19. For more on working women during World War I, see Carrie Brown, *Rosie's Mom: Forgotten Women Workers of the First World War* (Boston: Northeastern University Press, 2002).

20. The 1910s were a time of great shifts in American racial and social structure. New leaders and groups dedicated to fighting institutional racism grew out of the instability of the times. The National Association for the Advancement of Colored People (NAACP), for example, was founded in 1909. White Southerners perceived their lives as unstable as well, but their privileged position in society allowed them to take actions often impossible for African Americans. Some eugenicist theorists, such as Madison Grant, in his book *The Passing of the Great Race*, postulated that the white race was being eclipsed by more fertile nonwhite people. The release of D. W. Griffith's epic film *The Birth of a Nation*, ostensibly an antiwar movie, helped spark the resurgence of the Ku Klux Klan in 1915. Some whites took the law into their own hands in their effort to suppress black freedom: lynchings between 1910 and 1919 averaged sixty-five annually. See Mark Ellis, *Race, War, and Surveillance: African Americans and the United States Government during World War I* (Bloomington: Indiana University Press, 2001), xiii; Melvyn Stokes, *D. W. Griffith's* The Birth of a Nation*: A History of "The Most Controversial Motion Picture of All Time"* (New York: Oxford University Press, 2007).

21. Robert R. Weyeneth, "The Architecture of Racial Segregation: The Challenges of Preserving the Problematic Past," *The Public Historian* 27, no. 4 (Fall 2005): 11–44; Grace Elizabeth Hale, *Making Whiteness: The Culture of Segregation in the South, 1890–1940* (New York: Pantheon Books, 1998), 9.

22. *Confederate Monument*, Arlington, Virginia, 1914; Hilary A. Herbert, *History of the Arlington Confederate Monument* (Washington, DC: United Daughters of the Confederacy, 1914), 77.

23. Ibid., 77; Martin Binkin and Mark J. Eitelberg, and others, *Blacks and the Military* (Washington, DC: The Brookings Institution, 1982), 17.

24. "We of the colored race," wrote W. E. B. Du Bois in 1918, "have no ordinary interest in the outcome. That which the German power represents today spells death to the aspirations of Negroes. . . . Let us, while this war lasts, forget our special grievances and close our ranks shoulder to shoulder with our own white fellow citizens and the allied nations that are fighting for democracy." Bernard C. Nalty and Morris J. MacGregor, eds. *Blacks in the Military: Essential Documents* (Wilmington, DE: Scholarly Resources Inc., 1981), 77; J. Douglas Smith, *Managing White Supremacy: Race, Politics, and Citizenship in Jim Crow Virginia* (Chapel Hill: The University of North Carolina Press, 2002), 45–46.

25. *Confederate Monument*, Victoria, Virginia, 1916.

26. *Confederate Monument*, Prince George, Virginia, 1916.

27. *Confederate Monument,* Spotsylvania Courthouse, Virginia, 1918. The memorial was dedicated to those *"Who bore the flag of our nation's trust, and fell in the cause 'tho lost, still just."*

28. See Blight, *Race and Reunion.*

Chapter 7

1. Dell Upton, *What Can and Can't Be Said: Race, Uplift, and Monument Building in the Contemporary South* (New Haven, CT: Yale University Press, 2015).

2. Chris Grem, "Henry W. Grady (1850–1889)," *New Georgia Encyclopedia,* January 20, 2004, http://www.georgiaencyclopedia.org/articles/arts-culture/henry-w-grady-1850-1889.

3. David W. Blight, "'For Something beyond the Battlefield': Frederick Douglass and the Struggle for the Memory of the Civil War," *The Journal of American History* 75, no. 4 (March 1, 1989): 1159, https://doi.org/10.2307/1908634.

4. Ibid., 1164.

5. Southern Poverty Law Center, "Whose Heritage? Public Symbols of the Confederacy," Southern Poverty Law Center, April 21, 2016, https://www.splcenter.org/20160421/whose-heritage-public-symbols-confederacy.

6. Christopher Waldrep, ed., *Lynching in America: A History in Documents* (New York: New York University Press, 2006).

7. James Weldon Johnson and Sondra Kathryn Wilson, *Along This Way: The Autobiography of James Weldon Johnson* (New York: Penguin Classics, 1990), 341.

8. David Goldfield, *Still Fighting the Civil War: The American South and Southern History* (Baton Rouge: LSU Press, 2013), 312–13.

9. Jessica Bryce Young, "13 Ways of Looking at a Flag: A Post-Mortem of 'The Confederate Flag: A Belated Burial in Florida,'" *Orlando Weekly,* June 24, 2015, http://www.orlandoweekly.com/orlando/a-post-mortem-of-the-confederate-flag-a-belated-burial-in-florida/Content?oid=2406409.

10. Julian C. Chambliss, "Art, History, and Memory," The Hooded Utilitarian, June 4, 2015, http://www.hoodedutilitarian.com/2015/06/art-history-and-memory/.

11. See https://www.eji.org/ for more information about the work of the Equal Justice Initiative to track racial violence and to raise awareness around issues of social justice for racial and ethnic minorities.

Chapter 8

1. Lincoln quoted in James Lee McDonough, *War in Kentucky: From Shiloh to Perryville* (Knoxville: University of Tennessee Press, 1991), 61; number of monuments from Joseph E. Brent, "Civil War Monuments in Kentucky," National Register of Historic Places Multiple Property Documentation Form, United States Department of the Interior (January 8, 1997), 1.

2. For Kentuckians embracing the Lost Cause, see Anne E. Marshall, *Creating a Confederate Kentucky: The Lost Cause and Civil War Memory in a Border State* (Chapel Hill: University of North Carolina Press, 2010).

3. For information about the "proslavery capacity" of Kentucky Unionists, see Patrick A. Lewis, "'All Men of Decency Ought to Quit the Army': Benjamin F. Buckner, Manhood, and Proslavery Unionism in Kentucky," *The Register of the Kentucky Historical Society* 107 (Autumn 2009): 513–49. Lewis effectively expands this argument in his *For Slavery and Union: Benjamin Buckner and Kentucky Loyalties in the Civil War* (Lexington: University Press of Kentucky, 2015).

4. John T. Harrington to "Dear Sister," January 9, 1863, John T. Harrington Letters, 1863, KHS, Frankfort, KY. See also Stuart W. Sanders, "'I Have Seen War in All Its Horrors:' Two Civil War Letters of John T. Harrington, Twenty-Second Kentucky Union Infantry Regiment," *The Register of the Kentucky Historical Society* 105 (Autumn 2007): 657–77.

5. For Union enlistment of Kentucky slaves, see Richard D. Sears, *Camp Nelson, Kentucky: A Civil War History* (Lexington: University Press of Kentucky, 2002).

6. Marshall, *Creating a Confederate Kentucky*, 5.

7. Anne E. Marshall, "Historian on 'Confederate Kentucky': Time to Remove the Statues," *Lexington Herald-Leader*, August 16, 2017.

8. For Breckinridge, see William C. Davis, *Breckinridge: Statesman, Soldier, Symbol* (Lexington: University Press of Kentucky, 2010).

9. Advertisement reprinted in Wilma A. Dunaway, *The African-American Family in Slavery and Emancipation* (Cambridge: Cambridge University Press, 2003), 23.

10. "Unveiled," *Lexington Daily Press*, November 17, 1887.

11. Ibid.

12. Ibid.

13. For Morgan, see James A. Ramage, *Rebel Raider: The Life of General John Hunt Morgan* (Lexington: University Press of Kentucky, 1995).

14. "Morgan's Statue Unveiled," *The Bourbon News*, October 20, 1911, 8; "Veterans at Lexington for Unveiling of Monument to Chieftain," *Mt. Sterling Advocate*, October 25, 1911, 2.

15. Program, "Unveiling of the Monument to General John H. Morgan and His Men," United Daughters of the Confederacy Collection, Box 28, Folder 4, Kentucky Historical Society, Frankfort.

16. "Veterans at Lexington for Unveiling of Monument to Chieftain," *Mt. Sterling Advocate*, October 25, 1911, 2.

17. Percy Costello and Justin Sayers, "Confederate Statues in Lexington Removed Tuesday Night in Quick Move," *Lexington Herald-Leader*, October 17, 2017; Morgan Eads, Karla Ward, and Beth Musgrave, "In a Surprise Move, Lexington Removes Controversial Confederate Statues," *Lexington Herald-Leader*,

October 17, 2017; Kay quoted in Beth Musgrave, "Lexington Cemetery and City Finalize Deal to Move Confederate Statues," *Lexington Herald-Leader*, November 16, 2017.

Chapter 9

1. Sheffield Hale, "Finding Meaning in Monuments: Atlanta History Center Enters Dialogue on Confederate Symbols," *History News* 71, no. 4 (Autumn 2016): 20–24.

2. "No bill of attainder, ex post facto law, or law denying or impairing the right of property in negro slaves shall be passed." Confederate States of America Constitution, Article I, Section 9 (1861).

3. This figure is based on estimates of approximately 620,000 military deaths. Maris A. Winovskis, "Have Social Historians Lost the Civil War? Some Preliminary Demographic Speculations," *Journal of American History* 76, no. 1 (1989): 36–39; Darroch Greer, *Counting Civil War Casualties, Week-by-Week*, for the Abraham Lincoln Presidential Library and Museum (Burbank: BRC Imagination Arts, 2005); Drew Gilpin Faust, *This Republic of Suffering: Death and the American Civil War* (New York: Knopf, 2008), 250–66; J. David Hacker recently estimated a total between 650,000 and 850,000 in "Recounting the Dead," *New York Times Opinionator*, September 20, 2011; Gould B. Hagler, *Georgia's Confederate Monuments: In Honor of a Fallen Nation* (Macon: Mercer Press, 2014); J. Michael Martinez, William D. Richardson, Ronald L. McNinch-Su, eds., *Confederate Symbols in the Contemporary South* (Gainesville: University Press of Florida, 2001), 157; Gaines M. Foster, *Ghosts of the Confederacy: Defeat the Lost Cause, and the Emergence of the New South, 1865 to 1913* (New York: Oxford University Press, 1987), 273.

4. Martinez et al., *Confederate Symbols*, 59–63; Southern Poverty Law Center, "Whose Heritage? Public Symbols of the Confederacy," go.aaslh.org/SPLCforHN.

5. According to the 1860 census, the total population of the eleven states that formed the Confederacy was 9,103,332, of which 3,521,110, or more than 38 percent, were enslaved. The Confederacy also recognized Kentucky and Missouri, which brings the figures to 11,441,028 and 3,861,524, respectively, or nearly 34 percent enslaved.

6. The Peace Monument is a reconciliation monument erected in Piedmont Park in 1911 by the Gate City Guard. Like other reconciliation monuments of the time, the Peace Monument represents a partial reconciliation that left out the African American perspective due to the oppression of the Jim Crow era. The text from the Peace Monument reads as follows: "The Gate City Guard, Captain G Harvey Thompson, In the conscientious conviction of their duty to uphold the Cause of the Southern Confederacy, offered their services to the Governor of Georgia and were enrolled in the Confederate Army April 30, 1861. Inspired with the same sincerity of purpose and accepting in good faith the result of that heroic struggle, The Gate

City Guard, under the command of Captain Joseph F. Burke, Desiring to restore fraternal sentiment among the people of all sections of our country, and ignoring sectional animosity, on October 6th, 1879, went forth to greet their former adversaries in the Northern and Eastern states, inviting them to unite with the people of the South to heal the Nation's wounds in a peaceful and prosperous reunion of the states. This 'mission of peace' was enthusiastically endorsed by the military and citizens in every part of the union and this monument is erected as an enduring testimonial to their patriotic contribution to the cause of national fraternity."

Dedicated October 10, 1911, by Simeon E. Baldwin (governor of Connecticut) and Hoke Smith (governor of Georgia). A recording of the committee meeting can be found at City of Atlanta, Advisory Committee on Street Names and Monuments Associated with the Confederacy, (11/13/17). 1:19:00. Retrieved from https://view .earthchannel.com/PlayerController.aspx?&PGD=ataga&eID=901.

7. The Peachtree Battle Monument has the following inscription: "*On this historic ground where Confederate soldiery, defending Atlanta, met and disputed the southward advance of federal troops along Peachtree Road, July 19th 1864. This memorial is a tribute to American Valor, which they of the blue and they of the gray had as a common heritage from their forefathers of 1776, and to the pervading spirit thereof which, in the days of 1898 and the Great World conflict of 1917–1918, perfected the reunion of the North and the South. Erected by the Old Guard of Atlanta. Dedicated by Atlanta Post No. 1, American Legion. 1935.*"

8. City of Atlanta, "Report of the Advisory Committee on Streets and Monuments Related to the Confederacy," Advisory Committee on Streets and Monuments Related to the Confederacy, Submitted November 18, 2017, http://www.atlantahistorycenter.com/research/confederate-monuments/research-books-and-latest-news.

Chapter 11

1. Archaeological evidence shows that humans have lived in North America for at least twelve thousand years, likely arriving via the land bridge across what is today the Bering Strait from Asia. First contact between Europeans and native peoples may have occurred between the Norse and native groups along the eastern coast of North American as early as 900 CE. See James Axtell, *Beyond 1492: Encounters in Colonial North America* (Oxford: Oxford University Press, 1992).

2. There were fewer than five hundred Taino people left in the Caribbean by 1548, just over fifty years from their first contact with Christopher Columbus and Europeans. Kathleen Deagan, "Reconsidering Taino Social Dynamics after Spanish Conquest: Gender and Class in Culture Contact Studies," *American Antiquity* 69, no. 4 (2004): 597.

3. Axtell, *Beyond 1492*, 244.

4. Elena Goukassian, "Calls to Take Down Columbus and J. Marion Sims Statues at Public Hearing on NYC Monuments," Hyperallergic, November 22,

2017, https://hyperallergic.com/413383/nyc-monuments-hearing-columbus/sims on December 12, 2017.

   5. Ibid.

   6. Cleve R. Wootson Jr., "Why Police Have to Guard a Statue of Christopher Columbus in New York around the Clock," *Washington Post*, October 7, 2017, accessed December 17, 2017, https://www.washingtonpost.com/news/post-nation/wp/2017/10/07/why-police-have-to-guard-a-statue-of-christopher-columbus-in-new-york-around-the-clock/?utm_term=.04595bb1bd95.

   7. Elizabeth Kryder-Reid, "Sites of Power and the Power of Sight: Vision in the California Mission Landscapes," in *Sites Unseen: Landscape and Vision*, edited by Dianne Harris and D. Fairchild Ruggles (Pittsburgh: University of Pittsburgh Press, 2007), 181–212.

   8. Katharyne Mitchell, "Monuments, Memorials, and the Politics of Memory," *Urban Geography* 24, no. 5 (2003): 442–59.

   9. Veronica Rocha, "Decapitated and Doused with Red Paint: Vandals Target St. Junipero Serra Statue at Santa Barbara Mission," *Los Angeles Times*, September 14, 2017, accessed on December 27, 2017, http://www.latimes.com/local/lanow/la-me-ln-junipero-serra-statue-vandalized-santa-barbara-20170914-htmlstory.html.

   10. Ibid.

   11. Simon Romero, "Statue's Stolen Foot Reflects Divisions over Symbols of Conquest," *New York Times*, September 30, 2017, accessed on December 27, 2017, https://www.nytimes.com/2017/09/30/us/statue-foot-new-mexico.html?_r=0.

   12. Ibid.

   13. Laurie Pasteryak Lamarre, "Centuries of Memories: The John Mason Monument, Connecticut," unpublished notes to the author, December 26, 2017. In author's possession.

   14. Ibid.

   15. Ibid.

   16. Ibid.

   17. Ibid.

   18. Ibid.

   19. Ibid.

   20. "John Mason Statue Advisory Committee Final Report, October 20, 1993," from Laurie Pasteryak Lamarre, "Centuries of Memories: The John Mason Monument, Connecticut," unpublished notes to the author, December 26, 2017. In author's possession.

   21. The quote "amity for all Americans" is drawn from the final wording on the plaque commemorating the removal of the Mason statue. Ibid.

   22. Joseph A. Amato, *Rethinking Home: A Case for Writing Local History* (Berkeley: University of California Press, 2002).

   23. Chip Colwell-Chanthaphonh, *Living Histories: Native Americans and Southwestern Archaeology* (Lanham, MD: Rowman & Littlefield, 2010), 137.

24. Ibid., 8.

25. The National Parks Service has an informative website about the rules and regulations for NAGPRA that is found at https://www.nps.gov/nagpra/FAQ/INDEX.HTM#What_is_NAGPRA?

26. Rosemary Cambra, "Restoring Life to the Dead," in *Native American Testimony: A Chronicle of Indian-White Relations from Prophesy to the Present, 1492–1992*, ed. Peter Nabokov (New York: Penguin Books, 1991), 127.

Chapter 12

1. "As early as 1925, descendants of the Indian warriors in the battle, who were led by Sitting Bull, started petitioning for an Indian memorial at the battlefield. Although the monument is surrounded by the Crow Indian Reservation, successive monument superintendents did not encourage the effort to build it. Twenty-five years ago [1972], Russell Means, a founder of the American Indian Movement, renewed the call with a nationally publicized protest here." Quoted in James Brooke, "Controversy over Memorial to Winners at Little Bighorn," *New York Times*, August 24, 1997, accessed November 12, 2017, http://www.nytimes.com/1997/08/24/us/controversy-over-memorial-to-winners-at-little-bighorn.html.

2. In his plenary address at the 2010 AASLH conference, Baker said of this time, "We already had people there from the Crow Reservation because it was within the Crow boundaries. I wanted to hear the other side. I brought in elders as well. But there was a lot of mistrust, because the main interpretation at one time made George Custer a hero. What I wanted to do was bring people together and sit them down side by side so we could start telling our stories. I went to one reservation, and spoke to a crowd of about a thousand people, young and old. I invited them back to their national park, back to their homelands. . . . I encouraged their young people to work at Little Bighorn, to tell the stories that they heard, because you have two different versions of history there—the academic version and the personal version." AASLH *History News*, Winter 2011.

3. Roger G. Kennedy served as director of NPS from June 1, 1993, through March 29, 1997.

Chapter 13

1. *Memorials to Roosevelt: A Book of Suggestions* (Roosevelt Permanent Memorial National Committee, 1919), 9.

2. "Remembering Roosevelt," *Literary Digest*, April 12, 1919, 28.

3. *Memorials to Roosevelt*, 15–16, 50.

4. Colin Moynihan, "Protesters Deface Roosevelt Statue Outside Natural History Museum," *New York Times*, October 26, 2017; Hrag Vartanian, "#DecolonizeThisPlace Demands Removal of Natural History Museum's Roosevelt Statue,"

Hyperallergic, October 10, 2016, https://hyperallergic.com/329225/decolonize thisplace-demands-removal-natural-history-museums-roosevelt-statue/; Benjamin Sutton, "Over 120 Artists and Scholars Call on NYC to Take Down Racist Monuments," Hyperallergic, December 1, 2017, https://hyperallergic .com/414315over-120-prominent-artists-and-scholars-call-on-nyc-to-take-down -racist-monuments/.

5. Claire Voon, "Activists Splatter Red Paint on Roosevelt Monument at American Museum of Natural History," Hyperallergic, October 26, 2017, https:// hyperallergic.com/407921/activists-splatter-roosevelt-monument-amnh/.

6. Lesley Oelsner, "Six Indians Accused of Defacing Theodore Roosevelt Statue Here," *New York Times*, June 15, 1971.

7. *James Earle Fraser: The American Heritage in Sculpture* (exhibition catalogue), from the James Earle Fraser Estate, Syracuse University Art Collection, Thomas Gilcrease Institute of American History and Art, January 12–April 21, 1985.

8. Ibid., 11.

9. Sutton, "Over 120 Artists and Scholars Call on NYC to Take Down Racist Monuments."

10. Chloe S. Burke and Christopher J. Castaneda, "The Public and Private History of Eugenics: An Introduction," *The Public Historian* 29, no. 3 (Summer 2007): 6.

11. Theodore Roosevelt to Charles Davenport, January 3, 1913, American Philosophical Society, http://diglib.amphilsoc.org/islandora/object/letter-theodore -roosevelt-charles-b-davenport; Jelani Cobb, "New York City's Controversial Monuments Will Remain, But Their Meaning Will Be More Complicated," *The New Yorker*, January 12, 2018, https://www.newyorker.com/news/news-desk/ new-york-citys-controversial-monuments-will-remain-but-their-meaning-will -be-more-complicated.

12. See, for example, Kathleen Dalton, *Theodore Roosevelt: A Strenuous Life* (New York: Vintage Books, 2002), 152.

Chapter 14

1. David McCullough, *1776* (New York: Simon & Schuster, 2005), 225.

2. David W. Dunlap, "Long-Toppled Statue of King George III to Ride Again, From a Brooklyn Studio," *New York Times*, October 20, 2016, accessed November 15, 2017, https://www.nytimes.com/2016/10/21/nyregion/toppled-statue-of-king -george-iii-to-ride-again.html.

3. Arthur S. Marks, "The Statue of King George III in New York and the Iconology of Regicide," *American Art Journal* 13, no. 3 (1981): 61–82.

4. Krystal D'Acosta, "The History behind the King George III Statue Meme," *Scientific American*, August 23, 2017, accessed November 16, 2017, https:// blogs.scientificamerican.com/anthropology-in-practice/the-history-behind-the -king-george-iii-statue-meme/.

5. Ibid.

6. A notable exception to peaceful diplomacy being the border dispute that led to the Mexican-American War (1846–1848).

7. James H. Madison, *A Lynching in the Heartland: Race and Memory in America* (New York: Palgrave, 2001), 13. Clearly, the disproportionality of African American victims also shows that this violence derived primarily from the tragedy of racial animus lit by white supremacy in the United States.

8. Please note that I am not arguing that all scientific breakthroughs result in a better world. An unshakable belief in the power of scientific "progress" is folly. Very few people would argue that harnessing nuclear power to create devastating weapons or that the chemical solutions that propel industrial-scale agricultural practices that denude and poison rivers and soil are net benefits to our quality of life and healthfulness.

9. Now that the "extended universe" is no longer canon, I have plenty of work ahead of me to purge from my fan fic all the characters and references to scenes and characters that predated Disney Corporation's purchase of Lucasfilm. Germane to both controversial statues and *Star Wars*, please note that George Lucas, in his 1999 re-release of *Return of the Jedi*, edited in a scene in which the citizens of the "planet city" of Coruscant celebrate the Rebellion's victory over the Empire by pulling down a statue of Emperor Palpatine to the rambunctious cheers of a raucous crowd.

10. Jonathan Haidt, *The Righteous Mind: Why Good People Are Divided by Politics and Religion* (New York: Vintage Books, 2012), 221.

11. Wendell Berry, *Citizenship Papers* (Washington, DC: Shoemaker & Hoard, 2003), 85.

12. James Axtell, *Beyond 1492: Encounters in Colonial North America* (Oxford: Oxford University Press, 1992), 257.

13. Wendell Berry refers to the two parts of our minds as the Rational Mind and the Sympathetic Mind. Berry, *Citizenship Papers*, 88.

14. Steven R. Weisman, "An American Original," *Vanity Fair*, November 2010, accessed December 27, 2017, https://www.vanityfair.com/news/2010/11/moynihan-letters-201011.

Chapter 15

1. See South Carolina Statehouse Report, "Riley: Think Strategically and Expansively about Education," Statehouse Report, February 24, 2015, accessed December 24, 2017, http://www.statehousereport.com/2015/02/24/riley-think-about-education/.

2. To learn more about the Charleston Illumination Project, visit http://www.charleston-sc.gov/index.aspx?NID=1436.

3. F. Sheffield Hale, "Finding Meaning in Monuments: Atlanta History Center Enters Dialogue on Confederate Monuments." AASLH *History News*, Fall 2016.

4. John C. Calhoun Monument reinterpretation inscription text.

5. Robert N. Rosen, *Confederate Charleston: An Illustrated History of the City and the People during the Civil War* (Columbia: University of South Carolina Press, 1994).

6. Harold Holzer, "War by the Numbers," *HistoryNet Magazine*, 2017, access December 24, 2017, http://www.historynet.com/civil-war-casualties.

Chapter 17

1. *The Simpsons*, "The Telltale Head," season 1, episode 8, created by Matt Groening, originally aired February 25, 1990.

2. *The Simpsons*, "Lisa the Iconoclast," season 7, episode 16, created by Matt Groening, originally aired February 18, 1996.

Chapter 18

1. See Edmundo Edwards and Alexandra Edwards, *When the Universe Was an Island: Exploring the Cultural and Spiritual Cosmos of the Ancient Rapa Nui* (Santiago, Chile: Hangaroa Press, 2013), for more information about anthropologists' and ethnographers' interpretation of the meaning of the Moai statues on Easter Island.

2. As written in the Bible, the prophet Samuel wanted to memorialize the return of the Ark of the Covenant to Israel and Israel's defeat of the Philistines, so he set up a stone monument. 1 Samuel 7:12 reads, "Then Samuel took a stone and set it up between Mizpah and Shen and called its name Ebenezer [which means stone of help], for he said, 'Till now the Lord has helped us.'"

3. See Katharyne Mitchell, "Monuments, Memorials, and the Politics of Memory," *Urban Geography* 24, no. 5 (2003): 442–59. Writing about the pageantry of the Nazi regime, Mitchell notes that "the grand spectacle or 'monumental seduction' . . . is frequently recoded through time, but always contains the interplay of the 'fixed': monument, stage, building, flags or lights, and the 'mobile': commemoration, ritual, march, pageant, meeting, event" (444).

4. See William Sheridan Allen, *The Nazi Seizure of Power: The Experience of a Single German Town, 1922–1945*, revised edition (Danbury, CT: Franklin Watts, 1984). Allen presents a compelling narrative of the ways that the Nazi Party kindled a nationalistic pride that rested on pageantry and vitriol against anyone who was not of "pure Aryan" stock. See pages 48–52 in his book for descriptions of the rallies and parades that dripped with the rhetoric of Nazism.

5. Ibid., 444.

6. Ibid. Most historians assert that more than six million Jews were murdered during the Holocaust. Nazi Germany also killed homosexuals, Sinti and Roma, the disabled, and political opponents. See the Holocaust Memorial Museum website at

https://www.ushmm.org/wlc/en/article.php?ModuleId=10007329, accessed January 28, 2017.

7. See Siobhan Kattago, *Ambiguous Memory: The Nazi Past and German National Identity* (Westport, CT: Praeger Publishing, 2001).

8. Ibid., 4.

9. Ibid., 8.

10. Ibid., 7.

11. Ibid.

12. A. Taub and Max Fisher, "Germany's Extreme Right Challenges Guilt over Nazi Past," *New York Times*, January 18, 2017. This article spotlights Björn Höcke of the Alternative for Germany Party and describes a rally at which Höcke spoke: "Shouting to be heard over cheering supporters, many of whom stood, Mr. Höcke challenged the collective national guilt over the war that has restrained German politics for three generations." The Alternative for Germany Party is deeply opposed to multiculturalism and the recent influx of refugees to the country and has seen growth in popularity in Germany, mostly behind the support of millennials and young people.

13. Although the concept of identity in the context of a nation-state has become more deeply contested in recent years, underlying cultural proclivities and ways of thinking within a given nation can be perceived and deciphered through thoughtful ethnographic and sociological work. The example of Germany is particularly fascinating, as the long division between East and West Germany and the Iron Curtain estrangement meant that a uniquely *German* identity had to persist through four decades of artificial separation precipitated by Cold War politics.

14. Counter-memorialization arose as a "negative reminder" of the Nazi past in Germany in the 1980s and 1990s after reunification. Noam Lupu writes about these efforts in "Memory Vanished, Absent, and Confined: The Countermemorial Project in 1980s and 1990s Germany," *History & Memory* 15, no. 2 (2003): 130–64. "The counter-memorial project, as a collective memorial process, appropriated and historicized countermonuments as symbols of rupture for the ambivalent, always self-conscious, reunified (and thereby redeemed) Germany. Not only has memory (and re-memory) become a form of reconciliation, it has become an identity-forming process" (158).

15. See Alf Lüdtke, "'Coming to Terms with the Past': Illusions of Remembering, Ways of Forgetting Nazism in West Germany," *Journal of Modern History* 65, no. 3 (September 1993): 542–72.

16. Reports of Nazi victim memorial stones (gold-colored stones embedded into walkways with names of murdered victims of the Nazis on them) being stolen continue to surface. On November 7, 2017, an article mentioned that twelve of these memorial stones had gone missing in Berlin. This speaks to the ongoing struggles around commemoration, memory, and contested history. "Nazi Victim Memorial Stones Stolen in Berlin, Police Probe," *Reuters*, November 17, 2017, accessed November 17, 2017, http://www.reuters.com/article/us-germany-stones/nazi-victim-memorial-stones-stolen-in-berlin-police-probe-idUSKBN1D72LW.

17. Adam Taylor, "Why Japan Is Losing Its Battle against Statues of Colonial-Era 'Comfort Women,'" *Washington Post*, September 21, 2017, accessed October 27, 2017, https://www.washingtonpost.com/news/worldviews/wp/2017/09/21/why-japan-is-losing-its-battle-against-statues-of-colonial-era-comfort-women/?utm_term=.535660086164.

18. Ibid.

19. See Jackie Grobler, "Memories of a Lost Cause: Comparing Remembrance of the Civil War by Southerners to the Anglo-Boer War by Afrikaners," *Historia* 52, no. 2 (November 2006): 199–226.

20. Sabine Marschall, *Landscape of Memory: Commemorative Monuments, Memorials and Public Statuary in Post-Apartheid South-Africa* (Leiden: Brill, 2010).

21. Ibid., 4.

22. Cornel Verwey and Michael Quayle, "Whiteness, Racism, and Afrikaner Identity in Post-Apartheid South Africa," *African Affairs* 111, no. 445 (October 2012): 551–75.

23. Richard Wilson, *The Politics of Truth and Reconciliation in South Africa: Legitimizing the Post-Apartheid State* (Cambridge: Cambridge University Press, 2001).

24. Chana Teeger and Vered Vinitsky-Seroussi, "Controlling for Consensus: Commemorating Apartheid in South Africa," *Symbolic Interaction* 30, no. 1 (2007): 58.

25. See Heidi Peta Grunebaum, *Memorializing the Past: Everyday Life in South Africa after the Truth and Reconciliation Commission* (Piscataway, NJ: Transaction Publishers, 2011).

26. Official Truth and Reconciliation website, http://www.justice.gov.za/trc/, accessed November 26, 2017.

27. Ibid.

28. Jay A. Vora and Erika Vora, "The Effectiveness of South Africa's Truth and Reconciliation Commission: Perceptions of Xhosa, Afrikaner, and English South Africans," *Journal of Black Studies* 34, no. 3 (2004): 301–22.

29. The newest additions to the landscape are the digital augmented reality Pokémon Go! characters that lurk as a layer of catchable amusement throughout the world.

30. Town leaders and community members in the town of Bolzano in Italy recently superimposed the words "Nobody has the right to obey," from philosopher Hannah Arendt, in LED lights across a bas-relief fascist monument. In *The Guardian*, Carlo Invernizzi-Accetti writes of this superposed rejection of fascist ideas: "The transformed monument therefore invites people to reflect on the town's complex history in a way that is neither simply celebratory nor in denial, but rather contextualized—and for that reason all the more challenging and profound." See "A Small Italian Town Can Teach the World How to Defuse Controversial Monuments," December 6, 2017, accessed

December 9, 2017, https://www.theguardian.com/commentisfree/2017/dec/06/bolzano-italian-town-defuse-controversial-monuments.

31. It is worth remarking that thoughtful reflection and the attempts made in South Africa and Germany to memorialize the painful past have not been fully restorative, nor are they without detractors.

Chapter 19

1. Stolpersteine website (English version), accessed December 25, 2017, http://www.stolpersteine.eu/en/.

2. Ereshnee Naidu et al., *From Memory to Action: A Toolkit for Memorialization in Post-Conflict Societies* (Brasília: Amnesty Commission, Ministry of Justice, Governo Federal Brasil, 2014).

3. Frank Sap, "Sierra Leone Peace Museum—Background," Sierra Leone Peace Museum, accessed December 25, 2017, http://slpeacemuseum.org/about-us/background.html.

4. *The Memory Box Initiative: Seeking to Break the Cycle of Violence and Tragedy in Afghanistan* (Kabul, Afghanistan: Afghanistan Human Rights and Democracy Organization, 2013).

5. "Spaces of Hope," International Coalition of Sites of Conscience, accessed December 25, 2017, http://www.sitesofconscience.org/en/2016/06/spaces-of-hope/.

Chapter 20

1. Museums are implicitly trusted by the vast majority of the public. See *Public Perceptions of—and Attitudes to—the Purposes of Museums in Society*, BritainThinks for Museums Association (London: Museums Association, March 2013), 3.

2. Edwin Lawrence Godkin, "A Word about Museums," *The Nation* 1 (July 27, 1865), 113–14. Godkin's screed against P. T. Barnum's American Museum is fascinating for its fantastically demeaning view of the lower classes. A representative remark in which he mentions that the lower classes will not be able to go to P. T. Barnum's museum because it burned down reveals this disdain: "The worst and most corrupt classes of our people must seek some new place of resort" (113). Godkin continues by calling for a new "American Museum" in New York City that would hew to the standards of the British Museum and elevate the status of museums in the United States. The "American Museum" Godkin referred to eventually became the American Museum of Natural History (AMNH). The patrician sentiment that ignited AMNH's birth is still present visually in the form of the much-debated Teddy Roosevelt equestrian statue discussed at length in William Walker's essay in chapter 13 of this book.

3. See David Allison, "The Power of Amusement," American Alliance of Museums *Alliance Labs* blog, October 21, 2017, accessed December 25, 2017, http://labs.aam-us.org/blog/the-power-of-amusement/.

4. Colleen Dilenschneider, "Cultural Organizations Are Still Not Reaching New Audiences," *Know Your Own Bone*, November 8, 2017, accessed November 17, 2017, https://www.colleendilen.com/2017/11/08/cultural-organizations -still-not-reaching-new-audiences-data/.

5. Robert R. Archibald, *The New Town Square: Museums and Communities in Transition* (Walnut Creek, CA: AltaMira Press, 2004), 14.

6. *Public Perceptions of—and Attitudes to—the Purposes of Museums in Society*, 3.

7. John H. Falk and Lynn D. Dierking, *Learning from Museums: Visitor Experiences and the Making of Meaning* (Walnut Creek, CA: AltaMira Press, 2000), 28.

8. *Public Perceptions of—and Attitudes to—the Purposes of Museums in Society*, 3.

9. Sheila Watson, ed., *Museums and Their Communities* (New York: Routledge, 2007), 3.

10. Elizabeth Crooke, *Museums and Community: Issues, Ideas and Challenges* (New York: Routledge, 2007), 32.

11. Nina Simon, *The Participatory Museum* (Santa Cruz, CA: Museum 2.0, 2010).

12. Michael Frisch, *A Shared Authority: Essays on the Craft and Meaning of Oral and Public History* (Albany: State University of New York Press, 1990), 10.

13. Attributed to Denver's deputy mayor Allegra "Happy" Haynes.

14. For more information about appreciative inquiry, see Diane Whitney and Amanda Trosten-Bloom, *The Power of Appreciative Inquiry: A Practical Guide to Positive Change* (Oakland, CA: Berrett-Koehler, 2010). For details about design thinking, see Thomas Lockwood, *Design Thinking: Integrating Innovation, Customer Experience, and Brand Value* (New York: Allworth Press, 2009).

15. Katherine Mitchell, "Thinkwell's 2017 Guest Experience Trend Report," November 17, 2017, accessed November 25, 2017, https://thinkwellgroup.com/ news/thinkwells-2017-guest-experience-trend-report/.

16. Also important in this situation was food. Community members brought homemade green chili, noodle dishes, and desserts to the meeting. Food brings us together and reminds us that our shared humanity is given beautiful expression in relationships built around the breaking of bread. See Michelle Moon, *Interpreting Food at Museums and Historic Sites* (Lanham, MD: Rowman & Littlefield, 2015).

17. Crooke, *Museums and Community*, 32.

18. See Elif M. Gokcigdem, ed., *Fostering Empathy through Museums* (Lanham, MD: Rowman & Littlefield, 2016). In this collection of case studies and essays, Gokcigdem is able to make a compelling case that empathy is business and moral

imperative for museums. Empathy is the first step in developing transformational experiences at museums that also have the potential to transform society.

Chapter 21

1. University of Texas at Austin Archives.

2. Ibid.

3. Tommie Smith won gold in the 200-meter sprint in the 1968 Mexico City Olympics, and John Carlos won bronze. Australian Peter Norman won silver. Smith and Carlos raised their fists in a Black Power salute during the medal ceremony. Photographer John Dominis captured the iconic moment of their salute. This photo was the inspiration for a bronze statue that stands in the new National Museum of African American History and Culture in Washington, DC. See DeNeen L. Brown, "They Didn't #TakeTheKnee: The Black Power Protest Salute That Shook the World in 1968," *Washington Post*, September 24, 2017, accessed January 19, 2018, https://www.washingtonpost.com/news/retropolis/wp/2017/09/24/they-didnt-takeaknee-the-black-power-protest-salute-that-shook-the-world-in-1968/?utm_term=.df8dbfbe1746.

4. Statistics on numbers of Confederate statues in the United States are drawn from the Southern Poverty Law Center website. See https://www.splcenter.org/20160421/whose-heritage-community-action-guide, accessed November 27, 2017.

5. "In Praise of John Hope Franklin," *Harvard Gazette*, November 5, 2015, accessed December 24, 2017, from https://news.harvard.edu/gazette/story/2015/11/in-praise-of-john-hope-franklin/.

Chapter 22

1. The Chicano movement of the 1960s and 1970s was an organized response to racism and denial of civil rights in the United States to people of Mexican, mestizo, and Latino/a heritage.

2. See Yolanda Alaniz and Megan Cornish, *Viva la Raza: A History of Chicano Identity and Resistance* (Seattle: Red Letter Press, 2008).

3. Joe Contreras, "'El Moviemiento' Remembering Colorado Chicano History & Its Future, Forever," *Latin Life Denver*, October 2017, accessed December 19, 2017, www.latinlifedenver.com/community/el-moviemiento-remembering-colorado-chicano-history-its-future-forever/.

4. Many organizations similar to History Colorado have found that the word "society" is poorly received as being elitist. See Robin Pogrebin, "These Fusty Names Are History: Historical Institutions Update Their Brands," *New York Times*, October 23, 2014, accessed December 28, 2017, https://www.nytimes.com/2014/10/26/arts/artsspecial/historical-institutions-update-their-brands.html.

5. Referred to variously as Letting Go, Community Curation, and Radical Trust, many museum theorists and practitioners have championed this approach to working with community. See Bob Beatty, ed., *An American Association for State and Local History Guide to Making Public History* (Lanham, MD: Rowman & Littlefield, 2017).

6. Eduardo Diaz, "The People Who Weren't Kidding," *Huffpost*, June 2, 2015, accessed on December 19, 2017, https://www.huffingtonpost.com/eduardo-diaz/the-people-who-werent-kid_b_6994882.html.

Chapter 23

1. The Laundromat Project is a nonprofit organization that brings engaging and community-responsive arts, artists, and arts programming into local coin-ops and other everyday spaces, thus amplifying the creativity that already exists within communities to build networks, solve problems, and enhance our sense of ownership in the places where we live, work, and grow. See http://laundromatproject.org/ for more information about this organization. There is also a photo album of pictures from the *Not What's Broken; What's Healed* happenings at https://www.flickr.com/photos/thelaundromatproject/albums/72157674447393946/page2, accessed January 20, 2018.

2. See Ariel Zilber, "Protesters Now Demand Removal of Central Park Statue Honoring 'Father of Modern Gynecology' Who Conducted Experiments on Enslaved Black Women in the 1850s," *The Daily Mail*, August 20, 2017, accessed December 26, 2017, http://www.dailymail.co.uk/news/article-4808254/Protesters-want-removal-statue-controversial-doctor.html#ixzz52NwFGrtk.

3. Sarah Spettel and Mark Donald White, "The Portrayal of J. Marion Sims' Controversial Surgical Legacy," *Journal of Urology* 185 (June 2011): 2424–27, accessed November 4, 2013, http://www.jurology.com/article/S0022-5347(11)00227-8/fulltext.

4. Harriet A. Washington, *Medical Apartheid: The Dark History of Medical Experimentation on Black Americans from Colonial Times to the Present* (New York: Doubleday Books, 2006).

5. Ibid.

6. David R. Williams and Chiquita Collins, "Racial Residential Segregation: A Fundamental Cause of Racial Disparities in Health," *Public Health Reports* 116, no. 5 (2001): 404–16.

7. Francheska Alcantara is a multimodal artist from New York City who has created sculpture, performance art, and paintings as part of her portfolio. See http://francheskaalcantara.com/ for more information about her work.

8. See Nancy Ordover, *American Eugenics: Race, Queer Anatomy, and the Science of Nationalism* (Minneapolis: University of Minnesota Press, 2003). Note also that individuals with disabilities were often also the target of the eugenics movement.

9. See Lynn M. Harter, Ronald J. Stephens, and Phyllis M. Japp, "President Clinton's Apology for the Tuskegee Syphilis Experiment: A Narrative of Remembrance, Redefinition, and Reconciliation," *Howard Journal of Communication* 11, no. 1 (2000): 19–34.

10. See Iris Lopez, "Agency and Constraint: Sterilization and Reproductive Freedom among Puerto Rican Women in New York City," *Urban Anthropology and Studies of Cultural Systems and World Economic Development* (1993): 299–323.

11. Vernellia R. Randall, "Slavery, Segregation and Racism: Trusting the Health Care System Ain't Always Easy—An African American Perspective on Bioethics," *Saint Louis University Public Law Review* 15 (1995): 191.

Chapter 24

1. "Ferguson Protests: What We Know about Michael Brown's Last Minutes," *BBC News*, November 25, 2014, accessed December 24, 2017, http://www.bbc.com/news/world-us-canada-28841715.

2. IMLS grant number MA-10-16-0231-16.

3. NAACP is an acronym for the National Association for the Advancement of Colored People. CORE stands for Congress of Racial Equality.

4. The Double Victory campaign began during World War II as a way for African Americans to advocate for victory both abroad (militarily against the Axis powers) and at home (against segregation and discrimination in the United States). See Cheryl Mullenbach, *Double Victory: How African American Women Broke Race and Gender Barriers to Help Win World War II* (Chicago: Chicago Review Press, 2013).

5. See Lucy Delaney, *From Darkness Cometh the Light or Struggles for Freedom* (1890?), accessed December 24, 2017, http://docsouth.unc.edu/neh/delaney/summary.html. For information on Charlton H. Tandy, see the State Historical Society of Missouri Archives at https://shsmo.org/manuscripts/.

6. Robert Connelly and Elizabeth Bollwork, eds., *Positioning Your Museum as a Critical Community Asset: A Practical Guide* (Lanham, MD: Rowman & Littlefield, 2016).

7. For more information about the Black Artists' Group, see Liam Otten, "Rediscovering the Black Artists' Group," *The Source*, February 6, 2006, accessed December 24, 2017, https://source.wustl.edu/2006/02/rediscovering-the-black-artists-group/.

Chapter 25

1. See *Muscle Shoals*, directed by Greg Camalier (Dallas: Magnolia Pictures, 2013).

2. "Confederate Monument Unveiled," *The Florence Times* (Florence, AL), May 1, 1903, p. 1.

3. View the video at https://www.projectsaysomething.org/2017/09/confederate -monument-campaign/.

4. Allison Carter, "Project Say Something Wants Educational Dialogue about Monuments," *The Times Daily* (Florence, AL), October 1, 2017, p. 1.

Conclusion

1. I realize that I am in dangerous territory for historians here. Students of history are often reluctant to bemoan present times or to make reactive judgments about current events. Realizing that the troubles of the past are not quantitatively any worse or better than the troubles we face in the present is a key part of savvy historical understanding and vision.

2. For a deep explanation of the Sumner caning, see David Donald, *Charles Sumner and the Rights of Man* (New York: Knopf, 1970).

3. See Marcus Rediker, *The Slave Ship: A Human History* (New York: Penguin Group, 2007).

4. Bob Beatty, ed., *An American Association for State and Local History Guide to Making Public History* (Lanham, MD: Rowman & Littlefield, 2017), 206.

5. William Shakespeare, *The Tragedy of King Lear*, act IV, scene 6.

6. An apt quote from novelist Graham Greene is in collusion with Shakespeare: "Leaving the miraculous out of life is rather like leaving out the lavatory or dreams or breakfast."

SELECTED
BIBLIOGRAPHY

Allen, William Sheridan. *The Nazi Seizure of Power: The Experience of a Single German Town, 1922–1945,* revised edition. Danbury, CT: Franklin Watts, 1984.

Allison, David B. *Living History: Effective Costumed Interpretation and Enactment at Living History Museums and Historic Sites.* Lanham, MD: Rowman & Littlefield, 2016.

Amato, Joseph A. *Rethinking Home: A Case for Writing Local History.* Los Angeles: University of California Press, 2002.

Archibald, Robert R. *The New Town Square: Museums and Communities in Transition.* Walnut Creek, CA: AltaMira Press, 2004.

Beatty, Bob, ed. *An American Association for State and Local History Guide to Making Public History.* Lanham, MD: Rowman & Littlefield, 2017.

Berry, Wendell. *Citizenship Papers.* Washington, DC: Shoemaker & Hoard, 2003.

Bruggeman, Seth. *Here George Washington Was Born: Memory, Material Culture, and the Public History of a National Monument.* Athens: University of Georgia Press, 2008.

Castillo, Eric. "Expressions of Another Center: Borderlands Visual Theory & the Art of Luis Jimenez." University of New Mexico American Studies thesis, 2011.

Cook, Robert. *Troubled Commemoration: The American Civil War Centennial, 1961–1965.* Baton Rouge: Louisiana State University Press, 2007.

Coski, John M. *The Confederate Battle Flag: America's Most Embattled Emblem.* Cambridge, MA: Belknap Press of Harvard University Press, 2005.

———. "Historians under Fire: The Public and the Memory of the Civil War." *Cultural Resources Management* 25, no. 4 (2002): 13–15.

Crooke, Elizabeth. *Museums and Community: Ideas, Issues and Challenges.* New York: Routledge, 2007.

Davidson, James West, and Mark Hamilton Lytle. *After the Fact: The Art of Historical Detection.* New York: McGraw-Hill, 1992.

Dew, Charles B. *Apostles of Disunion.* Charlottesville: University of Virginia Press, 2002.

Dwyer, Owen, and Derek Alderman. *Civil Rights Memorials and the Geography of Memory.* Chicago: Center for American Places at Columbia College, 2008.

Eichstedt, Jennifer, and Stephen Small. *Representations of Slavery: Race and Ideology in Southern Plantation Museums.* Washington, DC: Smithsonian Institution Press, 2002.

Falk, John H., and Lynn D. Dierking. *The Museum Experience Revisited.* New York: Routledge, 2016.

Frisch, Michael. *A Shared Authority: Essays on the Craft and Meaning of Oral and Public History.* Albany: State University of New York Press, 1990.

Glassberg, David. *American Historical Pageantry: The Uses of Tradition in the Early Twentieth Century.* Chapel Hill: University of North Carolina Press, 1990.

———. *Sense of History: The Place of the Past in American Life.* Amherst: University of Massachusetts Press, 2001.

Gokcigdem, Elif M., ed. *Fostering Empathy through Museums.* Lanham, MD: Rowman & Littlefield, 2016.

Grobler, Jackie. "Memories of a Lost Cause: Comparing Remembrance of the Civil War by Southerners to the Anglo-Boer War by Afrikaners." *Historia* 52, no. 2 (November 2006): 199–226.

Haidt, Jonathan. *The Righteous Mind: Why Good People Are Divided by Politics and Religion.* New York: Vintage Books, 2012.

Horwitz, Tony. *Confederates in the Attic: Dispatches from the Unfinished Civil War.* New York: Vintage Departures, 1998.

Klosterman, Chuck. *But What If We're Wrong: Thinking about the Present as If It Were the Past.* New York: Blue Rider Press, 2016.

Kryder-Reid, Elizabeth. "Sites of Power and the Power of Sight: Vision in the California Mission Landscapes." In *Sites Unseen: Landscape and Vision,* edited by Dianne Harris and D. Fairchild Ruggles, 181–212. Pittsburgh: University of Pittsburgh Press, 2007.

Levin, Kevin, ed. *Interpreting the Civil War at Museums and Historic Sites.* Lanham, MD: Rowman & Littlefield, 2017.

Lowenthal, David. *The Past Is a Foreign Country.* Cambridge: Cambridge University Press, 1985.

Lüdtke, Alf. "'Coming to Terms with the Past': Illusions of Remembering, Ways of Forgetting Nazism in West Germany." *Journal of Modern History* 65, no. 3 (September 1993): 542–72.

Madison, James H. *A Lynching in the Heartland: Race and Memory in America.* New York: Palgrave, 2001.

Marschall, Sabine. *Landscape of Memory. Commemorative Monuments, Memorials and Public Statuary in Post-Apartheid South-Africa.* Leiden: Brill, 2010.

Mitchell, Katharyne. "Monuments, Memorials, and the Politics of Memory." *Urban Geography* 24, no. 5 (2003): 442–59.

Rentzhog, Sten. *Open Air Museums: The History and Future of a Visionary Idea.* Kristianstad, Sweden: Carlssons and Jamtli Press, 2007.

Rose, Julia. *Interpreting Difficult History at Museums and Historic Sites.* Lanham, MD: Rowman & Littlefield, 2016.

Rosenzweig, Roy, and David Thelen. *The Presence of the Past.* New York: Columbia University Press, 1998.

Schlereth, Thomas. "It Wasn't That Simple." *Museum News* 56 (January–February 1978): 36–41.

Sewell, Richard H. *A House Divided: Sectionalism and the Civil War, 1848–1865.* Baltimore: Johns Hopkins University Press, 1988.

Simon, Nina. *The Participatory Museum.* Santa Cruz, CA: Museum 2.0, 2010.

Synnott, Marcia G. "Disney's America: Whose Patrimony, Whose Profits, Whose Past?" *The Public Historian* 17, no. 4 (Fall 1995): 43–59.

Thelen, David. "Memory and American History." *Journal of American History* 75 (March 1989): 1117–29.

Tyson, Amy M. "Crafting Emotional Comfort: Interpreting the Painful Past at Living History Museums in the New Economy." *Museum and Society* 6, no. 3 (November 2008): 246–61.

Upton, Dell. *What Can and Can't Be Said: Race, Uplift, and Monument Building in the Contemporary South.* New Haven, CT: Yale University Press, 2015.

Upton, Dell, and John Michael Vlatch, eds. *Common Places: Readings in American Vernacular Architecture.* Atlanta: University of Georgia Press, 1986.

Vanderstel, David. "Humanizing the Past: The Revitalization of the History Museum." *Journal of American Culture* 12, no. 2 (Summer 1989): 23.

Vora, Jay A., and Erika Vora. "The Effectiveness of South Africa's Truth and Reconciliation Commission: Perceptions of Xhosa, Afrikaner, and English South Africans." *Journal of Black Studies* 34, no. 3 (2004): 301–22.

Wallace, Michael. *Mickey Mouse History and Other Essays on American Memory.* Philadelphia: Temple University Press, 1996.

Walsh, Kevin. *The Representation of the Past: Museums and Heritage in the Post-Modern World.* Abingdon: Routledge, 2002.

Warren, Robert Penn. *The Legacy of the Civil War: Meditations on the Centennial.* New York: Random House, 1961.

West, Patricia. *Domesticating History: The Political Origins of America's House Museums.* Washington, DC: Smithsonian Institution Press, 1999.

Wilson, Richard. *The Politics of Truth and Reconciliation in South Africa: Legitimizing the Post-Apartheid State.* Cambridge: Cambridge University Press, 2001.

Wineburg, Sam. *Historical Thinking and Other Unnatural Acts: Charting the Future of Teaching the Past.* Philadelphia: Temple University Press, 2001.

INDEX

ABOUT THE EDITOR AND CONTRIBUTORS

David B. Allison is the editor of *Controversial Monuments and Memorials: A Guide for Community Leaders* and author of *Living History: Effective Costumed Interpretation and Enactment at Museums and Historic Sites*, published in 2016. He is the onsite programs manager at the Denver Museum of Nature & Science and holds an MA in U.S. history from Indiana University–Purdue University Indianapolis (IUPUI) and an MBA from Regis University. Prior to moving to Colorado, Allison designed and developed experiences for audiences at Conner Prairie Interactive History Park, north of Indianapolis, where he worked for ten years.

Gerard Baker is a full-blood member of the Mandan-Hidatsa tribe and the highest-ranking American Indian in National Park Service (NPS) history. He appeared prominently in the Ken Burns and Dayton Duncan's film *The National Parks: America's Best Idea*. He is also a widely recognized public figure throughout Indian Country for his work as mediator and facilitator between the service and tribal governments on an exhaustive range of public policy issues. Baker began his NPS career in 1974 as a seasonal at Theodore Roosevelt National Park, Medora, North Dakota. His first permanent assignment in 1979 was as a park technician at Knife

River Indian Villages National Historic Site. In 1990, Baker transferred to the U.S. Forest Service serving several years before returning to NPS as superintendent of Little Bighorn National Monument. In 1998, he became superintendent of Chickasaw National Recreation Area in Oklahoma and in 2000 became superintendent of Lewis and Clark National Historic Trail. From 2004 to 2010, Gerard Baker served as superintendent of Mount Rushmore National Memorial. From April 2010 until his retirement later that year, he served as the assistant director, American Indian Relations, at NPS headquarters in Washington, DC.

Julian C. Chambliss is professor of history at Rollins College in Winter Park, Florida. He teaches courses in urban history, African American history, and comic book history in the United States. As a teacher-scholar concerned with community and identity, he has designed numerous public digital history projects that trace community development, document diverse experience, and explore the cultural complexity in Central Florida. He has been recognized for his community engagement work with a Cornell Distinguished Service Award (2014–2015) and Florida Campus Compact Service Learning Faculty Award (2011). Chambliss is one of the producers of "Every Tongue Got to Confess," a podcast exploring the experiences and stories of communities of color.

Vanessa Cuervo Forero is a Colombian cultural worker and creative facilitator who believes in the power of art as a social transformational practice and a form of critical thinking. As a dancer, producer, and curator, she explores the intersection of art, education, and social justice. Working with dance, theater, and film organizations in Toronto, Buenos Aires, New York, and Bogotá, she has collected a multiplicity of stories while programming theater festivals, facilitating workshops, producing plays, and supporting artists from Latin America. After completing her MA in arts politics at NYU, Vanessa has worked with cultural institutions including Creative Time, Elastic City, the New Museum, Laundromat Project, and Doc Society. She currently works with film teams strategizing on how to use their documentaries as tools for social change.

W. Todd Groce is president and CEO of the Georgia Historical Society. Born in Virginia and reared in Tennessee, Dr. Groce holds three degrees in history, including a PhD from the University of Tennessee and a certificate in leadership development from the U.S. Army War College. Before joining the Georgia Historical Society in 1995, Dr. Groce taught history at the University of Tennessee and Maryville College and was for five years the director of the East Tennessee Historical Society. He is the author of *Mountain Rebels: East Tennessee Confederates and the Civil War* and coeditor with Stephen V. Ash of *Nineteenth-Century America: Essays in Honor of Paul H. Bergeron*. He has written more than seventy-five articles and book reviews for publications ranging from *Journal of Southern History* to the *New York Times* and has made television appearances on the History Channel, Discovery Channel, and CSPAN. A graduate of Leadership Georgia and past president of the Rotary Club of Savannah, he has been listed by *Georgia Trend* magazine as among the "100 Most Influential Georgians."

F. Sheffield Hale is president and CEO of the Atlanta History Center. Prior to joining the Atlanta History Center in 2012 he served as chief counsel of the American Cancer Society and was a partner practicing corporate law in the firm of Kilpatrick Townsend LLP. Mr. Hale serves as a trustee of the National Trust for Historic Preservation, Robert W. Woodruff Library of Atlanta University Center, Fox Theater, Buckhead Coalition, and the Atlanta Convention and Visitors Bureau. He is a past chair of the Georgia Trust for Historic Preservation, the Atlanta History Center, St. Jude's Recovery Center, and the State of Georgia's Judicial Nominating Commission. Mr. Hale received his BA in history from the University of Georgia *summa cum laude* in 1982 and received his JD in 1985 from the University of Virginia School of Law. He is a member of the American Law Institute.

Modupe Labode is an associate professor of history and museum studies at IUPUI. She is also a public scholar of African American history and museums. Before joining the faculty of IUPUI, she was the chief historian at the Colorado Historical Society from 2001 through 2007. Her research involves representation of African American history in museums and monuments. She is researching a public art controversy in Indianapolis that resulted in the 2011 cancellation of Fred Wilson's proposed artwork, *E Pluribus Unum*. Labode wrote an overview of monuments commemorating the Confederacy and white supremacy, which appeared in *History News* in 2016.

George W. McDaniel is president of McDaniel Consulting, LLC, and lives in Summerville, South Carolina. McDaniel founded his strategy firm after having retired after twenty-five years as executive director of Drayton Hall, a historic site of the National Trust for Historic Preservation in Charleston, South Carolina, and of which he was named executive director emeritus. He holds a PhD in philosophy from Duke University and an MA in history from Brown University.

Brian Murphy is earning his MA in public history at the University of North Alabama. As a student, Brian has worked on five National Register Nominations, several exhibit panel designs, and an educator's resource packet for the Muscle Shoals National Heritage Area. As a board member of Project Say Something, Brian helped to implement the Florence African American Heritage Project, a community-based collection of artifacts, photographs, and stories of African Americans in the Florence, Alabama, area. Project Say Something recently launched a campaign aimed at supplementing the Confederate memorial in front of the Lauderdale County, Alabama, courthouse by starting a dialogue to envision a monument to justice in this space.

Linda Norris has been a leader for years in facilitating conversation and action surrounding the ways creativity can transform museums, shape more compelling narratives, and create deeper, more inclusive community connections. She is the coauthor of *Creativity in Museum Practice* and blogs at the Uncataloged Museum. In 2017, she joined the International Coalition of Sites of Conscience as the Global Networks Program Director. Linda holds an MA in history museum studies from the Cooperstown Graduate Program and has working relationships throughout the world. She was a U.S. Fulbright Scholar to Ukraine in 2009 and also served as a senior expert reporting on the state of Ukraine's cultural heritage sector for the Culture and Creativity Project of the EU-Eastern Partnership Programme. In 2016 she facilitated a series of museum practice seminars in Latvia. She is also an adjunct instructor in the Johns Hopkins University's online Museum Studies Program, teaching International

Experiments in Community Engagement and developing a new course on cultural heritage interpretation.

Elizabeth Pickard is director of education and interpretation at the Missouri History Museum, where she has worked in museum theater, education, and interpretation since 2007. She is the project lead for the ACTivists project, an interpretive theater program that supported and continues the interpretation of the #1 in Civil Rights: The African American Freedom Struggle in St. Louis exhibit by presenting performances about leaders in the continuum of work for African American equality in the nineteenth and twentiety centuries. She also led the museum's creation of the Teens Make History Program, a work-based learning program for teens that won the National Arts and Humanities Youth Program Award in 2014. Teens Make History has written plays about the teens' responses to Ferguson and the Stockley verdict in St. Louis. Elizabeth is a fellow of the Shannon Leadership Institute in St. Paul, Minnesota. She is a past president of the International Museum Theatre Alliance. She holds a BA in dramatic arts from St. Mary's College of Maryland and an MA in history and museum studies from the University of St. Louis, where she studied with Jay Rounds. Prior to moving to Missouri, she was a colonial interpreter at Plimoth Plantation in Plymouth, Massachusetts.

JJ Lonsinger Rutherford was an educator and exhibit developer at History Colorado from 2005 to 2017. A former social studies teacher, she holds a bachelor's degree in history from Princeton University and a master's degree in museum studies from the University of Colorado at Boulder.

Stuart W. Sanders is the history advocate for the Kentucky Historical Society. He is the former executive director of the Perryville Battlefield Preservation Association and the author of three Civil War histories, including *Perryville under Fire: The Aftermath of Kentucky's Largest Civil War Battle* and *The Battle of Mill Springs, Kentucky*. He has contributed to multiple anthologies about the Civil War and has written for *Civil War Times Illustrated, America's Civil War, MHQ: The Quarterly Journal of Military History, Hallowed Ground, Military Heritage, Blue & Gray, Civil War Quarterly, Kentucky Humanities, Journal of America's Military Past,*

Kentucky Ancestors, Register of the Kentucky Historical Society, Encyclopedia Virginia, and several other publications.

Thomas R. Seabrook is a public historian living in Richmond, Virginia. He received his BA from William & Mary and his MA in history from Virginia Tech. He has worked in museum education at Historic Jamestowne, Jamestown Settlement, and the American Civil War Museum. He is currently education and programs manager at Hanover Tavern Foundation in Hanover, Virginia.

Jill Ogline Titus is associate director of the Civil War Institute at Gettysburg College and co-coordinator of the college's public history minor. From 2007 to 2012, she was associate director of the C.V. Starr Center for the Study of the American Experience at Washington College in Chestertown, Maryland. Prior to joining the staff of the Starr Center, Titus worked seasonally for the National Park Service. She received her PhD in history from the University of Massachusetts in 2007. Her first book, *Brown's Battleground: Students, Segregationists, and the Struggle for Justice in Prince Edward County*, was a finalist for the Library of Virginia Literary Award.

William S. Walker is associate professor of history at the Cooperstown Graduate Program in Museum Studies (SUNY Oneonta). He grew up in Oyster Bay, Long Island, Theodore Roosevelt's hometown, and began his career as a seasonal park guide at Sagamore Hill National Historic Site.

Ben Wright is the Briscoe Center's associate director for communications. Prior to joining the center, he worked as a reporter covering the 2008 general election in New Mexico and the 2009 Texas legislative session in Austin. Later he worked as a communications director in both the Texas House and Senate. Wright earned an MA in modern history from King's College London. He hopes to pursue a PhD in the future, with his primary research interest being Texas between the Civil War and World War I. His personal writing focuses on history, curation, travel, and faith. Wright was also the curator of *From Commemoration to Education: Pompeo Coppini's Statue of Jefferson Davis*. Sarah Sonner, the center's assistant director for exhibits and curation, contributed to his piece in this volume and produced *From Commemoration to Education*.

Jose Zuniga is a Denver native who has been performing in the metro area for the last ten years. He studied theater at Metropolitan State University of Denver, where he graduated with his BA in theater. He began working at the Denver Museum of Nature & Science (DMNS) in 2010 and has portrayed a plethora of characters as an enactor in the exhibits *Travelling the Silk Road, The International Exhibition of Sherlock Holmes,* and *Vikings: Beyond the Legend.* Zuniga is a full-time educator-performer—and pop culture enthusiast—at DMNS.

Printed in Great Britain
by Amazon

18116601R00192